THE EPICUREAN'S
GOOD FOOD GUIDE

First published in 1999.
This updated edition published in 2013 by André Deutsch
An imprint of the Carlton Publishing Group
20 Mortimer Street
London W1T 3JW

10 9 8 7 6 5 4 3 2

A CIP catalogue record for this book is available from the
British Library.

ISBN 978 0 233 00384 9

Printed and bound in the UK by
CPI Group (UK) Ltd, Croydon, CR0 4YY

THE EPICUREAN'S GOOD FOOD GUIDE

Buying and using ingredients from around the world

ROZ DENNY

FOREWORD BY GORDON RAMSAY

ANDRE
DEUTSCH

Contents

FOREWORD
by Gordon Ramsay

In today's ever-changing food world, keeping track of up-to-date information on new foods, varieties, food safety and, increasingly, the impact of modern food production on our environment can leave us baffled, despite all the mixed messages we get from a deluge of papers, magazines and TV and radio programmes.

So the need for a definitive handbook on how to choose our foods has never been more acute. Especially for those who haven't had the benefit of a professional training.

With *The Epicurean's Good Food Guide*, Roz covers my own chosen subject and does not hesitate to inform and entertain. From everyday matters of food marketing, labelling, ethical concerns, etc., to the mysteries of speciality gourmet foods, she explains in practical terms how to choose and use the right ingredients. The contents are readable and personal, based on her long career in the food-writing world from a home cook's perspective.

Roz helped me write my early books based around what we cooked in our flagship restaurants, translating apparently complicated and daring recipes into a culinary language understood by the home cook without background help from sous chefs and assistants. Not only that, she tested them in her own kitchen (much to the delight, she said, of her many friends and family who enjoyed the results). So, may I suggest you clear a space on your kitchen bookshelf for this essential culinary ready-reckoner? It could help avert recipe disappointments.

Gordon Ramsay
London 2013

INTRODUCTION

The art of a good cook starts with being a savvy shopper; choosing good food in the first place means you don't have to fret about complicated recipes or tricky techniques. Let the food speak for itself. Think how wonderful a simple chunk of farmhouse cheese tastes with freshly baked crusty bread and maybe a few well-chosen olives and a sliced flavoursome tomato.

I buy first and foremost for flavour. Making the right choice in a shop comes largely from experience, although more and more retailers do give a limited guide on point of sale labels. Buying well does not have to mean spending a lot of money on food. If you are an omnivore, try and break free from the tyranny of always having meat and two veg each day. It is perfectly possible to eat like a prince on grains, vegetables and some dairy foods enlivened by a host of flavourings, sauces, spices and herbs. All of which are readily available fresh or in convenient store containers. The chapters of this book are laid out in categories that replicate sections of supermarkets and food stores so they are easy to refer to. If you are starting up a new kitchen stock then buy two or three new flavouring items each week, rather than panic and throw a motley selection into your basket without thinking how you might use them.

My most useful basics are: • quality oils (for cooking and flavouring) • a few dried herbs • some aromatic spices • a tub of good stock powder • pure sea salt • a couple of Chinese sauces • some vinegars, seeds and nuts • a bottle of dry vermouth. They are all to hand on one shelf just above the cooker. I treat them like an artist's palette and use them in splashes, sloshes, pinches and shakes. Nothing complicated there.

Fresh vegetables are a particular passion of mine. I could happily eat a plate of four or more types and forget the meat or fish or alternative veggie protein base. This accounts for the large section on vegetables in the book.

Homely vegetables are best cooked simply, but new species add variety.
One of the most interesting developments in fresh produce retailing is the
gathering momentum to bring out new varieties or flavours. In some cases
this has meant the re-introduction of older varieties bringing different flavours
to a new generation. Sometimes the choice of vegetables and fruits is quite
bewildering as new strains and hybrids jostle for space on the shelves.

Seasonality used to be the yardstick by which cooks would choose the best
available quality. In the main this was easy to judge – foods 'in season' were
bountiful and therefore cheaper. Then you knew strawberries were best in June
and September, sprouts after the first frost, game in the early winter months
and so on. Now, we have to ask which season in which hemisphere? I'll buy
home-grown Cox apples in November for a couple of months, but wait until the
early summer to buy equally good apples from New Zealand. Air freight brings
us raspberries and asparagus from Peru, mangetouts from Kenya and baby
corns from Thailand. Potatoes and carrots are dug up from Egyptian or Cypriot
soil and vast tracts of Holland seem to be under glass growing all manner of
vegetables for us from peppers to tomatoes. But this involves massive food
miles at what cost to our environment?

Alongside the growth in fresh food marketing has been a mushrooming in
the number of ethnic stores and products. Modern transport may have opened
up new exotic holiday destinations to tourists but it has also meant foreign food
companies are exporting to our stores. Not only do we have more authentic
versions of sauces and ingredients we may already be used to, such as soy and
oyster sauces, olive oils and hot pepper sauces but following in their wake are
completely new taste experiences such as unusual spice pastes, sea weeds, rices,
cheeses and sauces. Our multi-racial society and the global village has resulted
in a glorious rainbow of stores that cater for many tastes, from corner stores and
ethnic shops open all hours to high-tech Oriental and Asian superstores.

The impact of environmentally friendly produce is increasingly felt. Foods
grown with care and minimum use of artificial fertilisers or preservatives tend
to taste better. But we will have to get used to paying a bit more for these
qualities in our food.

Storing food correctly is important not only from a safety point of view,
but again to keep the flavour at its best. Don't store oils, herbs or spices
in daylight unless you use them frequently – they lose their pungency and
colour quickly in light. Some oils, such as nut oils, are best kept in the
fridge, while others will sit happily in a cupboard. There is no need to pack
your fridge full of sauces and jams unless of course they are low in sugar or
salt and will go off quickly.

The food retailing world – then and now

Food is no longer sold in the Western world, it is marketed. We buy food for many reasons, not just to sustain our bodies. The movers and the shakers in the food industry consider more than just flavour, texture and general wholesomeness. They need to bear in mind material costs, safety, distribution, image, advertising, packaging and most important, profit margins. Add other global factors such as trade barriers, climate change, war and revolutions and it's a wonder any food ever reaches us as Nature intended.

It is worth reflecting on the significant changes in the availability of foods in the last half century. There are lots of pluses and a few minuses. For most of us we have a far greater choice than our grandparents' generation. Price is no longer a critical issue. As a nation develops and becomes more prosperous so it spends proportionally less on food per capita. First World countries (that's us) now eat less meat and animal products than they did twenty years ago, chiefly because they can afford to choose a healthier diet. (Emerging developing countries ironically see meat, animal products and refined foods as a sign of increasing status and their health begins to show classic symptoms of the malnutrition of affluence – an increase in heart disease, cancers and obesity.) In the developed world we have a large variety of foods to choose from all year round as the seasons have become blurred and Third World countries become the market gardens of the West.

The austerity decades of the 1940s and '50s gave way to a period of reawakening in the '60s and '70s with the increasing imports of then exotic foods such as peppers, avocados, aubergines, chillies, mangoes and garlic – lots of them! Olive oil was still something you bought in small bottles from chemists for medicinal purposes and crème fraîche only encountered on French holidays. But people began to entertain more and give dinner parties. It was the era of cookery part-works and we all learnt to make boeuf bourguignon, quiche (with real Gruyère) and pavlova topped with passion fruit pulp and kiwis. Consumer power was gathering momentum, food companies spent an increasing amount on new product development and advertising while the growth of supermarkets squeezed out the high-street butchers, greengrocers, bakers and fishmongers. On the plus side, farmers started up PYO (pick your own) stores, farm shops and mail order, and once luxury foods such as smoked salmon could be sent by post.

During the '90s we entered a phase of ethical consumerism. We've had the food gluts and food scares. Our appetites for more exotic foods are becoming satiated and we are increasingly concerned about where our food comes from and how it is produced. Fair trading, food hygiene, animal welfare and most of all farming standards occupy the consumer press. Organic foods and concerns on genetically modified crops are shaping our attitudes. A state of 'war weariness' over food scares and health and nutrition leaves many bewildered about just who or what to believe. Eggs, beef, chickens, butter, sugar, white bread, milk, soft cheeses, coffee – they've all taken a battering and in some cases the distrust lingers on.

The good cook and the informed shopper

It is perfectly possible to eat well and economically without spending much time in the kitchen or buying packs of ready meals. Nor does one need to be technically skilled in cooking to eat well. What is more important is to know what to buy and what represents good value and quality. This book is intended to be an introductory guide to the foods coming at us from home and all over the globe and to give a little background knowledge about the foods we eat. It does not set out to be the ultimate authoritative work. I hope to explain some facts on food to stimulate your curiosity in food and tempt you to buy and try. It is aimed at the vast majority of us who shop mainly in supermarkets, but also to encourage you to venture further afield and support small producers, genuine farm shops, farmers' markets, markets and delis and the emerging number of independent fresh food stores that sell local produce.

Supermarkets dominate the food-buying scene and it would be naive to pretend that we can turn the clock back to rosy days of high street food shops, wonderful as that may be. Where these still exist they have, in the main, adapted to becoming specialised or catered for a more up-market clientele. Supermarkets have greatly improved the quality of the fresh foods they offer for sale. And the variety from small producers is slowly increasing, albeit tucked away on the end of aisle as speciality foods – just to show what jolly open-minded chaps the buyers are. Refrigerated transport and vacuum-packed smoked foods has brought in another type of retail outlet – online food companies. You can order direct from suppliers by phone, online or email for next-day delivery. And now that everyday food shopping can be done from the home computer it is quite possible to eat well without having to go out and shop. But, for me, the main pleasure of eating well is the joy of looking first and then deciding what to eat. I'm not good at weekly menu planning.

Food labelling

You don't have to plough through piles of books and newspapers to be clued up on what you are eating. More often than not the answer is on the label, or at least part of it. By law, manufacturers have to list the ingredients in decreasing order of importance. You will also be able to judge the amount of sugar or fat in a product in relation to the other ingredients just by looking at the order. A fruit yogurt that lists sugar before fruit will have a small amount of fruit. If additional claims (such as a high fibre content) are made on a label then these must be stated as a minimum amount. Many manufacturers are aware of their responsibilities to consumers and often give information with symbols or warnings: e.g. if the product contains nuts for those with allergies, or are vegetarian or vegan. If eggs are included, check to see if the word 'pasteurised' follows should you need the reassurance if you are elderly or pregnant.

E numbers are codes for long chemical names, but this can arouse suspicions so where possible a good manufacturer will spell out the full name – sometimes it can be innocuous. As a general guide, E100–180 are colours, E200–283 preservatives, E300–322 antioxidants and E400–495 emulsifiers and stabilisers.

If additives are listed the label must say what they are used for, e.g. stabilising, preserving etc. For products to survive a reasonable shelf life then stabilisers and preservatives are a necessity. They help the product look appetising by stopping it from separating out or losing colour. Having said that, if more of us were willing to buy products that looked more natural then these would not need to be added. If you make a French dressing at home, it will separate out into oil and vinegar until you shake it back together. Bought dressings with a homogenous texture have added stabilisers, which, I think, looks unnatural. How many seconds to shake a bottle?

If a product makes a reduced calorie, diet or 'light' claim then it must be significantly lower than the standard product. Similarly a product cannot make a claim that it is not known for anyway (e.g. no claims for low fat lettuce). But products can have their health attributes highlighted – such as high in fibre, low in fat/sugar/salt. In particular, watch out for low fat claims. A product may claim to be half the fat as the usual version but still be quite high in fat. For example, reduced fat crisps – they are still only suitable as occasional treats, not an OK food you can suddenly eat lots more of. It is worth bearing in mind that products labelled as 90% fat free are actually 10% fat.

Almost all foods must carry a date stamp (either best before or use by – see below) and a weight (in metric). The name of a product can be revealing. The word 'flavour' for example indicates the product can taste like an ingredient without actually having any of that ingredient in it (i.e. it is an artificial flavouring), while the word 'flavoured' means it contains some of the ingredient to give flavour. Strawberry *flavour* sweets for example cannot have pictures of a strawberry on the wrapper but strawberry *flavoured* yogurt can. And by and large the name of a product must live up to the impression it creates, unless it has been in use for many years (e.g. Swiss rolls don't have to come from Switzerland and cream crackers don't need to contain cream).

Date markings can be puzzling. What's the difference between Use by and Best before? *Use by* is a food safety instruction – that is, if the food in question is not used by the date it could be unsafe thereafter, although some items can be cooked or frozen beforehand which extends the storage life. *Best before* is a guide to eating quality applied to foods such as biscuits or canned foods. Biscuits may stale beyond a date but they are still edible. Canned or pickled foods may lose colour or crispness but they can still be eaten.

Nutrition labelling

Most packs and cans of food contain some form of nutrition labelling. If they do declare nutrition content, then it has to be in a standard form so you can compare like with like. Nutrients have to be listed per 100g but many products will also be more helpful and list nutrients per serving. Breakfast cereals (one of the best and most informative nutritional labellings) even give you figures assuming an added amount of milk. There are four basic categories which must be given – energy (kilocalories or kilojoules – more accurate), protein, carbohydrate and fat. If you are a diabetic then the amount of sugars subdivided under carbohydrates will be useful. If saturated fat causes concern this can be singled out too. Additional information can be lists of vitamins, fibre and minerals.

Our need for protein is actually quite small – just 75g a day for men and 65g for women. What our body does not need for growth and repair it converts into energy and what we don't use up in energy goes straight to our tums, hips and thighs. So following a low carb/high protein diet is a no-brainer, and could affect the health of our kidneys. We are also encouraged to eat at least half our daily calorie allowance in starchy, low G.I., carbohydrate foods, not sugars. End of lecture. I won't even touch on alcohol.

Dietary requirements

Average dietary requirements as suggested by the Government. Some supermarkets are already giving information on packs as DGAs (Dietary Guideline Allowance).

	MEN	WOMEN	CHILDREN ages 5–10
CALORIES	2,500	2,000	1800
FAT	95g	70g	70g
of which saturates should be	30g	20g	20g
SODIUM (salt)	2.5g	2g	4g
FIBRE	20g	I6g	15g
SUGAR	70g	50g	85g

For all aspects of sensible nutrition, log onto the British Nutrition Foundation at www.nutrition.org.uk. For labelling guidance from the Food Standards Agency, go to www.food.gov.uk.

Food safety

A quick rundown of official guidelines to minimise food poisoning:

1. Get frozen and chilled food home as soon as possible after shopping, or pack it in an insulated container.
2. Prepare and store raw and cooked food separately.
3. Check the fridge temperature regularly. The coldest part should run at no more than 5°C. A thermometer will help.
4. Wash chopping boards in hot soapy water and dry well. Wash up in clean hot soapy water.
5. Change tea towels and dish cloths daily.
6. Keep hot foods hot and cold foods cold. Bacteria breed rapidly at room temperature.
7. Always wash your hands before handling food.
8. Sorry, but pets should not be allowed to jump on worktops or tables. They may look clean and smell sweet but their fur, paws and soft licky tongues are alive with bugs.

Metrication

The UK and USA are the last countries to change over completely to the metric system of measurements, although technically and practically it makes sense for all countries to use the same scale, like time and weather. But political considerations slowed the changeover originally scheduled for 1975 right down and while we had a D-day for decimalisation in 1971, no M-day was forthcoming. All fresh produce must be sold in metric units. It makes sense therefore to bite the bullet and learn to cook and shop in metric without cumbersome conversions. After all – scales, measuring jugs, thermometers and ovens have been in metric measures for well over 40 years so it's just a question of looking on the right side of the scale. No need to convert.

Recent EU regulations have relaxed weight declarations on packs. No longer do they need to conform to standardised metric weights, such as 100g, 250g, 500g, 1kg, etc. This has already led to food companies selling products in smaller weights for the same price. If you think packs are getting smaller, they are! For practical advice on shopping and cooking in metric, log on to www.gfw.co.uk/metrication.cfm.

Ethical issues – the concerned shopper

Food issues have become front page news and a major political concern. Efficiency in farming, the growth of food companies and the impact of advances in biotechnology have led to a corresponding growth in consumer watchdog groups. For many food shoppers it's hard to decide which side of the fence to come down on. Are retailers and producers really devious or are campaigners scaremongering? Should we really leave it entirely to government departments to police the scientific advances? Most food campaigners say they are really only asking for more information to be made readily available in easy to understand language so we can all make an informed choice.

Animal welfare

There is no doubt animals are affected by their conditions and suffer stress for many of the same reasons we humans do. We don't enjoy living in close conditions with a poor monotonous diet and little access to fresh air, so why should they? Animal welfare groups say there are good business reasons for rearing animals in better conditions. You get a product with better flavour and texture but this won't happen with fast-track factory farming. Such ideal conditions increase costs, so prices have to rise accordingly and some campaigners argue that we have become too used to cheap food. If we buy first-class (e.g. meat and fish) protein products less often, we can then afford to buy better quality when we do. The largest animal welfare assurance scheme in the UK is the RSPCA monitored Freedom Food group (www.rspca.org.uk/freedomfood). Or try Compassion in World Farming to support an end to so-called factory farming (www.ciwf.org.uk).

Fairtrade

Many of the everyday foods we take for granted come to us from Third World countries – tea, coffee, cocoa, tropical fruits and the like – and it would be easy to assume that workers receive a reasonable standard of living as a result, after all there is always a ready market for such staples. But the reality is that many of the workers still live in poor conditions with few opportunities to improve their lot. In the late 1980s schemes began to be formed by aid organisations to work towards obtaining a fairer deal for the workers so that they could benefit more from the fruits of their labours. These organisations are now active in developing countries promoting better living conditions, education and welfare schemes. Products produced under these schemes carry the Fairtrade logo, so if you wish to enjoy a cuppa or a bar of chocolate with a clear conscience then buy brands displaying the trademark. You may well be surprised to see who's signed up! Check the Fairtrade website (www. fairtrade.org.uk).

Organic foods, farmers' markets and farm shops

The organic issue has been around for decades now, bubbling under the surface. Supermarkets toyed with the idea on and off but it was generally viewed as niche marketing for the well-intentioned. The often bedraggled look of organic fruits and vegetables next to their designer-grown counterparts (a look the consumer has come to expect) was always a drawback for the image-conscious supermarkets. But the last decade has seen quite a turn-around in the approach by supermarkets and attitude of the general public.

The organic movement started around 60 years ago, after World War II, in response to the emerging tendency of farmers to use artificial pesticides and chemical fertilisers to grow crops. It also extended to animal husbandry. Organic agriculture encourages sustainable methods of production using the biological cycles of natural flora, fauna and animals. In a sense it works with nature instead of riding roughshod over it. With the various food scares of the last decades more and more consumers are seeing organic foods as somehow more trustworthy. It also avoids the dangers of pollution, maintains the landscape and natural wildlife and gives food a comforting country aura, which, by nature, it should have.

But organic farming cannot be entered into lightly. There are very strict regulations to follow to ensure the land is completely free of pesticides and artificial fertilisers and this may take some years to achieve. Organic farmers have to be extra vigilant about their practices. First of all, farmers or growers must register with approved bodies and submit to regular inspections – the Soil Association, set up in 1947, is perhaps the best known. It is hard to tell just by looking at produce or meat if it is organic so trademarks, logos and symbols are the best guide.

Organic food should, in principle, taste better but this is not always the case. It is the variety that determines flavour, and I have to say I have had disappointing experiences especially with organic fruit. The best guide to flavour is to buy fresh, home-grown produce when it is in season. If it is also organic, so much the better. The Soil Association (www.soilassociation.org/buyorganic/buyfrom farmers) produces lists of organic farm shops and retail outlets.

As an impressionable teenager in the mid-1960s, I vividly remember my mother telling me about a book she had just read which fired her up. It was Rachel Carson's *Silent Spring*. One of the best sources of organic or environmentally aware produce is from farmers' markets. These pop up at least once a month in country towns, villages and inner city squares. They are a delight and a great way to get in touch with your inner rural soul (www. localfoods.org.uk).

Sustainable fishing

When we look out over the seas and oceans all appears to be just as we've always known it, the waves roll powerfully or lap gently. But beneath the waters lies a worrying and growing problem that will have a major impact on all life forms, and that means most of all us. It's hard to believe that the seawaters which cover over two-thirds of the vast Earth's surface are slowly and systematically being stripped of all life because of mankind's need to feed. And we are the prime suspects of this environmental time bomb. Large factory ships with their massive drag nets, mile-long fishing lines and satellite technology that scours the sea beds can pinpoint lucrative shoals of popular fish species and drag them onto their boats for speedy processing. The problem is that these high-tech commercial systems don't just capture the intended fish species; they also scoop up vital life of sea weeds, corals and bottom-feeding sea species leaving behind a trail of destruction that can take decades to regenerate. Not to mention the young fish that are too small, plus hapless turtles, sharks and sea birds that get caught up and are discarded dead.

Not only is this an environmental disaster, it seriously affects future fish stocks because the baby fish cannot grow into mature reproductive adults and that, in turn, can spell disaster to the fishing communities around the world that depend on fishing as livelihood. And so the cycle continues. International recognition of this problem has been slow to respond despite the many vociferous warnings of sea and fish experts. International co-operation to tackle this problem and protect our future with sea life requires all nations that thrive on the produce of the sea to agree on codes of best practice. There are too many national and commercial vested interests.

The Marine Stewardship Council is an international body that strives to rectify this by prompting sustainable practices. It is the link between producers, fishing communities and concerned consumers. They strive to ensure that all wild fish and seafood can continue to reproduce and thrive to replenish stocks and that commercial fish and prawn farms have minimal environmental damage to sea beds, sea shores, coral beds and mangroves. To play your part in improving the health of our oceans and seas and check on the sustainability of fresh and frozen fish or prepared meals look for the distinctive blue Ecolabel MSC or check online at www.msc/Sustainable-Fishing.

At a national level, the Marine Conservation Society (a charity that also helps protect UK beaches) issues a consumer guide to sustainable seafood (www.thegoodfishguide.co.uk) with ratings 1 to 5 from green (seafood you can consume with a clear conscience) to red, that which should be avoided if stocks are to be left to increase.

Other worrying commercial aspects are the quotas fixed by governments, including the EU, on the amount of species that can be legally landed. Anything over and above that has to be tossed back into the sea, as 'discards' which is often dead or dying. A shocking waste of good food. The TV personality Hugh Fearnly-Whittingstall has spearheaded a campaign, *The Fish Fight*, to get a change in the EU quota system and other fishing issues (www.thefishfight.net).

Geographical indicators

One way of guaranteeing the quality of a product is to ensure the name is not copied or taken in vain, so cheaper and inferior products cannot be sold using the same names. Many long established food products cannot benefit from legal patents, although their brand names can. Competitors will have to use different names to avoid confusion for the customer.

For decades the French had their Appellation Controllée system (AOC), the Italians and Spanish similarly. But it was felt there were hundreds if not thousands of well-established foods and products that have heritages and intellectual property worth protecting from unfair competition. Most of these were associated with specific regions. So the European Union (EU) set up a scheme of Geographical Indicators (GIs) to help protect not only food and drink within the Community but also imports of consumables from the rest of the world. This was to reassure consumers that what they read on the label was the same product inside. There are 3 GI's:

- Protected Designation of Origin, or PDO, ensures the product is traditionally and entirely manufactured (prepared processed and produced) within a region to be uniquely associated with it. (UK examples include West Country Cheddar Cheese, but not general Cheddar); Stilton cheese can only be produced in Derbyshire, Leicestershire and Nottingham but ironically Stilton the town is in Cambridgeshire although a magnificent blue cheese from there is now called Stichelton produced using raw milk and non-factory rennet. In effect regarded by many cheese aficionados as better. Cornish Clotted Cream is PDO as are Jersey Royal Potatoes and Yorkshire Forced Rhubarb

- Protected Geographical Indication (PGI) traditionally associated and partially manufactured within a region. Examples include Cornish Pasties, Melton Mowbray Pies, Abroath Smokies plus Ciders and Perrys from Herefordshire, Gloucestershire and Worcestershire

- Traditional Speciality Guaranteed (TSG) is a product that does not have to be manufactured within a specific area or region, just that it is traditional and different from other products. Eg, Traditional Farm Fresh Turkey

For full lists, go onto www.defra.gov.uk. Click on EU protected food names schemes.

FRESH MEATS

Shopping for fresh meat can be quite daunting to the novice cook. A slab of stewing beef can look like a sirloin steak, but the difference in eating quality is dramatic. Supermarkets have made things easier by categorising their cuts according to cooking method and many high street butchers are following suit. No longer do you have to know a best end from an aitchbone or possess an exact anatomical knowledge of a cow or lamb. Meat cookery is a vast subject and so it helps to understand a few of the basic principles.

BASICS

Cooks judge good meat on flavour and tenderness. These two properties are affected by several factors: species (some taste better than others); method of rearing and feed, (a calm animal reared outdoors fed as near a natural diet as possible will have more tender flesh and finer flavour); the method of killing (an over-stressed animal can have certain enzymes in its tense muscles which affect flavour); the length of hanging; and finally – fat. There is some debate among cooks on this point. Fat adds flavour and bastes the meat during cooking keeping it moist. But animal fat is high in saturates that can contribute to heart disease. Producers have responded by breeding leaner animals with thinner layers of fat and less marbling – some gourmets say this is at the cost of flavour.

When shopping for meat you have three choices – supermarkets, high street butchers and increasingly, mail order direct from farms. It requires great knowledge, skill and enthusiasm to be a good butcher and the meat trade takes great pride in maintaining high standards. Supermarkets extend their company control right back to the farmer, abattoir and distribution network. Their overhead costs include time, and time costs money. Hanging times for example will be keenly monitored. Hanging is essential, especially for beef, to develop flavour and tenderness. A speciality high street butcher may well hang his meat for up to three weeks with some superb results.

Supermarkets often hang for less time. Having said that, many chains are now offering high quality traditionally reared meats, with longer hanging times and in more gourmet-style cuts.

Animal welfare schemes are being actively promoted. The meat industry are developing quality schemes with accompanying logos. Top specialist independent butchers belonging to a nationwide network – The Q Guild – increasingly aim to satisfy a more discerning clientele. All independent butchers may well have more culinary knowledge and take great pride in supplying their meat, often from single farms. As ever with better quality and choice comes higher prices. However, many independent butchers. especially in country towns, source their meat locally and offer wonderful old-style service.

Quick-cook cuts

The trend these days is to sell ready trimmed and prepared meats for tipping straight into a wok or frying pan or slapping under a grill. Butchers now cut the meat by removing individual muscles, a technique they call 'seam butchery'. This gives leaner, quick-cook cuts. If you intend following a slow-cooked casserole or stew recipe then look for stewing or braising cuts. Ideally buy such meat in large pieces and dice it up yourself.

For roasts a larger bone-in joint may look better value but remember you will lose some of the weight to bone. A smaller ready-boned and rolled joint may actually feed more people. But meat cooked on the bone always has a better flavour. If you are feeding more than four people then a roast makes good sense. A roast for two is more fiddly, better to buy two quick-cook steaks. The larger the joint the more moist it will be, so ideally aim to cook at least a kilo at a time. You can always carve the meat cold for the next day. Meat is now sold by metric weight (often rounded up to the nearest 100g). This makes the old system of calculating roasting times tricky if you are following the old minutes per lb system. So here is a more user-friendly guide. As a rough guide allow about 125g a head, that's four people to a 500g pack of diced meat or mince. More for joints – 150–200g per person. I reckon on 1kg diced or minced meat to feed 6. A joint of 2kg is perfect for 6–8. The larger the joint, the better it cooks. Leftovers for the next day remain juicy to slice for salads or sandwiches.

MEAT ROASTING CHART

		gas mark 5 or 190°C (375°F)		
BEEF	rare	30 mins per kilo	+	20 mins
	medium	50 mins per kilo	+	20 mins
	well done	60 mins per kilo	+	30 mins
LAMB	medium	45 mins per kilo	+	35 mins
	well done	50 mins per kilo	+	35 mins
PORK		50 mins per kilo	+	30 mins
CHiCKEN + TURKEY		40 mins per kilo	+	20 mins

Mince

Gone are the days when mince was made from any scrap of meat. Nowadays, good leaner cuts are used with fat contents ranging from 15% right down to 3%. A lean red meat mince will look darker in colour than a higher fat one. Beef minces will be around 5–10% fat, lamb mince at 15%, pork at around 10%, venison at 5% and lowest of all, turkey mince between 3–5%. If you buy a high fat mince then dry-fry it in a hot frying pan, stirring until it is crumbly and pour off any excess fat that seeps out. Coarse ground mince makes excellent homemade burgers and chilli con carnes. Still, the best source of good mince is fresher ground butcher's mince.

BEEF AND VEAL

There are beef cattle and dairy cattle. Beef cattle are young beasts slaughtered around 18–24 months old. Meat described as 'cow beef' is from dairy cows too old for milking. The meat will be used in factory production (for pies, burgers etc). Veal is from young cattle (18–24 weeks old); some veal is very young known as 'milk-fed'. Controversy regarding veal rearing is well known. Young animals reared indoors in crates with restricted movement will have a lighter-coloured flesh and more delicate flavour, a quality required by top chefs and gourmets. But the moral price is too high for many. Veal calves reared in more open barns on straw beds with access to fresh air (a system known as 'loose house') have a pinker flesh and a deeper flavour. *West Country* or *Quantock veal*, now sold as *Rose veal* and a great favourite of mine, when I can find it, are good examples. Aberdeen Angus beef cattle are highly sought after, the ultimate in Scotch beef. Reared for generations in natural organic conditions, this is the beef for that special occasion meal.

Beef cuts

A beef carcass is divided into two by the meat trade – forequarter and hindquarter. There are legs and shins on both. In general, the leaner, more tender cuts come from the hindquarter and stewing/braising cuts from forequarter. Muscle length is longer in the forequarter and the muscles are firmer, so meat tends to be less tender but well flavoured. The fillet is the long round muscle from the centre of the hindquarter. Because it gets the least movement the muscle length is shorter and more tender. *Sirloin* follows on from the fillet and the sirloin leads into the *rump*, both lean and tender cuts with good flavour. *Rib of beef* leads down from the back bone and includes the popular *wing rib* roast joint, which traditionally was cooked on-the-bone for best flavour but is also sold boned and rolled. Joints sold as *top rump* are less tender than rump but are still lean and full of flavour. *Silverside, aitchbone* and *brisket* are best slow roasted. (If you look closely you'll notice the muscles are coarser.) *T-bone steaks* are from the rib of beef, like giant chops really. *Entrecote* steaks are similar to sirloin. A *Chateaubriand* is a double portion size fillet. Stewing and braising cuts are now rarely sold with specific names. Braising meat is more tender and has more marbling of internal fat which keeps the meat tender during cooking. Stewing meat will have more connective tissue (gristle etc.), which requires slow, gentle cooking to tenderise it. Adding acid ingredients like red wine or tomatoes helps too. Shin meat is very lean with little fat but much connective tissue. It makes meltingly tender stews and fine mince but needs good slow cooking. *Skirt* is lean, long muscle from the belly of the animal, which makes excellent stews – the cut for classic Steak and Kidney pies. This is also the cut for beef olives because you can get long thin slices for rolling. *Oxtail*, as the name implies, is tail meat sold chopped into neat bony rounds. Highly prized as a cut by French chefs. *Ox cheeks* (from the head of cattle) are long and lean, full of flavour, and wonderful for stews. Chefs will braise this cut slowly, then shred the meat. *Kidneys* and *liver* (for some reason known generally as ox not beef) are best cooked long and slow in casseroles. *Beef suet* (from around the kidneys) is hard to get now from butchers but it does makes excellent puddings and dumplings. And, of course, beef fat is the best hot fat for fat cut chips.

Veal cuts mirror beef cuts but on a smaller scale. Roasts are generally leg cuts or rolled rib cuts. *Veal escalopes* are cut from the fillet or top rump, which is slightly coarser, then beaten between kitchen paper until wafer thin.

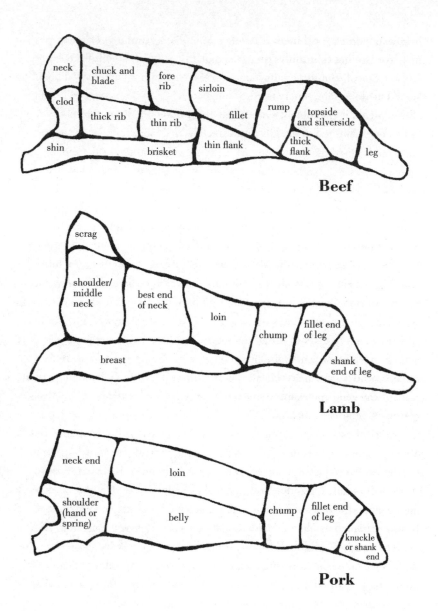

Beef

Lamb

Pork

Veal chops are like smaller T-bones, stewing veal is wonderful for blanquette de veau in a white wine cream sauce and veal shin is the cut for Italian osso bucco. Veal mince is lean and light in colour. It is frequently mixed with pork mince and makes very tasty meat balls.

Flash fry steaks are thin cut and lean steaks from parts of the animal that would be suitable for slow roasting or braising but they are packed with flavour. The French bavette or onglet has been a bistro classic for years and is now found in the cabinets of independent butchers. Marks & Spencer sell *flat-iron steaks* beautifully prepared and absolutely delicious for a modest midweek meal. But these cuts can only be cooked quickly on a good heat, then served medium rare, otherwise they toughen. The ultimate gourmet's choice of beef steak, it is claimed, comes from Japanese cattle known as *Wagyu*, or *Kobe, beef*. Farmed in the UK (www.freedomfood.co.uk).

LAMB

Lamb is sold when it is between 6 and 9 months old (depending on the season) when the meat is still tender but the animal has had time to develop flavour. Lamb meat is sweet and slightly aromatic. Mature lamb, known as mutton, was at one time popular in country-style cooking, then became hard to find but is now making a comeback – Renaissance mutton it is called. It has a distinctively strong flavour and was traditionally cooked by gentle boiling.

There are a number of breeds of lamb prized for fine eating. Canterbury lamb from Kent, Welsh lamb, Devon or West Country lamb and Scottish lamb. French lamb from the Pyrenees is regarded as the ultimate choice for top chefs while many good cooks are increasingly impressed by fresh New Zealand lamb reared on organic pastures.

Lamb cuts are less complicated than beef and modern butchers continue to fine tune new fashionable cuts such as *valentine chops* or *shoulder strips*. Lambs have two rear legs and two shoulders (front legs). Rear legs are lean and sold as whole legs or cut into smaller *fillet end of leg* (the part nearest the torso) and *shank end* (the shinny bit leading on to the hoof). *Gigot* is a French-trimmed whole leg popular in Scotland. Lamb shanks are a popular cut for Greek and Middle Eastern dishes. Shoulders are wide at the top with a shallow blade bone tapering to more sinewy shanks. Shoulder meat has a higher fat to lean ratio but the flesh is sweeter. Good for long slow roasting, in fact my favourite cut as the sweet meat can literally fall from the bone. Carving a shoulder is a challenge so ask the butcher to remove the blade bone leaving just the shank bone. Then after roasting you can slice the meat easily. You can also stuff the cavity left by the blade bone. Or try a ready boned and stuffed shoulder called *ballotine* tied in an attractive octagonal star. Running along the back bone the neck cuts start with scrag end cutlets, used for stewing to middle end and best end joints (aka *fine end* in some parts of the country). Sometimes the long round muscle called *neck loin fillet* is removed and sold whole. Ideal for slicing into medallions for stews or grilling on the BBQ. The best end is also trimmed neatly to make a French cutlet roast with neatly scraped bones. Best ends of neck should be chined (i.e. the rib bones are sawed through where they join the back bone. This is generally done for you, but do check, it makes for easier carving). *Loins of lamb* follow on from best ends – each side will have about 6 chops. A whole loin fillet of lamb will come from this cut. A *saddle* is a whole double-sided best end and loin combined. *Crown roasts* are two matching best ends of neck joints chined, bent round and tied together at the top of the chops to form a crown. Stuffing is spooned into the middle. A *guard of honour* is made from two matching best ends again but the scraped chop bones are interlocked at the top like a cocks comb. *Lamb rumps* and *chump chops* come next before finishing at the fillet end of a leg. *Breast of lamb* is from the belly of the lamb where it runs from the best end to the leg. Often sold boned and rolled round a stuffing as an economical joint. It is quite fatty. Breasts of lamb can be sawn into spare ribs for barbecuing but I find they need 30 minutes or so first in a medium oven.

GOAT

Rarely seen in your average butchers, but available through certain ethnic Halal or West Indian butchers. The meat is quite aromatic (like goat's cheese) and tastes a little like gamey lamb. Speciality organic producers sell kid. Cook it like lamb. Wonderful for a West Indian-style curry.

PORK

A truly versatile meat that is easy to cook until tender because it has a slightly higher fat to lean meat ratio. However, pork farmers are now breeding leaner pigs. The anatomical layout of pig is similar to lamb, but the cuts are slightly bigger. For roasts go for a leg or part of a leg. *Chops* are from the backbone. *Pork tenderloin* is the fillet running underneath the loin, while a *boned loin* of pork is from the middle of the rib cage. You can buy *saddles* and *best ends* of pork, and the classic *Chinese spare ribs* are from the belly. *Pork belly* also provides thick rashers of lean and fatty meat or can be sold as a piece to be boned, stuffed and rolled. The rind is sometimes left on roasting cuts to crisp into crackling during open roasting (in lamb it is called the bark and is stripped off by the butcher). If you intend to braise a cut of pork or marinade it then cut off the rind. Otherwise to make crisp crackling, ask the butcher to make deep score lines through the skin. If you have to attempt it yourself use a razor sharp Stanley (craft) knife but take great care. Score the skin every 1cm or so. Rub with fine sea salt and cook in a moderately hot oven, without basting for at least 1¹/2 hours. The crackling is done when it starts to blister and looks crisp and light. But, getting good crackling is a bit hit or miss. I sometimes, in despair, remove it after roasting and place the whole skin under a medium grill to crisp it up. Watch that it doesn't burn though. That's a dead give-away that you've cheated. My favourite cut of pork is from the shoulder. It is fattier than the leg (which can be a little dry) and if cooked long and slowly it becomes quite delicious and tender. *Shoulder meat* also makes good homemade pork pies and is sometimes sold cut into chops or diced for casseroles. Incredibly it is also one of the cheapest cuts of meat. *Pig's trotters* are generally only for chefs to tackle. They need slow pre-cooking then careful boning, stuffing and cooking again. *Suckling pigs* are piglets of about two months old, gutted, stuffed and best roasted over a spit. They have to be ordered ahead.

Slow-roasting and nose-to-tail cooking

The economic downturn has seen a change in cooking meat. Instead of top-quality, quick-cook cuts, we seek out leaner cuts from coarser grain or fat-marbled parts of animals and cook them for longer and more slowly, at around 145–150°C, until the meat is very tender and can be broken apart with a fork or even a spoon. Start these cuts off with flavoursome herbs or crushed spices and some sliced or chopped veggies on the base and a cupful or two of water, stock or dry wine. Cover lightly with foil or a butter paper and watch the juices ooze out. Then uncover for the last hour to brown and crisp.

CHICKEN

Probably the world's most popular meat and, with modern factory farming, the most readily available, although in the UK and Europe, we seek more humane farming. Like lamb, there are no religious taboos about eating it and chicken is invariably bound to please. *Poussin* (spring chicken is the old English expression, but rarely used) are baby birds, about 6 weeks old each weighing around 300g. Small chickens can be found at around 1 kilo, which are perfect for two. Otherwise sizes range from 1.5 kilos up to 3 kilos. Larger chickens are available from time to time. At one time, one could buy *capons* (castrated young cocks) of a size and tenderness that made them a good alternative to small turkeys, but they are no longer widely available.

For a rough estimate, allow 400–500g per head for bone-in-weight, about 150–250g per head when boned. In pieces, chicken is sold as bone-in and boneless breasts, thighs and drumsticks. *Chicken breasts* are actually two fillets bound together. The top fillet is sometimes called a *supreme* and can be sold with the wing bone attached; the smaller under fillet is generally sold 6–10 in a pack. Skinless, boneless thighs are becoming increasingly popular as they suit spicy slow cooked curries and Oriental marinades. Allow two per head. Boneless breasts are ideal for slicing as stir-fry strips. Chicken breasts sold bone-in and with skin are best for grilling and barbecues. (Marinade them first in soy sauce, sherry, honey and a trickle of sesame oil). *Drumsticks* are the lower part of legs, good too for the barbie and for casseroles

Now the question of eating quality. Like all animals their environment and feed affect the chicken. While there are strict controls regarding the amount of space to allow each bird, the more space it gets, the happier the bird and the tastier the flesh. A high grain or corn diet without growth promoters or unnatural foodstuffs gives a better flavour and creamy colour to the flesh. Birds that grow slowly have time to develop more flavour. But rearing birds in such near natural conditions costs money, so expect to pay a lot more than for intensively reared ones. Beware of weasel words on labels, they can be misleading. Farm Fresh or Farm Assured can simply refer to battery farms. Free-range may mean the birds have some access to fresh air but they can still be housed in barns at a certain density, not necessarily pecking happily around outside. Organically reared birds have the best of all worlds, happy pecking and freedom to roam, but they can take twice as long to grow to a commercial size. A good poultry farmer will shout about his good conditions, and as regulations are strict you can be sure he won't be allowed to make it up. Top chefs might buy black leg *Poulet Bresse birds* from France or other similar French breeds – you can track these down at up-market food halls.

TURKEY

Once a Christmas time special, turkey farmers have done a good marketing job and now supply this meat all year round. However, if you want a good quality naturally reared bird outside the Christmas period then you'll probably have to order it specially. Turkey is a lean, denser meat than chicken but can be a little dry if cooked carelessly. Because of its size, cuts are more varied. *Breasts* will be sold sliced into *steaks* or *escalopes*. *Thigh meat* can be bought ready diced for casseroles or curries, whole *drumsticks* make a good two person mid-week roast (but cook them slowly for tenderness) Boned and stuffed breasts make attractive dinner party meals. *Turkey mince* is particularly growing in popularity. And it cooks so quickly too; 500g can be ready in around 10 minutes if stir-fried.

At Christmas time, if you are looking to discover the joys of old-fashioned flavour, then place an order with a speciality butcher for a *Bronze turkey* or a *Norfolk black*. You might also spot adverts for mail order free-range and organic turkey farmers who will deliver fresh birds by courier.

REARING POULTRY

A very contentious issue. The most efficient and fast method of raising birds for eating does involve factory farming. There's no escaping that if you want to produce high-protein lean meat, and for those on restricted budgets there is little choice. A chicken can grow to maturity within 6 weeks but producers increasingly will take on board that birds allowed space, clean litter and fresh air (even if it is pumped into vast barns housing thousands of birds) does produce better eating quality – a halfway house to the proper and ultimate, near-natural conditions of organic-fed, outdoor-reared, farmyard-style birds. I am old enough to remember my Aunt Alice serving me Roast Chicken in the early 1960s and I can't recall eating chicken as good since. But that may be a romantic notion. For the price of a leg of lamb from a supermarket, you can buy a wonderful bird. You get what you pay for.

DUCK AND GOOSE

The rich meat of these two birds is making increasingly popular eating. The goose is popular for special occasions. It has a high bone to meat ration so a normal size 4-kilo bird will serve only six, while a turkey of that size could stretch to ten. So, not a cheap mid-week meal. Goose meat is rich and is covered in a thick layer of the most delicious fat. In fact, I buy goose for two reasons, the delicious meat for a special meal (try one on Michaelmas Day, September 29th the traditional day for goose) and the lovely fat that trickles out during roasting. Prick the goose well all over, roast it on a large trivet and pour off the fat that gathers every half hour or so. This makes the most wonderful fat for pâtés, roast potatoes and best of all fried eggs. Make sure in advance that your oven is large enough to take a goose in a roasting tin and don't cook it without someone to help you lift it in and out of the oven. The carcass makes excellent stock.

Traditionally, ducks were available as *Lincolnshire, Aylesbury* and the larger, more gamey-flavoured *French Barbary* breeds. (Barbary breasts are called *'magrets'* and one breast is sufficient for two modest portions.) But now the big duck meat is sold as *Gressingham* (originally from a village in Lancashire where the cross between a wild mallard with a plumper Pekin duck was first achieved to give a good-eating, crispy-skin bird now reared in East Anglia). Like geese, ducks are fatty birds and if roasted whole are best pricked well all over, cooked on a trivet and the fat poured off at least twice during roasting. The breast meat can be served slightly pink but the legs are better well cooked. Duck breasts on the other hand can be cooked medium rare like steak, or sliced thinly for stir-fries. Start them in a hot, preheated, dry frying pan, skin side down (which you can slash a couple of times to look good and stop the edges curling). As fat trickles out, tip it away into a cup (save it!). After 5 minutes flip it over and cook the flesh side until the breasts feel slightly bouncy when pressed with the back of a fork. Let the breasts stand for 5 minutes before slicing on the diagonal. Season well to serve. Duck leg portions make excellent small joints and are best slow-roasted, grilled or braised. You can buy excellent ready-prepared *Chinese Pekin* or *aromatic roasted Chinese* duck with a good authentic flavour. The meat is ready to roast until very tender and then stripped from the bone in the traditional way with two forks. Packs come complete with Hoisin sauce and pancakes.

GUINEA FOWL, QUAIL, PIGEON, PHEASANT AND PARTRIDGE

I refer to these as game-style poultry. Indeed, the last three are game birds, but they all suit the same styles of cooking and accompaniments. They are not generally available as portions. Guinea Fowl (*Pintade* to the French) are similar in taste to a well-flavoured chicken. They are around 1 kilo in weight and serve two people as a special roast. Cook like young chicken.

Quails are tiny, you need about two per head unless they are partly boned and stuffed. Surprisingly, the flesh is quite well flavoured for such little creatures. They're popular in Spanish cooking, nice cooked on a bed of saffron rice in the oven and ready in under an hour.

Pigeons farmed in France are called *squabs* – plump and tender to be pan-fried medium rare like duck breast. They also come wild as *wood pigeons*. They are best braised or casseroled slowly. Because of their full flavour they can take strong sauces or spices. A couple of squares of dark chocolate melted into a red wine sauce will add interest, if only as a talking point. Allow one per head and watch out for tiny pieces of shot. Old English Pigeon Pie is made from casseroled wood pigeons, no need to bone the meat first, but it does help to cut the carcasses into four.

Pheasants are generally sold in pairs (known as a 'brace') from speciality butchers (who have to be licensed to sell game). Supermarkets sometimes sell them singly, in their more up-market stores. Hen pheasants are smaller but more tender than cock birds, but I find there's not much in it. Sometimes, you can stretch them further if you have a brace by boning out the breasts to pan-fry, removing the legs for casseroles and making rich stock or soup with the body carcasses. Cook like young chicken if they are young birds, but braise older ones.

Partridges are like smaller pheasants but slightly more gamey. Allow one per head and cook like pheasants. Traditionally served roasted on a piece of buttery toast with the pan juices poured over. Game will be sold fresh in season but most freezes well, if carefully wrapped. (See Wild Game Seasons on page 35).

GAME

Though enterprising farmers are investing in building up herds of managed
'wild' animals, it takes several years of patient breeding to build up a profitable
herd. Truly wild animals are only available during limited periods dependent
on the breeding seasons.

One advantage of game meat is that it is naturally low in fat and cholesterol.
The meat is darker in colour with thinner more golden fat layers. Because of
the lower fat content, it has a tendency to dry out during cooking and needs
frequent basting or bathing with a rich stock or sauce. Or I cover them with
butter papers. Tender cuts are best served medium rare so they remain plump
and juicy.

Venison (deer) is perhaps the best known of the farmed wild meats.
Genuine wild venison can be found in season in speciality butchers. Farmed
venison is also imported from New Zealand. As a cooking guide, treat it like
beef for casseroles, pie fillings, roasts and even pâtés, burgers and sausages,
sometimes, as it is a dry meat, you may find it has been mixed with pork
fat. There are three breeds of deer: the *red deer*, introduced by William the
Conqueror after 1066 and fiercely protected by draconian forest laws; *fallow
deer*, found gracefully grazing in landscaped parks and the smaller *roe deer*.
The breed will rarely be given at the point of sale, but on a need-to-know basis
red deer is the most gamey, roe the most tender and fallow the finest flavour.

For roasting cuts choose a saddle joint (the loin) or the haunch (top of the
leg). Fillets are the most tender and should be treated like the best beef fillet
steak. Venison liver is a rare treat and said to be delicious. Most of it goes to
the keepers or farmers. Finders, keepers!

Finally, the question of hanging. Like most red meat, venison does need
some hanging, say one to two weeks to relax the muscles and develop some
flavour. Properly hung meat will not smell.

WILD GAME SEASONS

PHEASANTS	October 1st–February 1st
PARTRIDGE	September 1st–February 1st
GROUSE	August 12th–December 10th
ROE DEER	April–October (bucks)
	October–February (does)
RED DEER	August–April (stags)
	November–February (hinds)
WILD DUCK	September–February
PIGEON	All year round
RABBIT	All year round
HARE	August–February

WILD BOAR

Europeans have enjoyed true wild boar for centuries. In Britain, they were hunted into virtual extinction by the seventeenth century. Boars are now reappearing in breeding programmes both pure breeds and crossbred with domestic pigs. Sows only have one litter a year so herds are still small. The wild boar is a natural forager, it will eat almost anything it can so the meat is full flavoured and quite dark Think of it as gamey pork. It should be hung for one to two weeks and is nicest marinated first. In cooking, treat boar like pork – the cuts are very similar. The meat makes the most wonderful sausages.

OTHER EXOTICS

At the height of the beef crisis, some supermarkets offered *ostrich* steaks as an alternative. Now if you have a predilection for the more unusual meats, then you have a wonderful choice of domesticated wild meats from speciality farms. Many offer an excellent mail order service. Barrow Boar of Yeovil, Somerset (Tel 01963 441439) have an incredible range – from *kid* and *crocodile* to *peacock* and even *locust* (really just hopping shrimp). Other delicacies include *buffalo* (like sweet beef), *kangaroo*, *emu*, and *alligator* (tastes like a cross between chicken and seafood). I have cooked up Laverstoke Park Farm buffalo burgers to my partner for some time as 'beef burgers' and he loves 'em. Very tasty, he says.

RABBIT AND HARE

Tame rabbit is much enjoyed by gourmets because of its delicate slightly sweet meat, not dissimilar to chicken. You cook it in the same manner too – legs are best casseroled, saddles (loins) roasted. You can also buy long fillets from the loin that can be sliced and pan-fried. A number of supermarkets sell rabbit meat and it is certainly becoming popular on restaurant menus. Wild rabbits and hares have a more gamey flavour and slightly darker flesh. The younger the animal the more tender its flesh, but older beasts make excellent stews, pies and pâtés.

CURED MEATS

Until around the 18th century, farmers would kill their animals at the start of winter when grazing became difficult. Rather than eat the meat all at once, they learnt to preserve carcasses using dry salt, brine and smoking. Pork and beef were the most suitable turned into bacon, hams, sausages, hocks and boiling joints. Curing meat in these ways imparted a flavour and texture that is still popular even though we can now eat fresh meat all year round.

CURING METHODS

Wet and dry curing

Wet and dry curing both increase storage times. In wet curing, cuts of meat are submerged in a salt and water brine or nowadays the meat can be injected with a brine solution to speed up the curing time. The meat remains moist and weight loss is kept to a minimum. In dry curing, the more traditional method, meat is layered with rock salt, which is left to seep into the flesh by osmosis. Government food standards allow a small percentage of 'added water' in wet cured meats and you will notice, when you open a pack of ham or bacon, that the contents are slightly wet, almost sweaty. This has to be declared on packs as 'added water'. Dry cured meat, on the other hand, has no added water and will not have a sweaty feel – it's all meat, and is regarded as being of superior quality. Flavourings such as sugars or maple can be added to the cure to give *sweetcure* or *maplecure* bacon. *Tendersweet* is a mild cure that leaves the meat felling rather moist.

Smoking

Smoking is used not necessarily to lengthen storage times but to impart flavour to meat that has been cured. (Unsmoked bacon is sometimes called 'green'.) Smoking entails the slow burning of chips of green wood – usually flavoursome oak, apple, chestnut or hickory – to give smoke but no flame. The meats are hung for varying periods in smokehouses, where they acquire a distinctive flavour. Cold smoking is carried out on cured meat, leaving it still technically uncooked but not raw as such. Hot smoking is where the temperature of the smoke is sufficiently high to cook the flesh. Cold smoked meat and fish will be served thinly sliced and can be cooked briefly, like bacon, or raw, like *Parma ham*.

PORK AND BACON

Hams and gammon come from the rear of a pig; bacon rashers from the loin and ribs; boiling bacon joints from the forequarter; and hocks from the lower legs. Technically a ham is the hind leg of a pig that is removed from a whole side and cured separately, but the terms gammon and ham are interchanged so frequently that they have become blurred. Bacon pigs are different breeds to fresh meat pigs, with longer trunks for longer rashers! The pig is very sensitive to growing conditions and diet and thrives on access to the outside. Free-range, outdoor-reared or, even better, organic pigs have a far superior flavour so check the label or pack first. These days salt cures for raw bacon are quite light and need little to no pre-soaking. Follow pack instructions for guidance.

Gloucestershire Old Spot (or GOS pigs) is a new–old designer pork that grew in popularity over the millennium years. An old breed from two centuries or so ago, it is now perfect for new tastes. Full of piggy flavour and ideal for fresh meat, sausages and bacon.

Cuts of pork and bacon

Fine quality bacon comes from Britain, Holland and Denmark where the entire bacon industry seems to centre on satisfying the British love of eggs and bacon. Gammon cuts: a whole *gammon* (hind leg) can be divided into four cuts – corner, middle, hock and slipper, which is a small triangular cut at the side. Gammon steaks are cut from the top of the leg.

Forequarter cuts: these are taken from the collar or forehock and are generally boiling joints. The meat is a little coarser and needs gentler cooking. Occasionally you can find *collar bacon* in traditional butchers, but it is an old-fashioned cut decreasing in popularity. A pity because cold and sliced it is delicious and tender.

Bacon rashers: these are mostly sold as back rashers (from the loin) or streaky rashers (from the belly). Rashers sold as top back are from the cut nearest the shoulder of a pig. Middle back rashers are very long and combine back and streaky. *Oyster cut rashers* are from the end of the back. The trend towards American and Canadian bacon cuts means we are seeing a lot more long, thin, lean streaky-style rashers which cook to a light crispness: perfect for BLT sandwiches. Most bacon is sold rindless, but there is still demand for rind-on bacon and it does tend to hold the rasher in shape as it is cooked. Check the pack to be sure of what you're getting. The best bacon is considered to be outdoor-reared (or free-range) dry-cure, available smoked or unsmoked. The flavour reward is certainly worth the extra charge.

Lardons: these are a French cut of small cubes of cured bacon which can be dry-fried and tossed into salad with a vinaigrette or used in casseroles and stews. They're good simmered gently with beans and pulses.

Pancetta: Italian cured bacon that has been flavoured with herbs and certain spices, cured between boards that flatten the rashers and sold smoked or unsmoked. The rashers are very thin and need only the briefest of cooking. British pancetta rashers are excellent, and a light take on a British eggs 'n' bacon breakfast. *Pancetta coppata* is rolled pancetta, increasingly available as regional Italian cooking becomes more popular.

Spek (speck): this is a chunk of very fatty streaky bacon, sometimes almost all fat. It's popular in Polish, German and Dutch cooking. You buy it in a piece and cook it with lentils, in soup or with sauerkraut. A leaner Italian Speck (*Speck Alto Adige*) with a distinctive smoky-sweet flavour is produced in South Tyrol. Use it finely chopped up like small lardons or slice wafer thin and fried like bacon.

SPECIALITY RAW HAMS

Cured ham, sliced wafer-thin from specially reared pigs, has been a speciality of several continental countries for centuries. Italy, Spain, Germany and France all produce hams with great traditions of rearing, curing and maturing, protected by strict codes of practice and quality controls. You can buy them packed in supermarkets or have them sliced freshly with great aplomb in front of you. They are all best eaten as antipasto spread out on plates or scrunched into loose rosettes accompanied by black pepper or slices of fresh melon, figs or gherkins. Some people like to trickle over a little extra virgin olive oil and serve with a few capers. Incidentally, the fat is a very important part of these cured speciality hams so don't remove it.

Prosciutto di Parma, perhaps the best known, is from the north of Italy, encompassing the regions of Piedmont, Lombardy, Veneto and Emilia-Romagna. The producers are gathered into an association known as the Consorzio del Prosciutto di Parma, which has the familiar gold ducal crown as a logo, just so you can check. The pigs are a specially pampered breed, fed on a grain and whey diet to ensure the famous sweet, delicate flavour of true Parma ham. The hind legs are removed from the carcass and cured separately, first in a dry salt cure then washed and dried. The hams are then beaten to soften the flesh and hung in rooms with long windows open to the fresh air. After that they are covered with a thin layer of lard and transferred to cellars for the final hanging, in which special enzyme activity develops to produce the characteristic flavour of Parma ham. The whole process can take up to a year.

Prosciutto di San Daniele is a similar high quality Parma-style ham with a pronounced flavour and darker colour.

Serrano hams from Spain are increasingly popular and are served in the same way as Parma ham. There are a number of variations but perhaps the best known is the *jamón Jabugo* produced in the heart of Andalucia. This is truly the product of very happy pigs, a particular long-legged breed of black skinned and hoofed Iberian hogs allowed to forage freely on aromatic plants and fed a diet of acorns. The legs are dry cured in sea salt, then hung to mature in bodegas for up to three years. During this time the hams are pierced with a fine bone needle, which adds to the characteristic aroma.

Westphalian hams, from Germany, are characterised by large, relatively lean slices with a distinctive charcoal-colour edge. The flesh is tender, smoky and slightly sweet. The flavour comes from a combination of juniper and beechwood. Very enjoyable. *Black Forest ham* (*Schwarzwalder*) is another type of well-flavoured air-dried and smoked ham.

Prague ham, from Czechoslovakia, is a mild cured, beechwood-smoked ham generally eaten antipasti style.

French hams: these include the well-known lightly smoked *Jambon de Bayonne* from the Basses-Pyrénées, *Jambon de Toulouse*, and many other French country hams (*jambons de campagnes*).

COOKED HAMS

Hams that have been boned then pressed into neat shapes have invariably been brine-cured quickly, contain added water and given names to suit modern marketing – fine for making sandwiches or for everyday cooking. But there are still many fine traditional cured hams sold on- or off-the-bone and sliced on demand. Most of them are British or American in style.

York ham is the best known in the UK, particularly popular as a Christmas joint. Dry cured, matured for around three months and lightly smoked with a harmless pale green mould, the York ham has a tender, lightly sweet flesh. The name is sometimes used as a 'generic' name for good-quality lean ham and may not be the 'real' thing but it's still good for eating. (I just wish they would stop covering hams with artificial golden crumbs.) If you buy a whole ham raw to cook, then it will need just a light soaking overnight.

Bradenham is a traditional Wiltshire ham, cured in molasses, spices and juniper, giving it a dark skin and unique flavour. Worth trying.

Suffolk ham are also given a light sweet cure resulting in rather pinky flesh and a light blueish bloom to the skin.

Bath chaps are the cheeks of pigs cured and cooked like hams. The name refers to the best quality, said to come from pigs in Bath in the county of Avon.

American hams include the famous *Virginia ham* from a particular breed of pig called the razorback. In past times these pigs were fed a luxurious diet of peanuts and peaches. After dry curing, the skin is covered in molasses, pepper and saltpetre, the ham is matured for a year then smoked over hickory or apple wood. The *Smithfield* is another Virginia ham from pigs fed a foraging-style diet of acorns, nuts and corn. The skin is pepper-crusted and hickory smoked.

Kassler is generally associated with Polish meats though it's made in many European countries. Kassler uses the main muscle meat from a pork loin, which is then cured and sometimes smoked. It's delicious sliced, hot or cold.

DRY CURED MEAT

Dry cured meat is made by sprinkling cuts of pork with coarse salt and nitrates. It dehydrates the moist meat, and the salty moisture then helps to brine the meat further. Sometimes extra flavourings are added, such as juniper, sugar and coriander.

CURED BEEF

Joints of beef that have been cured in brine or dry cured are a feature of a number of country's cuisines. They're particularly popular with Jewish communities who will not eat pork. Salt beef sandwiches are one of the world's great take-aways. Sometimes the salt brine will contain spices to add flavour. Curing changes the flavour and texture of the meat as well as helping to preserve it for longer. It needs to be soaked in cold water for a period of about 24 hours before simmering gently in water with vegetables. Popular cuts include the coarse-textured joints such as silverside, brisket and ox-tongue.

Corned beef is the name given to two products: traditionally, beef was dry cured with large granules of salt called corns, then boiled and served as salt beef. This is still popular in America and Ireland. However, since the days of Argentinean imports of canned beef, corned beef has meant pieces of cooked, salt beef pressed into a tin to be served sliced in sandwiches and salads.

Bresaola is air-dried, cured and pressed beef from Alpine Italy, sliced wafer-thin and served as an antipasti trickled with a little olive oil and crushed black pepper. *Bundnerfleisch* is an air-dried cured beef from Switzerland served like bresaola.

Pastrami is another American speciality, once associated only with Jewish cookery but now popular as a sandwich meat. It is a cut of brisket dry-cured in salt, sugar and spices, coated in cracked black pepper and served cooked and thinly sliced.

Beef jerky is derived from the South African *biltong*, strips of game beaten to tenderise them, then salted, spiced and sometimes smoked before being laid out and sun-dried. It's a wonder there's much left to eat. They are popular snacks, eaten like crisps, but also good tossed into salads.

SALTPETRE

Saltpetre, or potassium nitrate, is a piquant, slightly bitter substance used by some salting industries to give a good colour to cured meats on in sausage making. Without it, for example, pork pies would be grey. You cannot buy it over the counter as it is also useful for making explosives! But online it is sold for mail order in small packs. Good for Christmas spiced beef.

CURED POULTRY AND GAME

Chicken, duck, turkey and venison are suitable for the salting and smoking technique generally carried out by enterprising small producers. Smoked venison is particularly good eaten cured and raw, served in wafer-thin slices like bresaola. Personally, I find smoked chicken overpowering in flavour; darker meats are better, I think.

SAUSAGES AND SALAMIS

This is a huge area with many hundreds of styles, flavours and sizes. The scope of this book means I can give only an outline guide, which is all the more reason to encourage you to buy and try some.

Pork is the main meat but beef and occasionally lamb are stuffed into casings. Fat is important to keep the minced meat moist and tender, otherwise the sausage would be tough and dry. Fillers such as rusk and oatmeal may be mixed in to help bind the meats: sometimes blood is added with the fillers to give a differently textured sausage called a *'pudding'* or **haggis**. These puddings are boiled whole or fried in slices. There are strict guidelines covering the meat content of sausages but by and large a good rule is that 'you get what you pay for'. Top-quality sausages with nearly 100% meat (which can include fat) are as much gourmet items as the best cuts of meat. There is now a flourishing market for top-quality, butcher-style sausages with catchy names, sold at the top end of the market, e.g. The Black Farmer and The Ginger Pig.

Mostly associated with European and American cultures, sausages are popular in all climates from the hot, dry Mediterranean to cold, temperate northern Europe. Sausages can be cured and smoked, to be served raw and thinly sliced or fresh made with minced meat (usually pork but it could include beef or veal), herbs and spices. The main basic styles are French, Italian, Spanish, North African, German and Middle European. The Chinese also have an air-dried sausage, a long, skinny salami-type made from duck liver, pork, soy sauce and Chinese spices.

SAUSAGE SKINS OR CASINGS

In the days when every last bit of a slaughtered animal was used, the intestines would be washed then stuffed with a mixture of minced pork, fat, offal, spices and herbs as sausages. But now artificial casings made of cellulose can be used – edible and safe, but not the real thing. You can tell natural casings by the characteristic u-bend to the sausage when cooked. To make your own casing, try caul fat, which is the thin, flavourless membrane lining the stomach of animals. Cleaned, it is wonderful for wrapping minced meats (like faggots) or even homemade sausages.

FRESH SAUSAGES

British fresh sausages

The good old banger is enjoying a long-overdue revival in popularity. Sausage makers are rediscovering old recipes or experimenting with new ones of their own – some might say with mixed results. Many butchers are also using foreign recipes to make such classics as fresh *Toulouse* or *Merguez* sausages. The growth in small-scale, high-quality free-range meat farmers that supply mail-order meat has resulted in a growth in speciality fresh sausages, and even Michelin-starred restaurants feature creative versions of banger and mash on their menus. It's all very exciting.

The meat content of fresh sausages is governed by law and has to be declared as a minimum content. Good sausages will have 70–80% meat plus fillers, preservatives and either herb or spice flavourings. The specific recipe will give a British fresh sausage its character – *Oxford*, the meaty *Cambridge*, sage-flavoured *Lincolnshire*, and *Cumberland* sausage – sold by length, with a very high meat content of 90% and best cooked in a coil. *Venison sausages* are becoming more popular but, because the meat is very lean, pork fat is added to help to moisten it. Chipolatas are thin linked sausages, great for children, the barbecue or for serving as a trimming with Christmas turkey. *Saveloys* are a chip-shop favourite of finely minced smoked pork and cereal – a good, cheap filler invariably served with chips. They are the English version of the French *cervalas* sausage, a short pork sausage flavoured with garlic.

Black pudding is pigs' blood mixed with fat, cereals, onions, barley and spices. It is sold whole and cooked to be served sliced and fried, generally with eggs and bacon. Black pudding is also good topped with fried apple rings.

Haggis is chopped sheep's offal mixed with oatmeal, onion, suet and spices packed into a sheep's stomach, then boiled. The best make is Macsweens of Edinburgh – my Aunty's flat overlooked their shop, so I have a fond childhood memory. Haggis is usually served with mashed 'neeps', i.e. Swedish turnips.

Fresh sausages from other countries

French fresh sausages include the *boudin noir* (a blood sausage sometimes served with sauerkraut) and the *boudin blanc*, made of finely minced veal, pork and chicken. Traditionally these are part of the French Christmas feast. Eat both very fresh.

Andouilles (served sliced) and *andouilletes* are much smaller. They contain a variety of meats including iripe, plus spices and can be salted and smoked. Creole cooks have their own *Louisiana* versions which they consider indispensable in true New Orleans food.

Merguez are Algerian or Moroccan spicy sausages made with minced lamb. The minced meat is quite chunky and the flavour often fiery. They're good with couscous and in tagines (a Moroccan stew).

Italian and Spanish sausages are full flavoured, well coloured and often contain noticeable amounts of garlic and spices. *Cotechino* is a large-sized Italian sausage with wine, cloves and cinnamon, generally cooked long and slow as part of the dish *bolito miso* or served with lentils and a sweet mustard fruit relish (mostardo di fruta). Can be lightly cured and smoked. *Zampone* is sausage meat stuffed into a boned pig's trotter. The huge garlicky, finely ground pork *mortadella* (sometimes with added pistachios) is eaten cold and thinly sliced with bread or chopped into stuffings.

Chorizos, from Spain, are now very popular. They're found in Mexican cooking, too. The meat is pork and the main flavourings are garlic and paprika, their spiciness varying according to the paprika used. Chorizos are also sold smoked for slicing. *Butifarra* are milder garlic sausages from northern Spain and *Morcilla* is a blood sausage sometimes served thinly sliced and topped with a quince paste as a tapas.

German, Polish and Dutch sausages grace many a deli counter or are sold ready-wrapped from chill cabinets. They have a finely minced texture and are made with pork, sometimes with veal too. *Bratwurst*, which can be grilled or boiled in stews, is the best known. *German frankfurters* are a finely minced blend of pork and smoked bacon mixed almost to a paste then lightly smoked in the skin: they're popular throughout Europe and America. *American frankfurters* are pork and beef mixed and some of debatable quality. *Dutch smoked pork sausage* is sold packaged in a u-shape. It's already cooked for salads and is also very useful for adding flavour to stews and beanpots. They're popular with children. *Kabanos*, from Poland, are long, thin and smoky – good hot with beans or cold in salads. *Kielbasa* are a blend of pork and beef used in the hunter's stew pot called bigos, and *Krakowska* is a slicing sausage.

Kosher sausages are made frankfurter-style but with kosher beef. They're sold cooked and cured and need warming in hot water before serving.

Liver sausage is also known as *Leberwurst*. It's wrapped in a cylinder shape and sold in slices. It's paste-like texture means it can be spread like a pâté, but it can also be cut into chunks and mixed into a sausage mixture which, when sliced, has an attractive random pattern. *Zunenwurst* is a tongue sausage from Germany.

Brawns are pressed mixtures of a variety of chopped meats blended with pork fat, spices etc. and set in aspic like a mould. It's a somewhat old-fashioned (but tasty) way of using small pieces of pig meat. They're often seen in butchers shops. The French have a version called *fromage de tête*. Another old-English pressed meat cold cut is haslet, still found in pork butchers in the north of England and in supermarkets.

TIP: NEVER PRICK A SAUSAGE

Sausage makers plead with us to treat a fresh sausage with respect and

never prick it for cooking. If you prick the skin, you let out not fat but

moisture. The best way is to grill or gently fry sausages over a medium

heat and until they feel firm when pressed. Baking sausages is fine but the

skins wrinkle unless you eat them quickly. Let a cooked sausage stand for

5 minutes before you stick your fork in.

CURED SAUSAGES AND SALAMIS

Another vast subject. If you wish to improve your knowledge then try one or two new sausages at a time, tracking down traditional varieties in good Italian or Continental delis.

Some are made of finely chopped or minced meat giving a dense texture, others consist of bigger chunks including fat, making for a coarse texture almost like crazy paving. In between may be whole spices, peppercorns and seeds which, when sliced wafer-thin, add an attractive speckled look. Flavours can be gentle, perhaps with wine, or fiery with spices. Most contain garlic.

A salami is made from uncooked meat which is then smoked, or air-dried or even pickled. Some will have added colouring making them bright pink, others are rolled in cracked pepper: some have edible casings, others need to be peeled. You can buy them sliced or small and whole, which you slice yourself. Mostly they are eaten cold with crusty bread, gherkins, olives, baby onions, tomatoes or salad. Sometimes they can be cooked, sliced on top of pizza, layered into lasagnes or simmered with beans and vegetables.

Italian salamis

The Italian word *salame* comes from sale, meaning salt. There are countless Italian salamis from mild *Milano* to pungent *Napoletano* in the south. Textures range from fine through to coarse and chunky, depending on the proportion of lean meat to fat, the breed of pig (in some cases beef, wild boar and even horse flesh is included, a perfectly good quality lean meat), what it has been fed on and the spices and flavourings used.

Salami afficianados rate the *salame felino* as the best. It is made in the Parma region from the same pigs as the famous ham. It's finely minced, with a little garlic and only 20% fat, and is cured for just two months. Cremano is said to be the 'birthplace' of salami and the sausage here is coarse textured and large. A richly flavoured pork and beef salami called *salame di Fabriano* comes from central Italy. The best known, certainly outside Italy, is *Milano salami*, made from Lombardy pigs fed on a whey diet. It is quite finely textured and can be made with all pork or pork and beef mixed. Garlic, wine and spices are added and the stuffed casings matured for up to twelve months. *Salame toscano* has small visible pieces of fat, is very garlicky and studded with whole peppercorns. It is traditionally aged in local caves where it acquires a characteristic flavour. *Salame finocchiona* is speckled with fat and flavoured with fennel seeds: *Fiorentino* is similar but without fennel and larger in diameter. *Salame romano* is slightly squared, *napoletano* long and thin flavoured with red and black peppers, and *genovese* is a mixture of pork and veal.

TIP: SLICING SALAMIS

Italians suggest the larger the salami, the thinner it should be sliced,

which makes sense. Smaller salamis can be little thicker. For attractive

presentation, lay salami slices overlapping on a plate. Larger slices can

be folded in half or even in quarters to make cornets.

Other salamis

The most famous non-Italian salamis (though now also made in Italy and called *ungherese*) is Hungarian salami, made with finely minced pork, beef and pork fat flavoured with paprika, garlic and wine, then stuffed into casings that have been smoked before filling. It is then cured for about six months. *Danish salami,* made with pork, beef fat and veal, has a very distinctive bright pink colour and a definite salty flavour. The texture is finely minced. *Cervelat* is a German smoked sausage with finely minced pork and beef.

Pizza salamis

These are more American-Italian than Italian. They are thinly sliced small cured pepperoni sausages to sprinkle over pizzas flavoured with chilli or paprika. Sold ready sliced in packs, you'll find them in supermarket chill cabinets along with the long, skinny snack-size *pepperami* sausages popular with children.

French sausages

French sausages – *saucisse* – are a variety sold fresh or cured. Perhaps the best known fresh sausage is from Toulouse. It's made with coarsely chopped pork and lots of garlic and is delicious cooked in stews though best known in cassoulet with chunks of goose or duck and topped with breadcrumbs. The French have a number of salami-style cured sausages, known as *saucisson – de Lyon* is a cured mixture of pork, fat, white peppercorns and mixed spices. *Rosette de Lyon* is a rosy pink in colour and is made with finer quality pork shoulder. *Jésus* is a larger, coarsely chopped cured sausage deemed to be one of the best quality – almost heavenly, as the name suggests.

FOIE GRAS

I include notes on this expensive contentious delicacy on a need-to-know basis in case you ever find yourself cooking fresh foie gras or pondering the difference between various products called 'foie gras'. Foie gras (fat livers) are the artificially enlarged livers of geese and ducks. The former is more expensive than the latter, but many leading chefs use duck foie gras, considering it just as fine and delicious as goose.

There are two main areas of production in France: the Perigord and around Strasbourg. Fresh foie gras has to be ordered in advance from top-quality butchers. In southwest France (the old province of Gascony) farm-reared geese are hand-fed excessive amounts of grain a few weeks before slaughter. It is a sideline perk for the farmers' wives. They claim their free-range geese waddle happily towards them to have corn poured down their throats. It's probably not unlike some of us who gorge on doughnuts or pizza. In factory conditions, the geese have little option but to swallow.

One of the benefits of cooking fresh foie gras is the delicious fat that seeps out. The birds are fed a very rich diet that includes eggs, barley, potatoes and milk. They must think themselves in a foodie's paradise until the time comes for boiled maize to be funnelled down their throats (the farmers say their birds enjoy it) and they are also kept in a restricted space to minimise energy. This causes their livers to expand with fat.

The foie gras season is mid-November to January, peaking around Christmas and New Year. It's sold in lobes that should be carefully opened and any membranes, veins and blood spots gently picked out without damaging the delicate flesh. The most delicious and simple cooking method is to fry thick slices in a medium-hot pan for a few minutes until lightly browned and still bouncy to the touch. Season lightly and serve on hot toast with the pan juices poured over. Foie gras products are many and varied – in terrines layered with duck or pork or as pâté de foie gras (the best brands will contain 80% liver and flecks of black truffle) and mousse de foie gras (at around 50% liver). Spoonfuls of this pâté or mousse can be blended into sauces – divine over chicken or plump juicy steaks of fillet mignon.

FISH

There has been a noticeable revival of interest in fish, judging by the many TV programmes and books on fish, seafood restaurants, supermarket wet fish counters and new fish 'ready meal' ideas on offer. Fish farming, air transport and a willingness to try different species have seen fish counters displaying more colourful and lively displays than ever before. But this has been at some considerable cost to the health of our oceans and seas (see pages 19–20).

Fish is a first-class protein food, high in vitamins and minerals. White fish is low in fat and oily fish high in heart-friendly omega-3 fatty acids. Buy fresh fish from good traditional fishmongers where possible. Supermarkets have larger branches with wet fish counters but quality is variable, though steadily improving – they are making a determined effort. Really fresh fish will have a light slime on the skin and feel quite firm. They will have bright, glassy eyes and won't smell too 'fishy' – just sweetly of the sea. Otherwise buy fillets in packs that have been gas flushed (quite harmless) or shrink-wrapped to extend the storage life. Quality frozen fillets can be better value. Frozen at sea, they're often fresher than so-called fresh.

Much fish is sold ready filleted but if it isn't simply ask the fishmonger to fillet, and skin it if necessary. Fish is very simple and quick to cook: it cooks well on the bone under the grill, whole in the oven or just dropped on top of a barbecue. Fish is cooked when it feels firm and springy. That's it – don't overcook or it will become tough and dry.

What fish to eat that is sustainable and not endangered changes almost overnight, it seems, and also depends on where you live. I am lucky in that I live within 30 minutes of England's south coast, where I can buy beautiful fresh fish off the beach from small-scale, day-catch fishermen – fat juicy plaice, sea bass (wild), real Dover sole and cod – but that is not the case everywhere.

FRESH FISH

Flat fish

Plaice is a long-time favourite, but a little dull. Instead, try *sole* – lemon or Dover if you can afford it. *Halibut* and *turbot* are very large flat fish sold in steaks. *Brill* is in between, a manageable size with a delicate but meaty texture – a delicious fish that lives up to its name!

Oily fish

Oily doesn't mean greasy, just firmer and richer in flavour. The best-known oily fish is *salmon,* now so wildly available as farmed salmon it has become cheaper than cod. Wild salmon or *sea trout* (and the younger *grilse*) are very seasonal (February to the summer) and not cheap. *Mackerel* is rich, delicious and excellent value: try it grilled, soused or barbecued. *Herrings* are very good value too. *Farmed trout* is nearly always on sale. If you buy direct from trout farms the fish will have shiny blue hues to the skin – cook it quickly and taste a really fresh fish.

Warm water fish

Air freight has meant that we can have a choice of fish from around the world but many of these now can be endangered (see pages 19–20). Even farmed fish and prawns may not be sustainable. There are different coloured *snappers, swordfish, breams, red mullets, squids, tilapia, parrot fish, pornfrets, mahi-mahi (dolphin fish)* and *marlin* – the list is almost endless.

White fish

The flaky chunky round fish loved on both sides of the Atlantic, such as cod and *haddock,* is becoming increasingly expensive as stocks become overfished. So, expect to pay a premium price or, better still, experiment and switch to other species such as *hake, whiting, pollock, dogfish* (rock salmon), *conger eel* and *coley.* The gourmet's choice is sea bass, but its price will make it for special occasions only.

CURED FISH

Wherever there are fishing communities there are traditions of salting, smoking and drying excess catches. Curing fish changes textures, natural flavours and sometimes colours.

Salting and drying are logical means of preserving because of their connection with the sea: fish is speedily filleted, then packed in salt to extract moisture and prevent bacterial growth. Air drying prolongs the storage life into years. Smoking adds flavour and also extends storage times. The simplicity of these methods has encouraged the growth of many cottage industries in remote island and coastal communities, to our great benefit. Many suppliers are owner managed, surely a guarantee of commitment to quality.

Salting your own fish

You can salt fish at home – it doesn't take long. Simply place a large thick fillet of cod, haddock or salmon in a long dish and cover with about two good handfuls of rock salt or sea salt flakes. Add some crushed fresh parsley stalks and lay a platter or tray on top of the fish to hold it down gently. Store in the fridge for 24 hours, after which time you will note much moisture has exuded. Rinse the fish well in cold water, then poach it gently until just firm. You will notice how the texture has changed and the flavour is quite delicious, not at all salty. Flake the flesh and use it in fish cakes or pies.

Smoked salmon

Salmon is a rich, oily fish that preserves well. After filleting and trimming, whole sides of salmon are packed in layers of sea salt until cured, then rinsed and hung up to smoke at a low temperature so the flesh remains uncooked. The variations depend on the recipe for the cure (some contain sugar or honey), length of curing and the mixture of wood shavings or, sometimes, peat. Cheaper smoked salmon has been injected with a salt brine and given a light smoking, or even covered with a liquid smoke. Quality smoked salmon is more selective.

The smoked salmon industry owes much to Eastern European Jewish immigrants to 19th-century London, who brought with them techniques of salting and smoking Baltic salmon. Finding fresh Scottish salmon considerably superior, they started up smokehouses in London's East End, importing perfect wild fish from the Highlands. The canny Scots then applied the same techniques to their own salting traditions, developing a fuller-flavoured smoke. The London cure still remains more subtle and the Scottish richer. Few London smokehouses remain. The best is Forman's, (www.formanandfield.com) with a high-quality connoisseur's product supplying leading hotels, good food halls and a large international market, particularly in Italy and the Far East, where fat-belly salmon is the preferred choice. Located near the Olympic Park in London's East End, Forman's is one of the few houses still smoking wild salmon, using sides they have frozen during the season. Freezing makes the darker lean flesh more receptive to curing and smoky flavours and is regarded as the gourmet's choice.

Farmed salmon has certainly changed the whole industry and producers are now concentrating on rearing fish on feedstuffs as near to a wild diet as possible and in lochs with currents to encourage the fish to swim and develop lean muscle. Around the Scottish islands, farms are placed to benefit from the strong natural currents swirling around the shores. Individually named smokehouses will supply a better product, so check packaging carefully. Look for lean slices unless you prefer the belly slices with wider fat lines.

You can find at speciality food halls super trimmed salmon fillets (the fillet steak of salmon) and royal fillets or the *Tsar's fillet*, which are cured and lightly smoked in the old Russian style to be served cut into half-moon slices.

Hot smoked salmon is a relatively new idea followed by a number of smokehouses. After curing, sides or portions of salmon are smoked at a temperature high enough to lightly cook them. They're rather good, actually – certainly more tasty than boring poached salmon.

Other cured fish varieties

Gravadlax is another Baltic speciality, associated with Sweden. Sides of salmon are salted with a mixture of sea salt, sugar, crushed dill and spices. It's served in D-cut wafer-thin slices, usually with a sweet mustard dressing.

Smoked sturgeon: the sturgeon is a primeval-looking fish with a tough snake-like skin and flesh not unlike that of the catfish, to whom it is distantly related. The flesh is rich and not terribly exciting, but smoked it is quite enjoyable and something of a novelty. After all, there has to be some use for the flesh of the fish after we take the eggs for *caviar*. Slice it thinly and serve like smoked salmon.

Smoked halibut, a product of Greenland, is served in the same way as salmon – that is thinly sliced and uncooked. The curing is light and uses a little honey. The smoking is light too and over juniper, which imparts a golden colour. A combination of smoked halibut and smoked salmon makes an attractive party platter.

Haddock, cod, *bloaters* and *kippers* are also cold smoked fish. Unlike salmon they all need a light poaching in water, although kippers are nicest grilled and brushed with melted butter, or they can be microwaved on a medium setting. Haddock and cod are cured in the same way as salmon but, because they are white fish, the texture is drier and not so amenable to slicing. They develop a yellow hue when smoked naturally but this can also be applied artificially with dyes which you can tell easily if you look at a cut section – the colour will be a thin yellow line on top of the flesh and won't extend through to the white underneath. Golden fillets are dyed cod fillets. Naturally cured dyed haddocks have a superior flavour and smell faintly of wood smoke. The top choice is whole *Finnan haddocks*, split and opened up. Poach them in mixed milk and water topped with knobs of butter and grated fresh nutmeg. It's the best fish for a good kedgeree and good, too, topped with a poached egg for a special supper.

Boning kippers

A whole kipper is much easier to bone than you might think.
(Boned fillets may still have many annoying pin bones in them.)
After cooking you simply scrape off the thin layer of cooked flesh
on top of the long central bone, ease the point of a fish knife under
the bone at the tail end, then gently lift up the whole skeleton with
the tail. Most of the bones attached to the central bone will come
away easily. Any that do not can just be pinched off.

Bloaters are a speciality from Yarmouth in Norfolk. They are lightly salted and smoked herrings. They're good grilled or fried. Or cook them, remove the flesh and as many bones as possible, then mash with butter for a quick pâté – the old-fashioned bloater paste. *Sprats* are small herrings, cured and smoked. Just serve them whole. Kippers are also cured and smoked herrings but they're given a longer salting and fuller smoking, depending on the individual style of the area in which they're cured. Kippers hail from many old fishing centres: those remaining are Craster in Northumberland (slightly sweet flavour, lovely mahogany colour), Manx on the Isle of Man and Loch Fyne from Scotland. At one time it was fashionable to marinate uncooked kipper fillets in vinaigrette to serve as a starter with salad.

Arbroath smokies are another variation on the cured and smoked haddock theme but these are small, filleted fish sans head and tails. After curing in salt they are hot smoked over peat, at a temperature sufficiently high to lightly cook the flesh. A speciality of the Aberdeen area around Abroath.

Smoked eel: though a traditional product in that we have enjoyed smoked eel for some time, it is becoming fashionable as a starter in restaurants, and small-scale smokeries are springing up. Demand is also building up through quality mail-order catalogues. The eels are smoked still in their skins, unlike fresh eel, which is skinned first. The flesh is rich and well flavoured, so you don't need much. And as they are hot smoked you don't need to cook them either: just skin and flake. They're very tasty with scrambled eggs on toast.

Smoked trout is a hot-smoked fish sold in handy-serve fillets. It's good with a little horseradish cream and salad.

Hot-smoked mackerel fillets are richly flavoured, sold as whole fillets or in long strips. Pepper-crusted fillets are one of my favourites, especially flaked into a crusty roll with tomato. Try smoked mackerel flaked and mixed into pasta or rice salads with a mayonnaise dressing.

Quick smoked fish pâté

Skin and flake about 300g (10½oz) of hot smoked fish, checking carefully for pin bones. Place in a bowl and mash with a fork. Melt about 50g (1¾oz) of sunflower or olive oil spread and mix into the fish along with 1tbsp of thick set natural yogurt. Add a crushed garlic clove or 2 finely chopped salad onions (or both). Add lots of freshly ground black pepper, a little fresh grated nutmeg and a good squeeze of fresh lemon juice. Spoon into a small bowl or dish and fork the top attractively. If liked, you could sprinkle over some smoked paprika to garnish. Chill until lightly firm. Good for healthy hearts.

CANNED FISH

Where would we be without one or two cans of fish in the storecupboard, ready to fall back on when times are hard or we've forgotten to shop? Canned fish is cheap and nourishing but very tasty. Canned fish is sometimes whole fish, or more usually prime cuts of wild ocean fish layered into a can with a little added salt for flavour, then sealed and heated to a temperature sufficiently high to cook and sterilise it. Even bones soften under the pressure and can be eaten to provide calcium. Inside the can the fish makes its own cooking juice, which you should try to use as well. Whole rich fish can be sealed in oil – cottonseed, sunflower or occasionally olive. Please do check that canned fish (especially tuna) is pole and line caught.

Canned fish varieties

Big fish-eating nations can many fish, chiefly oily fish like herrings, *sardines*, *sild*, *pilchards* (the same family, just different sizes), mackerel and tuna.

Sardines are the best-known canned fish but are fading from fashion which is a pity as I find them delicious. Spanish sardines are sold canned in tomato juice or lemon oil to add variety.

Tuna is the most contentious canned fish. Drag netting is far too efficient a method of catching fish for many, who say we are in danger of leaving sterile seas empty of life. We may get a lot of cheap food from the sea but at the cost of sustainable fish stocks. Dolphins are one of the many natural casualties. Pole and line-caught tuna is more acceptable with less damage to other species. So check the label on the can. *Skipjack* (yellowfin) tuna is lighter meat from the Pacific *bonito* tuna. Canned tuna is available in oil (soya, sunflower or olive) or the rather dreary brine.

Shellfish can be canned, and preparation requires removal of hard shells. The flavour and texture are different from the fresh originals, but I still find them excellent for homely meals. Look for canned *prawns*, *crab meat* (especially good-quality white crab meat), *smoked oysters* and *smoked mussels* (both oriental specialities, and both nice on toast).

Alaska wild salmon, with the characteristic 'US Salmon' logo, will be familiar to many families. The Pacific teems with wild salmon, a different species from Atlantic salmon but they make good eating. Middle cuts of salmon are sealed in cans with just a little salt. Red salmon is the high-grade *Sockeye salmon:* pink is another variety. Both can be used in the same way – for salads, sandwiches, mousses, even pasta sauces and fish cakes.

Caviar and roes

For thousands of years gourmets have enjoyed the roes (or eggs) of certain fish, from the humble herring roe to taramasalata.

Caviar is the roe of sturgeon fish and is simply salted and packed to preserve it. It is taken only from mature fish of at least ten years old (some sturgeon can reach 100 years old). There are varieties of sturgeon all over the world but the ones that produce the finest caviar are locked into the inland Caspian Sea, some 900 miles long and bordering Russia in the north where the waters are chilly down to the warmer shores of Iran in the south. Because of the collapse of the former Soviet Union and strict controls, Russian production was suspended until 2011 to allow stocks to regenerate. The Iranians are now thought to have more control over the consistent quality of their caviar. Look for blue tins with the brand name Caspian caviar. If you can, check that the caviar eggs are not sold bruised or oily. Once opened, keep the tin chilled and use within a few days – if it lasts that long uneaten!

There are four main varieties of caviar and their value depends on rarity factors. Top of the rarity stakes is *Beluga caviar*, with its delicate texture, silver grey colour and creamy, almost buttery taste. *Imperial caviar* is a brilliant gold colour with a mild, nutty flavour and produced only by albino Caraburun sturgeon. *Osietra* (pronounced 'o-cee-tra') is popular with caviar aficionados for its firmer texture and nutty texture, while *Sevruga* is the most widely available. Caviar from farmed sturgeon is now produced in southwest France, where these fish were fished in the rivers for generation.

Salmon eggs, from Atlantic or Pacific salmon (also known as keta) are a translucent orangey-red, slightly larger than caviar. They're nice as a garnish or on blinis. An affordable alternative to caviar.

Lumpfish roe is the red or black eggs of lumpfish (whose only commercial purpose seems to be as a provider of eggs). It's quite salty and a bit runny, but good as an all-purpose quick garnish.

Smoked cod's roe: the whole roes of female cod are cured and smoked still encased in their membrane. Peel off the membrane, then eat the thick, slightly sticky roe spread on thin toast. Or blend it with fresh white breadcrumbs, olive oil, garlic, lemon juice and a little water to make a homemade taramasalata, much nicer than the lurid pink, grainy, salty cream sold in supermarkets. In Greece, taramasalata is traditionally made with the smoked roe of grey mullet, also known as 'tarama'.

SALTED FISH

The award-winning American author Mark Kurlansky called his book *Cod: The Fish That Changed History*. The central theme is the consequences of the great demand for salt cod in many communities on both sides of the Atlantic. In the days prior to refrigeration and freezing, salting cod was the only sure way of ensuring a year-round supply of good, cheap protein. Even today *salt cod* is a mainstay of Iberian and West Indian cuisines.

Basically, salt cod (also known as bacalao) is simply filleted or split cod, salted and dried. In Spain you can buy the whole fish split open, otherwise salt cod is sold in slabs of varying sizes. Buy chunky pieces because they are better value and have more flesh than tail pieces and look for creamy-coloured flesh: yellow flesh is ageing. To soak, cover in cold water for 24–48 hours, changing the water frequently. Be warned, it can smell very unappetising but once cooked and flaked it takes on a delicious flavour and texture. Really good used in fish and tomato stews, fishcakes or brandade, a classic French fish and potato 'pâté' made with salt cod.

Stockfish is large white fish (cod, hake or ling), split and gutted, head removed, then left to dry without prior salting until very dry and hard (so hard that in Italy it is beaten to break it up before soaking, and in parts of Germany and Scandinavia it is soaked for days in several changes of lye water).

Anchovies, another member of the herring family, are part of a long tradition of salting tiny fish to use as a flavouring. The Romans had 'rotting garum', the Thais have their *nam pla* (see pages 271–2) and the British anchovy essence and Gentleman's Relish. Dishes using anchovies don't actually taste 'fishy' but they are delicious. Anchovy is the English name: in Spain they are *boqueron*, in Italy *acciughe*, and in Turkey *hamsi* where they're cooked with rice, currants, cinnamon, sugar, onion and anchovies to make an unlikely but memorable pilaff. In the south of France, Spain and Sicily anchovies are sold in coarse salt, loose in boxes. You open them up, rinse and use them tender and full of flavour. In Britain, we are mainly confined to little fishy strips in small cans, swimming in oil which causes the flesh to harden. Though these are fine for cooking, you can find jars of salted anchovies in good food halls and delis; they can be rinsed, then dressed in oil and lemon juice and tossed into green salads. Anchovies add a mysterious flavour to a dish if first sautéed slowly in olive oil with garlic until they melt into a paste. Try this paste mixed with chopped black olives and tossed into pasta with a few fennel seeds. My personal favourite is anchovies cooked slowly with sliced red onions as a dressing for crisp green cabbage or lightly boiled broccoli. You can buy anchovy as in tubes or as a bottled sauce for adding a quick bite to cheese sauces.

Salted herrings and *matjes* are Eastern European specialities popular in Jewish homes. Salted herrings are covered in coarse salt and have to be soaked and rinsed before use. Matjes are preserved in a lighter brine and can be eaten after a quick soaking in either water or milk. Serve them dressed with lemon juice, sliced onions and soured cream.

SEAFOOD

Like fish, this can be a large area for study, so I'll just outline principles. Seafood from icy cold waters tastes sweeter, and some would say has a finer flavour. Certainly cold water prawns are preferred for many seafood dishes to warm water ones, which are more suited to hot spicy sauces. Chefs prefer to buy *lobsters* reared in cold Atlantic waters, crabs and *langoustines* (Dublin Bay prawns) taste better and thick king-sized scallops have a sweeter flavour from the cold Scottish Highland waters (even better if hand dived). Having said that, seafood from tropical waters has good, firm flesh and tempting bright colours which suit stir-fries, char-grilling and aromatic steaming. Much tropical seafood is reared on fish farms, so quality is consistent, but there are concerns about environmental damage to the coastlines. Certainly, the great variety of warm water prawns has increased competition and made it more affordable.

When buying seafood from fishmongers' counters check whether it is genuinely fresh or previously frozen. It should say on the price tag. You need to know because, while seafood freezes well, it does leech water on thawing which can affect cooking. The more moisture that seeps out, the less there is to keep the flesh succulent, so the quickest and lightest of cooking should suffice. This is fine for prawns but not for scallops: I find I can rarely get a nice caramelised browned colour on thawed small queen scallops – they just seem to get more watery. So keep thawed scallops to drop into creamy sauces.

Lobsters and crabs

Crabs and lobsters are daunting for first-time buyers but most are sold ready cooked. When buying lobsters, ask for hen lobsters as they have a greater flesh to shell ration so are better value. Don't feel they have to be perfect specimens unless you intend using them for show: many chefs buy cripples missing the odd claw or two – the shell meat is still sweet. A fishmonger will go through the intricacies of extracting the meat for you, or you can just cut them in half lengthways, in which case you just need to remove the olive-green brain and dark intestine line.

If faced with cooking a live lobster, first ensure the claws are well muzzled with bands. The RSPCA suggested humane cooking method is to place the lobsters in the freezer for about 2 hours. They then go into hibernation and can be boiled or split and grilled according to taste.

Crabs are tricky: best buy them ready dressed. After all, the meat is all you need them for. European crabs have white and brown meat – the brown is from the body shell, the white from the claw. American crabs are all white meat. Mix the brown meat with some fresh brown breadcrumbs plus seasoning and lemon juice, or do as I do and save it to add to fish sauces or mix into a quiche.

If you like exploring at weekends, let me recommend a trip to the crab capital of Britain – Cromer on the Norfolk coast – or further south at Selsey, near Chichester, where you can buy them from the beach huts. It's a charmingly genuine seaside town with old tractors hauling small fishing boats up on to the beach and, best of all, fish shops selling fresh dressed crabs at very tempting prices. Buy two each and a crusty loaf of bread and enjoy a beach picnic in the tradition of a bygone age.

Oysters

Oysters are enjoying a revival too. In the 19th century the poor of the industrialised cities were nourished on a surfeit of oysters. The British cast them aside as our living conditions improved: the French sensibly would not let snobbery come before their love of good food and continued to enjoy them. France, especially along the southwest coast, is Europe's biggest supplier, with oyster beds (or *parcs*) stretching from the Charente estuary in the north or the Marennes-Oléron and onto the Archacon Basin. Here, tidal waters refresh the oysters twice a day.

Oysters are mostly farmed (and have been since Roman times), like mussels but on raised beds to keep them off the sandy bottom. Many oyster beds were established by the Romans – in Colchester and Whitstable, for example. Now we have two types – *natives* (or *belons*, as the French call them) and *rock* or *Pacific oysters*, with their slightly elongated craggy shells. The latter are the most popular on sale – the hinges are slightly easier to snap open, which helps.

Oyster opening is more about skill and cunning than brute strength. Buy a short stubby oyster knife (or a special opener that will prise a shell open). Wrap your left hand well in a double thickness of tea towel and hold the oyster cup-side down. Stick the point of the knife in at the edge of the hinge at the narrow end and firmly wriggle it in, taking care not to chip the shell or you will get pieces in the oyster. You will find there will be a moment when the hinge seems to relax, at which point you can stick the knife in further and quickly run it under the top shell to lever off the lid. Don't tip out the juices; these are to be swallowed too. Slip the knife under the lower part of the flesh and loosen it.

Serve oysters on a bed of crushed ice or rock salt or an oyster plate, with a wedge of fresh lemon, a dash of Tabasco sauce or, my favourite, a little red wine vinegar mixed with chopped shallots. The French like them with thin spicy sausages, their idea of surf and turf. Swallow whole, if you like, or bravely chew. They are delicious either way.

Seafood in shells

Mussels, clams and *oysters* are becoming more readily available and we seem less frightened to use them. There is also a good selection of ready-cooked seafood like squid rings, whelk meat and seafood cocktail mixtures that should encourage use. A favourite buy for a pasta sauce is a frozen seafood mixture of mussels, squid, prawns and clams, which my children greatly enjoyed tossed into a tomato sauce.

A 1kg bag of fresh mussels may look daunting to the novice, but give them a quick steam in a large covered pan with a little white wine, onion and butter and the shells obligingly open after a few minutes. Within another 10 minutes you'll have picked the meat from the shells (there's no need to fillet, bone or skin a mussel) and you'll have a good hearty meal for two within 20 minutes.

Ireland and France have farmed mussels on ropes for decades in quite clean sea inlets, keeping them sand free. During a holiday visit to Bantry Bay I imagined the sweet flavoured mussels quietly and contentedly growing under the tranquil waters. New Zealand fish producers export large greenshell mussels by air, generally on sale on the half shell and cooked to be eaten cold, but also ready to be reheated topped with some garlicky butter and Parmesan crumbs.

Clams range in size from baby ones about 3cm across to the larger 8cm across, and to long razor clams, depending on the season. Supermarket wet fish counters have helped to bring them to our attention but often some of the clams will have started to open, which means they are not suitable for eating. However, at least we are beginning to see what they look like and perhaps we'll be encouraged to buy a few next time.

Squid

Squids are farmed in many parts of the world, and supplies come to us from as far away as the Falkland Islands. Most are ready-prepared either whole (with tentacles tucked into the cleaned body cavities) or sliced into rings. Cook squid very quickly or it will turn tough and chewy.

EGGS, DAIRY AND TOFU

HENS' EGGS

In the United Kingdom we eat an average of two eggs a week per person, which, considering their nutritional value, ease of cooking and good value, is a surprisingly low figure. Eggs are the cook's best friend – invaluable in so many dishes and recipes, adding richness and lightness, and they are good emulsifiers for sauces such as mayonnaise and custard. So, why aren't we eating more?

Before intensive egg farming, egg laying was seasonal and supplies dropped during the winter. Chickens were reared in back yards or on small farms, pecking around in yards, orchards and fields, fed whole grains or gleaning food from a wide variety of whatever sources were available. This varied diet gave eggs flavour and made strong shells. Small-scale producers or 'good life' rural folk may still deliver eggs with the flavour of a bygone age, but in general our egg supply is in the hands of an industry that is highly efficient and heavily regulated. But we can break free of this if we look around. If you want truly free-range/organic eggs, buy from local small holdings.

The quality of hens' eggs depends on the method of rearing, about which there is never-ending debate. Basically, the closer to nature hens are reared, the less stressed they are and the finer the flavour of the egg. However, the colour and quality of the shell – white, brown, speckled, fragile or hard to crack – depends on the breed and feed and is not an indication of the nutritional value of the egg inside. The yolk colour is determined by the feed. But we all have a cosy idea of the 'wholesomeness' of an egg and associate brown-speckled shells and deep yellow yolks with happily pecking hens. Some of these perceived qualities can, anyway, easily be manipulated by breeders. In the USA eggs are sold white and in the UK they are brown. Inside, they are the same; one is no better than the other.

Large-scale egg producers can appeal to our better nature by using terms like 'Farm Fresh', 'Cheerful Chickens', etc, but modern poultry farming still rears egg-laying birds by the thousands throughout the seasons. Battery birds are now described as 'cage birds'.

Egg production

Battery-farmed eggs are the cheapest and the most contentious. Critics have long expressed concerns about rearing conditions for the birds, the quality of their formulated feed (which can include animal protein), the number of birds reared per square metre, hygiene and flavour of the eggs. But, for those on a limited budget, these eggs provide a good cheap source of protein, vitamins and minerals.

Deep-litter eggs are laid by birds on straw or other litter that is sufficiently deep to protect the newly laid eggs from damp or infestation. But the birds are still housed indoors, and fresh straw or sawdust is just sprinkled on top.

Barn eggs are laid by hens reared in large 'barns', not cages, so they are able to move about more freely and their conditions are slightly better. But they may be fed a diet similar to that of battery hens.

Free-range eggs are from hens that are allowed access to outside runs with a lower density of birds. It can still be a highly intensive system but with further refinements to combine the attributes of old-fashioned rearing techniques with modern feedstuffs and limited access to the outside.

Some supermarkets will have their own requirements of egg producers, such as 'farm-assured' labelling to regulate flock size, access to natural pasture, good housing and natural light. Beak trimming (to stop stressed hens pecking each other) and growth promoters in food are banned and visits for inspection and medication are carried out by independent vets. It's a better halfway house.

Grain-fed eggs have been laid by birds fed as near as commercially possible to a natural grain-based diet. This may not necessarily mean the birds are happy, clucking, farmyard hens but a good grain diet does give a better-tasting egg with nicely coloured yolk.

Organic eggs are becoming more prevalent and score highly on the nice person's eating guide. They are all free range, with lower stocking densities, fed a natural diet, reared by farmers who subscribe to organic principles – and probably talk to their hens each day to boot. Although more expensive, when you consider what good value an egg is in relation to its usefulness and nutrition, the cost for half a dozen or so organic eggs is still much cheaper than many other foodstuffs. It's the way to go.

Storing and using eggs

Clever technology means that all eggs can now be individually marked with their packing date by means of an ingenious device that air-puffs an imprinted figure on each shell. So it's easy to check and buy the freshest you can. In general, eggs will store well for a good two weeks so long as the shell is not cracked, dirty or wet. Eggshells may seem fragile and porous but they are also good filters of airborne bacteria, though not necessarily bacteria from close contact, if shells are cracked.

Intensively reared/battery farmed eggs have thinner shells and so are more prone to cross-contamination from salmonella and other bad bugs. *These eggs are best stored at the bottom of the fridge*, not in the door where they might become too cold and even freeze. If used in baking or boiled, they should be left out at room temperature for a good half hour then they will not crack when boiled and will whisk to a better froth, incorporate more easily into a cake mix, make a smoother mayonnaise and so on. *Fresh free-range or organic eggs can be stored out of the fridge* in egg racks or their boxes, so long as they are used within their date marking.

Should you have the luck to get eggs the same day they are laid they will be absolutely wonderful eaten boiled or scrambled, but fiendish to cook with. I once gathered three warm just-laid eggs from a hen house to make mayonnaise and could not understand why it kept curdling. I realised later they were just too fresh to emulsify with the oil. Very fresh eggs are also difficult to peel when hardboiled.

An egg in the peak of freshness will have a yolk that sits proud of the white when cracked on to a plate. As an egg ages the albumen proteins in the whites start to break down and spread thinner, while the yolk gets flatter. It will still be safe to eat but won't taste as good. Mind you, slightly stale eggs do bake better because they will have evaporated slightly and the proteins will be more concentrated. In fact, chefs prefer to use older egg whites for meringues and soufflés as they whisk to a firmer foam. Another test of an egg's freshness is to drop it gently into a deep glass of cold water: if it sinks quickly it's fresh; if it floats the air sac at the top of the shell is increasing so it's not as fresh as it could be.

Eggs out of the shell can be frozen – useful if you have separated yolks or whites leftover. Yolks need to be lightly beaten with a little salt or sugar to stabilise them. But do remember to label them: one blob of golden thawing yolk looks the same, sweet or salty and you won't know whether to use it in a custard or a quiche!

Eggs for children, the frail, the elderly and pregnant women must be well cooked. For everyone else, in dishes that require raw or lightly cooked eggs, e.g. cold soufflés, mayonnaise or crème anglaise, use top organic or quality free-range eggs. Yet even with high-quality produce, there always remains a slight risk of contamination with raw eggs.

Egg size and quality

It's all so confusing. At first we had pullet, small, medium, large and extra large/giant sizes. Then, for a few years, eggs were given size gradings. Now, we are back to large, medium, etc. The general sizes are from 58–63g medium, and 63–73g large. Very large eggs are 73g and over (sometimes sold as 'Biggies'), and much smaller eggs below 53g. Farm shops and roadside egg sellers may have a variety of egg sizes. At the end of the day, unless you are a precise cake baker, medium or large are interchangeable.

The British egg industry has introduced the lion symbol as a guarantee of eggs produced to the highest quality, a description that embraces welfare and hygiene but not necessarily flavour or organic rearing conditions. Class categories for eggs refer to their freshness: most eggs sold are Class A, the freshest; class B may have been stored for longer but at low temperatures so they're still edible but not as fresh; class C go straight to manufacturing.

OTHER EGGS

The vast majority of eggs sold are hens' eggs. But there should be a great choice of size, flavour and richness because, of course, all poultry lay eggs – ducks, geese, gulls, quails, even turkeys.

Duck eggs

Duck eggs are good country fare, increasingly sold at farm gates, with their white or pretty 'duck-egg blue' shells and rich flavour. Reckon on sizes one and a half times bigger than hens' eggs. Because the shells of duck eggs are thin they are prone to contamination from the salmonella bacteria so, if you use a duck egg, make sure it is well cooked. Duck eggs are brilliant in homemade cakes, scones and lemon curd. And they make delicious scrambled eggs.

Game bird eggs

Gulls' eggs are totally wild, plucked from seaside or marsh nests, and have a slight fishy taste. They are only allowed to be collected from the first of May for three or four weeks. They are traditionally served boiled and shelled to dip into celery salt at picnics or parties. *Pigeon eggs* can be found in Chinese restaurants. *Plovers' eggs* are now not allowed to be sold. *Quails', pheasants' and partridges' eggs* are available from certain game bird suppliers. Check out online.

Goose eggs

Goose eggs are up to twice the size of hens' eggs and have very tough white shells. Treat them as you would duck eggs. They, too, are rich and eggy and make the greatest cakes. But make sure they are well cooked.

Quails' eggs

These very small and dainty eggs are sold in boxes of twelve. Their speckled grey shells are devilish to peel but very decorative. For some reason you'll find them nestled in the cold cooked meats or cheese cabinets in supermarkets. They take 3 minutes to hardboil, 1 minute to softboil, but mostly they are served hardboiled and halved as a garnish, or made into baby Scotch eggs. Chef's trick: soak quails' eggs in vinegar water for five minutes before boiling for easier peeling.

COWS' MILK

Doorstep sales of milk have fallen dramatically in recent years, which is deeply regrettable, although one benefit is not being waken at 4am by the clink clink of rattling bottles and happily whistling milkmen. But farm-gate and local dairy sales are very much alive, including old-fashioned raw or unpasteurised milks.

Fat levels in milk

Whole milk has a fat content of 4%: *semi-skimmed milk* contains 1.7% fat; *skimmed milk* is virtually fat free at about 0.1%. Fat levels affect the mouth feel of milk, which in turn affects the flavour. There are those who find the creamy taste of whole milk too rich and sickly, and others who think skimmed milk tastes thin and watery. Semi-skimmed is the more popular option. Skimmed milks have proportionally higher levels of calcium, but should not be given to children under the age of five years – they need the extra calories from the fat for energy. At the luxury end is a higher fat milk which contains 5–8% fat. It comes from Jersey and Guernsey cows and used to be sold as *'gold top'*: it's sometimes sold now as **breakfast** or **Channel Islands milk**. *'Half-and-half'* is an American name for a half-cream, half-milk mixture that is usually added to coffee.

Types of milk

Most milk sold in the UK is *pasteurised*, including some *organic*, that is heat treated to destroy harmful bacteria.

Unpasteurised or *raw milk* has a fresher, sweeter flavour and a number of passionate devotees. The herds have to be certified as brucellosis-free and strict hygienic dairy practices ensure the milk is safe to drink. However, as a precaution, do not give raw milk to young children, the frail, elderly people or pregnant women.

Homogenised milk has been forced through a fine aperture to distribute the fat globules evenly throughout the liquid, giving it a whiter colour and uniformly creamy taste. Most milk sold now is homogenised.

Triple-filtered, lactose-free, etc, milk is very obliging. It can be processed to suit a variety of lifestyles. For example, if you are a single or small household, then fresh milk that keeps for 7–21 days is a plus. Production dairies can filter out bacteria or potentially allergic lactose.

Sterilised milk is homogenised milk that is bottled and then given a further heat treatment just below boiling point for 20 minutes. This helps it to keep without refrigeration until opened.

UHT/longlife milk is a homogenised milk that has been heat treated at temperatures higher than those reached for pasteurisation but for only one second, after which it is cooled rapidly and packed. Unopened, it will keep for a good year without refrigeration: once opened you should treat it as fresh milk. It's useful when camping and in emergencies, but some people dislike the slightly caramelised flavour.

Evaporated milk starts as fresh milk that has had up to 60% of its water removed by evaporation. This gives it a slightly toffee flavour and thick, glossy texture. Evaporated milk now comes in lighter-fat versions.

Sweetened condensed milk is a sweetened milk with added sugar that is boiled for more than 2 hours until sticky and reduced. It's good for making into homemade sweets. Like evaporated milk, it's now available in lighter-fat versions. The popularity of one dessert – banoffee pie – which requires cans of condensed milk boiled for up to 2 hours until caramelised, has spawned a new niche market: toffee or caramelised condensed milk. Argentinian cooks have used this for decades, ready-reduced as *dulce de leche* – sweet milk. So, cut the boiling and buy a jar, then just scoop out into a baked pastry case over a layer of sliced bananas and top with whipped cream and dusted drinking chocolate.

Buttermilk is still popular in certain parts of Britain and in the USA. It's the liquid that drains from butter making, so the fat has been removed. It makes a very refreshing chilled drink but also has a use in traditional baking because it is acidic and when mixed with alkaline bicarbonate of soda becomes a raising agent. It makes wonderfully light scones, soda bread and cakes. However, most of the buttermilk sold these days is specially cultured to resemble traditional buttermilk and is slightly thickened. It does keep for some time in the fridge.

OTHER MILKS

Concerns about cows' milk allergies, coupled with a rise in small-scale dairy farming have led to a rise in the availability of *goats'* and *sheep's milks* plus milk-like soya and rice drinks. *Goats' milk* in particular has proved a godsend to many an anxious parent of an allergic child. It's similar in structure to cows' milk but more digestible, albeit a bit sharper. Sheep's (or ewes') milk is richer than cows' milk and slightly sweeter.

Our human food culture includes the consumption of milk from cows, which can cause problems for those who find it hard to digest the milk sugar (lactose) contained in it because we may be low in the enzyme lactase. Symptoms include bloating, cramps, nausea and flatulence. Some sufferers find that *lactose-free milk*, treated with added lactase, helps ease their symptoms. It's worth a try, especially if you have IBS (irritable bowel syndrom).

Rice milk is completely dairy-free, with added vitamins D ad B12. It has a refreshing light sweet taste, and makes a nice alternative 'treat' drink when chilled for children.

CREAMS

In farming days of old, the cream that settled on the top of milk was simply scooped off. But some fat still remained in the milk. Nowadays, in the interest of commercial efficiency, the cream is separated from the milk by means of centrifugal force in a mechanical separator. Then it is made into creams of varying thickness depending on butterfat levels.

Single cream is the lightest, with 18% fat. It's a good cream for pouring or enriching custards and milky puddings. It cannot be whipped.

Soured cream is also 18% fat but has an added souring culture. It's good for spooning, but not for cooking unless it's stirred in at the end. Incidentally, do not confuse this with cream that has gone sour: that has a bitter 'off' flavour – not nice. For recipes that give sour cream, use fresh soured cream.

Whipping cream is 35% fat. It can be whipped but will never get stiff, which to my mind is a plus. The whipped texture is light and easy to fold into other mixtures or oozes just nicely when spooned on top of a pudding. It cannot be piped.

Whipped/squirty cream can be up to 35% fat. It's generally sweetened and has added stabilisers. It's also sold in an aerosol can. After squirting from the can, the nozzle must always be washed clean in cold water so you can use it again. This whipped cream soon fizzles down to a liquid, so use only to serve.

Double cream, so called because it nearly doubles in size when whipped, is 48% fat. It's a good all-purpose cream, slightly milky sweet in flavour. Use it in sweet and savoury cooking. It can be cooked without curdling if no lemon juice or vinegar is present.

Extra-thick creams (single or double) have been heat treated and homogenised to increase viscosity. They're good for pouring or spooning but not good whippers.

UHT cream (single or double), as found in corner shops, will be separated into very thick cream at the top of the pot and thin milky liquid underneath. Mix the two together to blend it. It has a slightly caramel flavour and is acceptable in emergencies.

Clotted cream. This is cream heated to a temperature of nearly boiling (82°C), then the cream crust is spooned off. It has a nice buttery taste and is good for spreading straight from the carton or pot. It's a robust product, and can even be sent through the post as a holiday souvenir.

TO WHIP CREAM

Make sure the cream is well chilled and, ideally, the bowl and beaters or whisk too. Whipping cream whips to soft floppy peaks, perfect for spooning but not piping. Double cream can easily be overbeaten and turn to buttery curds so watch as you whisk, particularly if using an electric whisk. To lessen the risk, add 2tbsp of milk to each 300ml (10fl oz) of double cream first before beating. You will find it takes time to get the cream to start thickening, but thereafter it thickens quickly. If sweetening cream with caster sugar, add it before beating: if using honey, stir it in afterwards. Cream sweetened with caster sugar and a little vanilla essence becomes Chantilly cream. Grated lemon rind, lemon juice, etc. are best stirred in after the cream starts to thicken, then you can continue whipping, but cautiously in case it suddenly curdles.

Crème fraîche

If you let unpasteurised double cream ripen a little to develop a touch of acidity you will have a deliciously refreshing product with a multitude of uses. Crème fraîche has a slightly similar, gently tangy flavour because, although it is pasteurised, the natural lactic acid it has been allowed to develop gives it just a hint of sharpness. This also stabilises it and makes it a dream for cooking. Its colour is more buttery than ordinary cream. Slight acidity in a thick cream is a plus: it blends better with more flavours. Dark chocolate, for example, tastes better, as do sweet strawberries or a trifle topping. Crème fraîche also cooks in sauces and casseroles without curdling, so add a good dollop whenever you want to finish off a gravy, or stir some straight into hot vegetables instead of butter. Many supermarkets now sell their own branded crème fraîche but you can also buy classic French crème fraîche from Isigny that even carries its own AOC (appellation).

Half-fat crème fraîche generally has an added culture to thicken and add a little tang. (Vegetarians beware though, as some companies use pork gelatine as a thickener and give no warning). At 15% fat, it is lighter in texture (and calories) yet can still be added to hot sauces without curdling. I like to have a 200ml pot in the fridge at all times as it is so useful to add that little *je ne sais quoi* when finishing off a dish. For example, to make a quick pan gravy, swirl some wine, or dry sherry into a pan in which you've just cooked steaks or chops, and a splash or two of water. Heat for a few seconds to bubble down, then mix in 1 tbsp of half-fat crème fraîche. Season and pour over the meat immediately, just enough to moisten. Half-fat crème fraîche is also nice mixed in equal amounts with a vinaigrette dressing for creamy green-leaf salads, or tossed with hot new potatoes plus a little wholegrain mustard.

Mascarpone

Is this a cream or a soft cheese? Technically, it's a cream to which a culture has been added then heated and left to mature and thicken. In Italy the cream is taken off the top of milk used to make Parmesan cheese. It's spoonable, like soft clotted cream, with a beautiful white colour and very slight hint of caramel. This is the cream to use to make tiramisu but it's also good used for any sweet or savoury dish. For a simple pud, sprinkle sliced fresh peaches with a little brandy or rum, dust with icing sugar and spoon on some marscapone. Or blend some ripe apricots to a chunky purée and mix with mascarpone, then top with crushed amaretti biscuits.

Smetana

A lower-fat, spoonable soured cream made from skimmed milk, single cream and a souring culture to give a slight tang and clean, refreshing taste. Originally from Eastern Europe and Russia, smetana is available in larger supermarkets. Use it in hot or cold dishes, but if it's a hot dish add the smetana off the heat so it doesn't curdle.

YOGURT

Yogurt is not simply sour milk – milk left to its own devices would not turn into yogurt, it would just go off. It needs to have added bacteria cultures that break down milk sugars (lactose) into lactic acid, rendering the new milk product easy to digest and giving it a distinctive, tangy flavour.

Although yogurt has been known about for centuries, indeed even millennia, it wasn't until early in the 20th century that a scientist working at the Pasteur Institute in Paris managed to cultivate the two bacteria responsible and so paved the way to make yogurt commercially. Danone was the first company in this field. The proliferation of yogurts and desserts seems to grow almost daily.

It is the added cultures that determine the nature of yogurt. The general ones are *Lactobacillus bulgarius* and *Streptococcus thermophilus*.

Lactobacillus is the culture that gives a sharp yogurty tang. The gentler bacteria *Lactobacillus acidophilus* and *Bifidobacterium longum* are particularly beneficial to digestion with the added advantage that they impart a mild, creamy texture: these are known as bio yogurts.

TIP: MAKING YOGURT

You can make your own in a more homely way by adding a big spoonful of

live yogurt, ideally organic, to tepid milk and storing it in a vacuum flask

overnight. Homogenised milk makes good smooth yogurt.

Types of yogurt

All yogurt (except UHT, which has been heat treated to kill all the cultures) is to a certain extent, live. Yogurts labelled as *'live'* simply contains more alive bacteria than almost-dead yogurt, for want of a better phrase. To stabilise most yogurts, growth inhibitors are mixed in to halt the work of the lactobacillus. *Natural yogurt* has no added anything – no stabilisers, sweeteners or preservatives. *Smooth creamy yogurts* can contain fruit, sugar, colouring and added modified starch. Yogurts with a pouring consistency have been stirred while they are incubating. Set yogurt is made from homogenised milk and allowed to set in the pot: it will have a thin clear liquid on top which you can pour off or stir in. This is the popular French-style yogurt, sometimes sold with a thin layer of cream on top too. Yum!

Strained yogurts are those that have been slightly drained of excess liquid to make them thicker and creamier: you can actually achieve the same result at home simply by spooning a 'normal' yogurt into a muslin-lined colander and letting the mass drain overnight in the fridge. *Greek yogurts* are described as strained. They also taste creamier because they are made with whole milk – traditionally ewes' (sheep's) milk, which is naturally sweeter anyway, but also whole cows' milk. *Low fat yogurts* use semi-skimmed milk and very low fat yogurts use fat-free milk. When buying flavoured yogurts, check the label to see what's been used: sugar or sweeteners, fresh fruit or flavourings.

Drinking yogurts have added fruit juice or water. Some are marketed specifically as dietary supplements. The Yakult brand is described by its makers as a fermented milk drink with healthy 'good' bacteria to assist digestion. It's sold in little bottles and you take one 'shot' a day. Useful for people who aren't wild about yogurt but recognise its health properties – like me.

Cooking with yogurt

You can cook with yogurt but if heated on its own it will curdle. However, yogurt mixed with a little flour and maybe an egg yolk can be stirred over a gentle heat to flavour a hot simmering stew, but watch that it does not boil. It will give you a light, creamy, smooth texture. Yogurts also make good marinades when mixed with garlic, spices or crushed herbs because the lactic acids act as tenderisers, e.g. for tandoori chicken or prawns.

LASSI

Lassi is an Indian drink made by mixing yogurt with water and served sweetened or lightly salted. It is very refreshing, particularly with a little chopped fresh mint and pinch of ground cumin – the drink for curries. Or blend with a mango purée for a sweet lassi.

BUTTERS, MARGARINES AND SPREADS

In the trade they call these 'yellow fats' which sounds rather unappetising. To understand the differences between them it helps to have a very basic 'shopping' knowledge of fats.

Saturated fats are solid at room temperature. These also happen to be the fats doctors associate with health conditions like heart disease. Chiefly these are animal fats such as suet, meat fat and cream but also certain vegetables fats such as palm oil and coconut oil. *Monounsaturated fats*, as found in olive oil, and *polyunsaturated fats*, from many seed oils, are liquid but can become solid if they undergo a process called hydrogenation in which hydrogen is pumped into a water and oil emulsion. This converts polyunsaturated fatty acids into mono-unsaturated and saturated fatty acids, known as *transfats*, so one is almost back to square one in health terms. All fats and oils contain all three types of fatty acids: it is the proportion of each that determines the nature of the spread. Still with me?

BUTTER

Butter is an 80% milk fat product (i.e. saturated fat), with milk solids and water making up the remaining percentage. It is made from pasteurised cream that has been left for eight to twenty-four hours to age to develop some flavour, then it is churned and separated out into buttergrains and liquid buttermilk (see page 70). The 'grains' are then worked into a smooth mass and salted if necessary. Recently, with the growth of the real food movement, it has become possible to track down some small-time butter makers who make farmhouse butter the good old-fashioned way. There will be a lot of character in the flavour, just like fine cheese and wine. The difference is quite apparent and will reflect the seasonal quality of the milk – summer milks tasting richer than winter ones.

Butter can be made in two styles of flavours: *sweetcream* and the more continental lactic, with an added lactic culture. Both of these can be salted or unsalted. *Salted butters* can have up to 2% salt added (e.g. Anchor): *slightly salted butters* have around 1%. An easy-to-spot guide is that sweetcream butters are often sold in gold-coloured foil wrappers and lactic butters in silver-coloured foil (e.g. Lurpak, Normandy and Dutch).

Concentrated or *cooking butters* will have a much higher fat content. *Butter ghee* is 100% fat, heated for some period to caramelise the flavour slightly – the water and milk solids are left behind. This is a similar to the process followed by many chefs when they clarify butter. *To make clarified butter*, melt a pack of butter gently until you notice milky deposits separate out at the base. Pour off the yellow pure fat and leave the milky part behind. (Don't waste this – it can be used in milky puddings or mashed potatoes.) Then cool or chill. Ghee, concentrated and cooking butters can all be heated to a higher temperature for frying without over-browning. Concentrated butters also make crisper, shorter pastry because of the higher fat content.

Spreadable butters have added liquid and vegetable oils. They taste buttery but check the label for fat percentages. In the main they are not ideal for baking or frying.

TIP: REAL BUTTER OR LOWER-FAT SPREADS?

After all the years of swapping between lower-fat spreads and butter, my

chosen preference now is to keep a pack of (real) butter out at spreadable

room temperature in an old-fashioned butter dish and use it thinly like a

spread. No need to chill.

MARGARINE

Margarines can be hard baking margarines sold in a block (e.g. Stork) or soft, sold in tubs (e.g. Flora). It is the blend of fats, oils, emulsifiers, stabilisers, flavourings etc used that determine the nature of a margarine. A French chemist, Meges-Mouries, first patented imitation butters – his original blend was beef suet and milk. The idea soon caught on and it was sold under names such as 'oleo' and 'butterrine' but the Margarine Act of 1887 finally sorted out the name. Margarines made with a higher amount of saturated fats are more solid and suitable for pastry, cakes etc. *Soft margarines* will have a higher blend of mono-unsaturated and polyunsaturated fats and will be softer, although still around 70–80% fat. Soft or tub margarines (with a little help from food processors) revolutionised home baking with the all-in-one cake recipes. There was no longer any need to leave butter out of the fridge to soften and to beat it laboriously with caster sugar until 'pale and creamy'.

REDUCED-FAT SPREADS

These fats have a lower fat content and more water and milky flavourings than butter or margarine. The fat content of these ranges from 63% to as low as 25%, though the very low fat spreads have a mousse-like texture – in fact quite unpleasant, so why not simply eat really fresh bread without spread? I prefer the taste of olive oil spreads but it is mostly a matter of personal choice, so taste a few before deciding which will be a regular item in your shopping basket. If you are concerned about hydrogenated fats (trans-fatty acids), buy margarine spreads. There are a number of brands on offer.

PLANT STEROLS

These are plant extracts that are similar in structure to cholesterol in our blood. They have to be blended with foods such as dairy yogurts or fat spreads to make them suitable for our bodies. When they enter our digestive system, they effectively block the absorption of harmful cholesterol into our blood stream, especially the more harmful LDLs (low-density lipoproteins) that can clog our arteries. Any chilled dairy product that claims to lower blood cholesterol will contain plant sterols, which it will say if you look at the back of the pack.

OTHER COOKING FATS

Shortenings are 100% fat products of hydrogenated fats (e.g. Cookeen, Trex, White Flora) that blend better into flour for lighter pastries, smoother cakes etc. Healthier hearts shortenings will have a higher proportion of polyunsaturated fats but will not be lower in fat.

Vegetable ghee is suitable for vegans who will not eat milk products, and is made from hydrogenated vegetable fats.

Coconut fat can be treated like any cooking fat. It looks white and creamy and naturally gives a coconutty flavour. *Lard* is clarified pork fat. It has been largely superseded by many other cooking fats but is still popular in many ethnic and European cuisines. Try frying potatoes or pancakes in lard – you'll find them surprisingly tasty. Old country cake recipes sometimes use lard – like lardy cake. The name says it all.

Suet is clarified beef fat. It is associated with traditional British puddings, especially Christmas pud, but in parts of rural North America they still enjoy suet biscuits (scones) and milk gravy. Like lard it is the fat taken from around the kidneys and other internal organs. First these pads of solid fat are cleaned of membranes and veins, then boiled with water. The hard fat solidifies on top and can be scraped off. Other solid matter remains in the water and is not used. The hard suet is then minced or shredded and tossed in a little flour to coat and keep it separate.

Vegetarian suet is made with hydrogenated vegetable and saturated vegetable fats. Again, it is not 'healthier', or lower in calories unless labelled as being lighter in fat, in which case it would have added water to reduce the fat content. Use in the same way as beef suet.

LATKES

These are grated potato pancakes cooked in lard, and good with bacon and eggs.

Peel two or three large waxy potatoes and grate them coarsely. Rinse in a bowl of cold water then drain well and pat dry in a large clean tea towel. Mix in a small handful of plain flour, enough to bind the grated potato together lightly, and season well with salt and (ideally white) pepper Heat a good knob of lard in a frying pan until hot and almost smoking, then scoop up dessertspoonfuls of potato and press into the hot lard like flat, roundish pancakes. Cook on a medium-hot heat until golden brown underneath, then flip over and cook the other side. They should take about 5 minutes each side to cook.

CHEESES

Cheese and cheesemaking is a vast subject and one that constantly changes. After all, mankind has been making cheese for thousands of years as a way of preserving milk. Small wonder there is such a diversity, and it helps to have a basic knowledge so you can understand what you are buying.

The character of the milk, the processes and techniques applied after the first curds are made, the amount of moisture eliminated in subsequent processes, the skill of the cheesemaker, the storage conditions and the length of maturation all contribute to the end result. It is a combination of these factors that shapes the cheese.

All cheese starts as curds and whey on day one. Both hard and soft cheeses are coagulated by means of rennet, a substance once found only in the stomachs of calves but now produced artificially. Fresh soft cheeses are set with a bacterial culture.

HARD CHEESES

Hard cheeses such as **Cheddar**, have much of the liquid drained from them by cutting the fresh curd into tiny pieces so more whey can be drained – a process known as 'cheddaring'. These curds are pressed into rounds and left to mature. As cheese matures so it loses moisture and firms up, depending on the length of time, into smooth hard and semi-hard cheeses. The texture becomes more crumbly and the flavour fuller, with a sharp, tangy bite, and a hard rind develops. British farmhouse hard cheeses are shaped into drum-shaped truckles, traditionally wrapped in muslin cloth and sealed in hard fat. They are turned frequently for even maturation – it's quite an experience watching a strapping dairy maid toss a huge truckle as if it was no heavier than her shoe! In Europe, young pressed hard cheeses will be left to soak in brine to seal the rind.

Mild cheese can be only around three months old. It has a smooth, slightly rubbery texture.

Mould rind cheeses are fresh curds pressed in perforated moulds and left to drain naturally in an atmosphere of high humidity. As they drain and mature, natural penicillium moulds form on the outside and over a few weeks a soft, velvety rind develops. The moulds also start to break down the curds inside to a smooth, creamy, almost runny texture. This is the process used to make **Brie, Camembert, crottin** and so on. Further processes with mould-

ripened cheeses change the character again, such as washing in wine.
A light pressing after moulding gives a semi-soft cheese.

Pressed cheeses can be coated in wax before mould develops, which
effectively seals them (e.g. *Edam*, traditionally from north Holland,
raclette from France, and *fontina* from Italy). If the fresh young curds are
cut, mixed with salt, hung up and left to drain, they form into a feta cheese.

Blue cheeses (e.g. Stilton, Roquefort, Danish blue) are made from milk
with a Penicillium mould added before the fresh curds form. The crumbled
curds are then scooped into perforated stainless steel drums, left there for up
to two weeks and turned frequently. The curds are demoulded and rubbed with
salt. The young cheeses are pierced with fine rods to let in air and when air
comes into contact with the latent Penicillium blue streaks develop. Some blue
cheeses are frequently wrapped in foil to keep them moist.

SOFT CHEESES

If you take fresh, unripened cows milk and add a lactic culture, you will find it
settles within a few hours into soft curds and liquid whey, which is drained away.
The remaining curds become a very fresh cheese and the style will depend on
the richness, or otherwise, of the milk. All cheeses prepared this way will have a
soft, smooth texture. The richer the milk, the creamier the flavour: cheeses from
fat-free milks have a sharper, more tangy taste. Rich double cream will yield a
thick, almost buttery *cream cheese:* whole milk will produce a medium-fat *curd
cheese*; and lower-fat milks will make *reduced-fat soft cheese.*

Soft cheese varieties

Cottage cheese (0.4–1.5% fat) is made from semi-skimmed or skimmed milk
that has been heated before the lactic starter is added. This causes the milk to
form into characteristic little soft curds. Much cottage cheese is flavoured with
additional ingredients – chives, pineapple, ham, prawns – as most of it is eaten
straight from the pot as a snack meal. Cottage cheese is too grainy to cook with
successfully but it's fine in salads or spooned onto jacket potatoes or pittas, or
onto crackers, particularly tasty sprinkled with spices, peppers and sea salt.

Quark or skimmed milk soft cheese has a smoother texture than cottage
cheese because the milk is not heated beforehand. Quark is the traditional
cheese used for baked cheesecakes. It can be seasoned and flavoured with
fresh chopped herbs or onions to serve with salads, in baked potatoes or
blended into light vegetables pâtés or mousses.

Curd cheese is a medium-fat soft cheese also used in cheesecakes. Many cooks like curd cheese because it is not as rich and cloying as cream cheese but creamy enough to blend well into sauces or with sugar and eggs.

Fromage frais, also known as *fromage blanc*, comes in two fat levels – 8% and 0%. Basically these are curd-style cheeses that have been homogenised, so the fat and set milk are inextricably mixed together. It's deliciously refreshing on a summer's day mixed with a little honey or seasoning and chopped fresh herbs and it makes a good fat-free salad dressing too. Fromage blanc from small producers seems to have a cleaner, fresher taste.

Triple cream cheeses are the very rich, soft and crumbly cheese sold wrapped in foil drums. The most famous is *Boursin*, named after its creator in the late 1950s. It is mainly sold in the lightly tangy natural, garlic, and cracked pepper flavours, though there are other varieties. Possibly the only cheese with an advertising slogan that has passed into legend – 'du pain, du vin, du Boursin'.

WHEY CHEESES

Little Miss Muppet's 'curds and whey' would have been a homemade soft cheese before draining. In cheesemaking, the whey is never wasted: it's too good to discard. Over the years, cheesemakers have found ways of making further cheese with it and many are now popular choices in their own right. Two of the most well known are *ricotta* and *mozzarella*.

Ricotta is made by boiling whey used in the making of other cheeses until small curds form on the top. These are scooped off and drained in baskets. There are a number of styles of ricotta, from salted, crumbly feta types (*ricotta salata*) to *smoked ricottas* and ewes' milk ricottas. The nicest is *Fior di Maggio*. Ricottas are classed as fresh cheeses and should be used within days. Ricotta has a slightly gritty soft, moist texture that falls apart into soft curds when forked. But it is one of the nicest cheeses to cook with as it blends well with other ingredients like a thick cream. Mix it with chopped cooked spinach and nutmeg to roll into pasta sheets as cannelloni and serve with a spicy fresh tomato sauce, or beat it with eggs, sugar, cinnamon and raisins and bake as a lovely filling in sweet open curd tarts.

Mozzarella is described as a stretched whey cheese. Curds are heated in whey, then kneaded until they become stretchy. This means they can be pressed into shapes such as balls (medium-sized or small) or even plaited, then sold stored in water, which can be drained. *Pizza mozzarella* is a Danish product made with mozzarella pressed into blocks, which is sufficiently hard to either grate coarsely or slice thinly – almost a different product from the original mozzarella. *'Farmhouse mozzarella'* in Italy is made and served very fresh, almost within a day: you can really buy it only in speciality Italian delis – it is too fresh for even the might of modern distribution. In the south of Italy they use water buffalo milk *(mozzarella di bufala)*, which makes a very clean tasting young cheese with a soft, forkable texture. It's wonderful with ripe sliced tomatoes, a trickle of fruity olive oil and some torn basil leaves. You can buy buffalo mozzarella in sealed packs.

CHEESES FOR COOKING AND SALADS

Most cheese is best eaten as it is, one chunk at a time, as a quick light meal with or without bread, for instant nourishment. It doesn't need to be cooked – in fact if you overheat cheese you toughen the proteins and render them indigestible. Some cheeses are more suitable in cooked dishes than others, including several of the world's greats – *Parmesan, Gruyère, Emmental* and *Cheddar* – though many others, like creamy *Lancashire*, salty and tangy *halloumi* and *pecorino*, sweet nutty *comté* and *crottin* and the Mexican *Queso*, also suit hot dishes. Many are good eaten as part of a light main meal with salad and the soft fresh cheeses above are ideal as ingredients in recipes.

In general, good cooking cheeses have a high fat content, so they melt to a smooth creaminess. The exception is Parmesan, but then that is mostly used finely grated as a flavouring or in shavings.

Varieties of cheeses for cooking

'Parmesan' is a collective name that needs defining. In fact, there is no one cheese called Parmesan but the name is so instantly recognisable in recipes and food stores that we carry on using it. The generic name is grana, and two cheeses in particular – *Parmigiano Reggiano* (see page 84) and *Grana Padano* – have their own official DOC classification which you can check stamped on the rind.

Parmesan might seem very expensive but because of its full flavour a little fresh Parmesan goes a long way. Buy a good chunk and keep it loosely covered with a food bag in the fridge and simply grate how much you need freshly each time – over pasta, risottos, soups and hot, buttery vegetables. The harder the cheese, the more finely you can grate it. Newly cut Parmigiano Reggiano can be shaved with a swivel vegetable peeler to scatter over salads or eat with ripe pears.

PARMIGIANO REGGIANO

This is the cheese cooks think of when a recipe calls for 'Parmesan'. It has been made for centuries in a clearly defined area that includes Bologna, Modena, Parma and Reggio Emilia. Its name is stamped in red dots all over the rind of the huge drums it is shaped in, so there can be no mistake.

The milk is always unpasteurised and semi-skimmed. (The cream that forms on the top after the first day is scooped off to make mascarpone.) The very young cheeses are soaked for three weeks in brine, drained and then the long maturation that can last up to four years begins. At the end of the maturation, the huge drums of cheese are so dense they are best cut not with a cheese wire but with two short, heavy knives that almost pull the cheeses into ragged chunks.

The unique flavour, sweet fragrance and texture are entirely the result of very strict regulations, from specifying the fresh feed of the cows to the production processes, storage and distribution. Even grated fresh Parmigiano Reggiano must carry the DOC symbol (see EU classifications on pages 20–1). Fortunately, those small cylindrical containers of dried grated Parmesan cheese that used to be the way we bought this cheese are becoming a rarity; the stale, musty smell was the ruination of many a spaghetti bolognese.

Grana Padano has a thick, yellow, slightly oily rind and a hard, grainy texture. Use it in the same way as Parmigiano Reggiano.

Pecorino is a collective name for Italian sheep cheeses, which have been eaten since the days of the Roman Empire. It has a sweet flavour with a sharp, salty bite. The texture is softer than a 'Parmesan' because the cheeses are aged for about a year and so it is slightly easier to grate. Some cooks even prefer it to Parmesan, but use it in the same way. Out of Italy we can find up to three main types of pecorino cheese in delis and larger supermarkets – *romano, sardo* (from Sardinia) and *toscano*.

Gruyère is Swiss and, like Grana and pecorino cheeses, has been made for centuries by increasingly defined production methods. It is made from unpasteurised milk and pressed into huge wheels and has the most flowery, sweet bouquet when you first cut into a wedge. The texture is both smooth and slightly grainy, with a light elasticity and small holes. It grates cleanly and when melted it stretches into long wires. Gruyère makes delicious quiches, soufflés and of course fondues. It is also good eaten as a table cheese. The rind will be stamped with 'Gruyère' and 'Switzerland' in red so there's no mistaking.

French Gruyères are called *comté* and **Beaufort:** both are AOC cheeses made in the French Alps and are used like Swiss Gruyère. The rinds of French Gruyères are not stamped with names but are a textured light brown.

Emmental is the holey one, from Switzerland. It is a medium-hard cheese, with a flavour and aroma fruitier and sweeter than Gruyère. Other countries make Emmental-style cheeses but they cannot carry the same AOC mark. Also known as 'Swiss cheese' when used in recipes.

Raclette, formerly known as Valais, is another Swiss cheese of unpasteurised milk. The newer name means 'the scraper', which is how the cheese came to be used by the locals. They would hold the cut side of the cheese before an open fire over a pot of freshly cooked potatoes. As the cheese softened it would be scraped off with a knife into the pot and served as a melted blanket with pickled gherkins. Obligingly, some Raclette producers sell their cheese in ready-sliced portions so you can just place them on top of hot new potatoes or toast.

Provolone, like mozzarella, is a stretched cheese but it's firmer, with a thin rind and pale yellow inside. It comes in a variety of sizes and shapes, according to the mood of the cheesemaker. It's often seen as long sausages and I've even seen little Provolone pigs hanging up in deli windows. A young, sweet Provolone will bear the word dolce.

Provolone Piccante uses goat kid's rennet as a coagulant, which gives it a sharper, goaty flavour. It can also be aged for up to two years.

Crottin (or crottin de Chavignol) are small fresh goat's cheeses with natural rinds that have developed because the new fresh cheeses were stored in drier conditions. Older cheeses are matured for up to three months and have a pungent flavour and darker, more wrinkled skin (which French speakers will recognise as a descriptive translation of the name). Crottins are most often seen grilled and served with a rocket leaf salad. Allow one cheese per head.

Cheeses labelled as *chèvre* must by French law be 100% goats' milk. Their age can be very young (just a couple of days old) to a few weeks. Goats' milk can also be mixed with cows' milk but the cheese must not be called chèvre. It's sold in many shapes and sizes, with rind or dusted with ash, dried herbs or even paprika.

Cheddar is one of the world's most famous cheeses and possibly the most imitated. A great Cheddar will have a clear, sweet, slightly walnut flavour and smell of a clean dairy. A mild Cheddar will be softly firm and slightly elastic. As it matures (up to 24 months), the texture will become lightly crumbly, almost palette-puckering, and the flavour very intense. Canada, New Zealand, Australia and Ireland all produce excellent Cheddars that can rival the best of British. It's the ultimate all-purpose cheese, from simply sliced on crusty bread to toasted rarebits, macaroni cheese and cheese soufflés. When you want to introduce a child to fine cheese, start him or her with a finger of early matured fine farmhouse Cheddar. A wedge of very mature Cheddar is a good alternative to expensive Parmesan in cooking, so if you have a slightly dried-out chunk, just grate it finely and use it in cooking. Unpasteurised Cheddars are among the best cheeses on the planet.

Paneer is a lightly pressed full-fat cheese made with a souring agent (acetic acid) and is chiefly used in Indian cookery. By itself the flavour is bland, but it does crumble when stir-fried and absorbs strong curry spice flavours well. It's rather similar to tofu in use.

Farmhouse cheeses – as the name suggests–are made in individual farms (which can still be quite commercial in size) and so have more character than factory cheeses. There are nine territorial cheeses in Britain – Cheddar (of course), *Cheshire, Red Leicester, double Gloucester, Caerphilly* (from Wales), *Lancashire, Derby, Wensleydale* and *Stilton.* Stilton is the king of British cheeses: its makers organised themselves early on into an effective marketing group to protect the use of the name and the quality of the cheese – a diligence that has paid dividends. Lancashire is a particularly good grilling cheese: pale, slightly crumbly yet very rich and almost buttery, it is made in a quite unique way mixing milks from different days. Most Lancashire cheese is eaten locally. Double Gloucester is traditionally made in a similar way, mixing milk from first milking with second, hence the name Double. True double Gloucester uses milk from heritage Gloucester cows, e.g. Daylesford. Daylesford sells the authentic cheese.

British and Irish cheesemaking is undergoing an exciting renaissance, with cheeses using cows', goats' and sheep's milk that rival many of the best from the continent. The British Cheese Awards held each September are increasingly helping to reward the new young British cheesemakers. Hurrah!

TOFU (DOU-FOU)

The Chinese developed this digestible, animal-free, low-fat , high-protein bean curd from soya beans and from there it spread to many parts of the Far East. It was embraced enthusiastically into Japanese cuisine and hence into our own Western food production, chiefly as a high-protein, vegetable-based ingredient. We find it sold as a semi-hard curd packed in water in health-food shops. As such, it is an acquired taste being almost flavourless, but those in the know use this blandness as a base for wonderful flavourful creations because it is so absorbent. A light tasty vegetable and noodle soup might have small protein-packed tofu cubes tossed in just before serving. Mainstream supermarkets sell semi-firm toasted and floured tofu cubes for stir-fries, and if you are looking for a creamy soft substitute for a small carton of light cream, search out Japanese silken tofu.

VEGETABLES

ASPARAGUS

Availability: all year round, but best home-grown season is May–June.

Asparagus is a native European plant, a member of the lily family. Asparagus has been a highly prized plant for centuries in Italy (the north-east), France, (around Argenteuil), Germany (around Lake Constance) and England (Norfolk and, curiously, Battersea). Asparagus spears are now imported from the Americas and Far East, notably Thailand. A 'crown' of asparagus takes about three years to reach the point when the shoots (spears) are ready for harvesting. It is quite a labour-intensive crop, which is reflected in the price.

Eat asparagus as fresh as you can, ideally the same day it has been picked. However, now that much of it is flown in from abroad that may be a vain hope. Certainly, asparagus spears should be so fresh that they snap when bent. The British and Americans like *green asparagus*, the Europeans *white spears* that have been forced or blanched. Both are preferred for flavour reasons, so the choice is very personal.

Tiny, tiny spears of wild asparagus grace plates of ultra haute cuisine plates, more for garnish than flavour. The first shoots of the new season's asparagus is known as sprue, which is really nice blanched and tossed in salads. You can also buy tender *purple asparagus*, flown in from Australia, which can be eaten raw in salads. Sliced asparagus can be stir-fried nicely. Asparagus has an affinity with eggs – try cooked spears topped with a tasty fried organic egg.

TO PREPARE ASPARAGUS

Trim the woody bases or snap them off, then peel the bases using a swivel vegetable peeler. How far up the stem you go depends on how tough the skin is, about halfway is the norm. Tie the stems together in bundles of six to eight with kitchen string and boil for about 5 minutes in a wide saucepan. You can go to the trouble of using a special tall asparagus cooker if you have one, but as we now all like vegetables crisp, including asparagus stems, I don't see the necessity. Just make sure the tips are not overcooked.

AUBERGINES

Availability: all year round.

The glossy, plump purple aubergine (also known as egg plant) that we see glinting on the supermarket shelf is only one of many worldwide varieties. The aubergine plant is thought to have originated in Asia, but now a great many varieties proliferate all over the world. In Thailand they use a wonderful selection of aubergines in clusters as small as peas to the size of white eggs – hence their alternative name of pea aubergine. West Indian cooks like their aubergines orange in colour, while the Chinese and Japanese prefer long, thin, striped purple and white varieties. All cooked aubergine tastes about the same – creamy, sometimes sweet, with a touch of bitterness. Raw aubergine flesh is springy and slightly sweaty when cut.

Some aubergine varieties contain juices that are quite bitter, so many cooks recommend that the cut flesh is placed in a colander and sprinkled with a little salt and left for about 20 minutes to draw out (degorge) these bitter substances. The tip-top fruits we import from Holland are quite mild and don't really need degorging, but it does help soften the flesh and makes them easier to cook. One problem with cooking sliced aubergines is that they absorb a lot of oil, but of course you don't have to fry them first, though it does give them extra flavour. If making a ratatouille, you can simply pop slices or chunks into the pan with a tomato-flavoured sauce. If I need to 'pre-fry' aubergine slices, then I brush them each side lightly with oil and grill them until they start to soften – ideal for a less greasy moussaka. The Middle East, especially Turkey and the Levant, have many memorable aubergine recipes, a favourite is a starter served cold called Iman Byaldi – halved aubergines filled with softly caramelised onions, tomatoes and garlic cooked long and slow in olive oil.

The flesh of large aubergines makes delicious creamy dips or caviar, as smart chefs call it. To make your own is really easy. In Greece, they add chopped hard-boiled egg for a salad, in Turkey, finely chopped walnuts and pomegranate seeds. Up-market restaurants use aubergine caviar as a base on which to place pan-fried meats and fish.

AVOCADOS

**Availability: all year round depending on country of supply
and variety.**

One of the New World fruits introduced to the West after Columbus but now
grown all over the world from Australia to South Africa, Israel, the Far East
and West Indies. Modern airfreight has enabled the avocado to become a
popular Western food. Once known as the alligator pear, the pale green,
creamy flesh is very nutritious and great for mashing up for baby food.

Depending on the time of year, there are about three main varieties on
sale. The *hass*, which comes as dark brown or dark purple, the smoother
green *fuerte* and the rounder *nabal*. Hass avocados are ripe when the skins
turn dark in colour, but even this is not the best indication. Feeling them is
the only real test. The ideal way to get a ripe avocado is to buy it firm about
three days before you need it and store it in a warmish cupboard. Cup the fruit
carefully in you hand and squeeze very gently. If there is some resistance, then
the fruit is ready.

Halve the avocado lengthways right through the centre, twist the halves in
opposite directions and pull apart. The big stone inside can be levered out
with a teaspoon or, of you have a heavy cook's knife (and nerves of steel) whack
down firmly on top of the stone as if trying to chop it in half. The stone will
stick to the blade, which can then be yanked smartly up pulling the stone with
it. To scoop out the flesh slip a large tablespoon between the skin and flesh and
try and remove it in one go. Despite all the helpful information about how to

stop avocado flesh turning brown, there is no remedy: lemon or lime juice will stop it only temporarily; putting the stone back into the mashed flesh doesn't do the trick either – sorry.

Treat avocados in cooking like a cream cheese. They have an ameliorating effect on spicy, fiery food – think of chilli chicken with sliced avocado in fajitas. I remember my father eating them for breakfast every morning, with the hollow in each half filled with neat Worcestershire sauce, sometimes sprinkled with a drop or two of hot pepper sauce for good measure. A true colonial.

GUACAMOLE

Guacamole has become one of the most popular of dips, but the ready-made versions bear no resemblance to a fresh homemade one. It's very easy to do and useful for fruit that's slightly over-ripe. Halve, stone and scoop out the flesh. Mash it with a fork but leave it slightly chunky. Grate a little raw onion on top or add a crushed garlic clove, Skin a large tomato and finely chop. Mix all together with the juice of a lime, some sea salt, ½tsp of ground cumin and freshly ground black pepper. Sprinkle some chopped fresh coriander over if you wish. Guacamole is good spread on soft wheat tortillas with chilli-grilled chicken, or use as a dip with chilled vegetable sticks and crisp tortilla chips.

BEANS

Availability: all year round, mid-to late summer for home-grown varieties.

The names peas and beans are interchangeable and sometimes confusing. For example, a black-eyed pea is really a bean. While peas are podded, most beans are eaten with pods intact. The home-grown season ranges from June through to September, depending on varieties.

Broad beans and fava beans

Broad beans are eaten shelled. To open the pods, press down firmly on the base of the pod with your thumb until it pops, then press out the beans out with your thumb. Broad beans in the early season are young and tender and can be eaten lightly boiled in their skins. Older beans later in the season are best popped from their inner skins after cooking, otherwise they taste very tough. Frozen broad beans are excellent, but again I find it is worth taking time to pop them from their translucent inner skins.

Fava beans are the delicious and nutritious main bean in Middle Eastern and Egyptian cooking. In fact, they are one of the earliest recorded beans and have an ancient and illustrious history. But do boil them well as they possess a mild toxin that can give rise to a medical disorder known as favism.

Fresh green beans

Whole green beans are sold under a variety of names – *runner beans, scarlet beans, stick beans, yard-long beans* (popular in Asian cooking), *French beans/haricots verts* and *fresh kidney beans*. Many of these are now grown in Spain, Thailand, East Africa and South America, so supply is nearly all year round, but at a premium price.

To check on the freshness of beans bought loose, bend them – fresh ones will snap. They will need topping and tailing by pinching off the ends (unless ready prepared) and larger beans may need stringing too. In fact, I find even beans sold topped and tailed may need additional stringing before you use them otherwise their skins are tough. Fresh runner beans are best thinly sliced on the diagonal so you get an equal amount of bean and pod in each slice. Yard-long beans do indeed grow very long (up to 45cm). Treat them as you would runner beans, that is thinly sliced on the diagonal.

Haricot beans, haricot verts and flageolet beans

These are all variations of the common bean, *Phaseolus vulgaris*. They are the inner beans from French bean pods that you can buy either dried in packs or still in their pods and semi-dried. They will range in colour from white to pale green and speckled pink or red. Fresh, they will need popping from the pods but not the inner skins. They are wonderful blanched in boiling water, then cooked in the juices of a lamb or pork roast. Dried variations include *kidney beans, pinto beans, borlotti beans, cannellini beans* and need special treatment (see pages 194–6).

Sprouting beans and seeds

Certain beans and seeds are more suitable for sprouting than others, although technically all of them can sprout so long as they have not been heat-treated in any way. Make sure the beans and seeds are well within their use-by dates; older specimens will not germinate readily. Ideally, use a stacking sprouting tray, otherwise a large jar, a thin muslin cloth or clean J Cloth and a stout elastic band will do.

Cover 2–3tbsp of the beans or seeds in tepid water and leave to soak, overnight if possible, then drain and rinse in a sieve under cold water. Place in the sprouting tray or jar. If using a jar, cover with a thin porous cloth, secure with an elastic band and lay the jar on its side. Keep the beans out of direct sunlight and rinse them twice a day in cold water to moisten and wash away any toxins. In two days you should notice new life (if there's no sign, then throw them away). Once the beans have started to sprout, continue watering until they are the length you require, but certainly no longer than it takes for the two cotyledons (leaves) to appear. After that the sprouts will start to taste bitter. Store the sprouted beans covered in a food box or bag in the fridge for up to a week.

SPROUTING SEEDS

Try the following beans and seeds for sprouting: lentils, mung beans, chickpeas, soya beans, aduki beans, alfalfa seeds and fenugreek seeds. Or experiment and try your own favourites.

BEETROOT

Availability: fresh in autumn and early winter.

Once regarded as an old-fashioned root vegetable grown by elderly gardeners, beetroot is creeping back into the recipe charts. In Europe it always occupied a more hallowed position as a versatile accompaniment. Here we still tend to find it sold vacuum-packed, reeking of harsh vinegar and fit only for the most boring salad plates. However, during the early winter and spring, supermarkets are increasingly offering raw, uncooked beetroot sold in small bunches. Snap these up because, although they look unprepossessing, the flavour of fresh, hot beetroot is quite a revelation. If you have a 'proper' greengrocer, then persuade him to sell you uncooked beets before he boils them: the old-fashioned way was to sell it ready cooked, hot and steaming, probably because raw beetroots do seem to go soft quicker than other roots.

Store fresh beetroot like other root vegetables, but they may not keep for so long. The downside of beetroot is the high level of the natural pigment anthocyanin, which colours everything it comes in contact with. The best advice is not to peel beets before you cook them. Simply scrub them if they need it, trim off the top stalks and roots, then boil in their skins. When cooked, cool in the colander then peel them, wearing rubber gloves if necessary. They are delicious dressed with a light white sauce flavoured with a pinch of fresh thyme, particularly good with roast lamb or pork.

Beets also make good salads, cooked or raw and coarsely grated. Dress with either vinaigrette or fresh orange juice and olive oil. Chopped and cooked, it's wonderful mixed into pasta salads with a creamy mayonnaise dressing. There is a growing trend for other coloured beets, too – golden and pink. Use them like the reds.

BORSCHT SOUP

To me, the nicest recipe for beetroot is a Russian classic – homemade borscht soup. You do need to peel raw beets for this, then chop and sauté them lightly with onion, a stick of celery and some chopped mushroom. Add stock or water to cover and 1tsp of ground cumin – the classic spice for sweet beets. Cook until soft, then purée for a cream soup or leave chunky. Check the seasoning and serve with a nice trickle of soured cream or fromage frais.

BROCCOLI

Availability: all year round, though traditionally April–December.

Broccoli comes as two types. The classic broccoli has lots of purple-green sprouts on a stem (marketed as tenderstem), which turn green once cooked. The other broccoli, sold in large firm green heads, is actually *calabrese*, originally an Italian vegetable but now popular the world over. It's high in beta-carotene vitamins and so is imbued with many nutritional virtues. Firm-headed purple broccoli is called *Cape broccoli* though it's actually a cauliflower, and pointed lime-green cauliflowers are sold as *romanesco*. As with cauliflowers, broccoli goes limp if stored too long. Also, green broccoli/calabrese should always have bright green spriggy heads. If you see any yellowing, don't buy it – it's a sign of age.

BRUSSELS SPROUTS

Availability: traditionally August–March.

Brussels sprouts are simply lots of little buds that grow up a single cabbage stem that culminates in an open terminal bud, sometimes sold separately as sprout tops. There used to be a saying: 'Don't buy sprouts until the first frosts have sharpened them up', but not anymore. They are very much a winter vegetable and, though we now import them from around the world almost all year round, there is nothing to beat a bowl of freshly boiled sprouts when the new season starts in November. I also adore them cold the day after cooking – wonderful fridge picking on Boxing Day!

Give sprouts a brief boiling just a few minutes before you need them. Rinse them quickly in cold water to stop overcooking, then toss in butter. Don't let them hang around in a warm oven before serving – the enzymes develop an awful stale smell.

CABBAGES

Availability: all year round depending on variety.

Very generally these are first categorised as either spring-sown or
autumn-sown depending on whether the plants form a firm heart or not.
Within these two categories there will also be round-headed and conical
cabbages, then further divisions of spring cabbage which can be cut
as 'spring greens' or, if grown on to become medium-hearted, summer
cabbages. In other words, our cabbages are all variations on a theme that
can be prepared and cooked in the same manner. The actual cabbage we
buy is referred to as a terminal bud, and specific flavours and textures vary
according to the variety.

Cabbage varieties

Firm white cabbage, popular with the Dutch, is a good winter variety that
seems to last and last in the bottom of the fridge, as indeed it did in days of
yore in farm outhouses and barns. There is little waste on such a cabbage, you
just cut off a wedge when required, cut out the hard central core and shred the
tightly packed leaves thinly. The cut edges may turn a little grey on standing,
but these are easily shaved off the next time you want some fresh cabbage.
White (or Dutch) cabbage is the variety used for coleslaw and sauerkraut.

 Red cabbage is a colour variant of white, containing the familiar
anthocyanin pigments. Use it in the same way you would firm white cabbage,
although many cooks like to serve red cabbage braised with apple and spices
as an accompaniment to pork or winter game casseroles, or soak raw shreds in
a pickling vinegar.

 Savoy cabbage in a tightly packed flower shape is highly prized by chefs
and home gourmets alike. The crinkly two-tone green leaves have a deliciously
sweet flavour that benefits from just a few minutes' light boiling. It is mainly in
season during the winter but some growers are able to extend the season well
into the summer.

 Spring greens are a conical variety of cabbage sold as either just the outer
leaves or with the inner cones as well. A very traditional use of spring greens
is to serve them lightly boiled and tossed in butter as an accompaniment to
spring lamb.

 Sugar loaf cabbage is a pale green cone with a sweet succulent flavour.

 Curly kales are a darker green and have a more pronounced flavour. The
leaves look like outsized curly-leaf parsley. They were originally hardy cottage

garden greens that survived harsh winters, but recently growers are picking the leaves young and selling them bagged at speciality prices. Green and purple kales are popular in Creole and Cajun cuisine and are often used as a garnish.

Now we are experiencing a blossoming of green leafy cabbages as growers experiment with more and more decorative varieties. *Cavolo nero* is a Tuscan green-black cabbage that looks a little like curly kale. Oriental cabbages are becoming increasingly commonplace too, such as *pak choi, pe-tsai, won bok, mustard cabbage, flowering cabbage* (choy sum), *Chinese leaf* (Peking cabbage) and *water spinach*. These you either steam whole (if they are sold in single heads) or shred and stir-fry. No need to stick to Oriental-style dishes, just use them as simple accompaniments.

CARDOONS

Availability: traditionally September–November.

Cardoons are ones to watch. Like globe artichokes, they are a thistle. Popular in southern Mediterranean cooking, they resemble heads of celery with white fleshy ribs. They need a lot of labour for growing as the plants are blanched in long pots to keep the stems white. Remove the outer stalks, and slice the stems. Cook like artichokes and serve dressed with buttery or tomato sauces.

CARROTS

Availability: all year round; baby carrots chiefly in the spring.

The orange-coloured carrot as we know it today was developed in the 16th century by Flemish refugees who fled to Elizabethan England, though the early varieties were often red, purple and even black. Pigments called anthocyanin, also found in peppers, tomatoes, beetroot and red cabbage, are responsible for these varied hues. Carrots are also a good source of beta-carotene, which our bodies synthesise to make vitamin A, one of the nutrients that helps our sight.

Carrots are available all year round, as new crop and main crop, but you will rarely find a variety name used in stores. Growers like nice straight roots that peel easily. (Carrots are grown in light sandy soil so the roots stay straight.) Generally speaking, the older and larger the carrot, the fuller the flavour, so if you want to make a good carrot soup, use large old carrots. For an elegant vegetable dish, choose young slender roots. Baby carrots have little flavour, but they do look good as a garnish. Carrots sold with leafy tops will be fresher than those trimmed, but you don't eat the tops anyway.

The best-flavoured varieties originated in France. One of the tastiest is the *Supreme Chantenay*. *Nantes* is an early crop variety, while stumpy little *Parisiennes* have a really nice, sweet flavour. If you are into juicing, then seek out and try the sweet and juicy *Zino* carrot.

There's not much new to say about this popular vegetable except that it makes a wonderful range of dishes, from creamy light soups to lunch-box salads and even cakes. One really nice and nutritious salad is to dress coarsely grated carrots with a trickle of olive oil, the juice of a fresh lemon, some sea salt and a good sprinkling of either poppy, black mustard or roasted cumin seeds or just lots of chopped fresh mint and parsley.

Store carrots in dark, clean and dry conditions. The bottom of a fridge is fine, but keep them loosely covered otherwise they dehydrate and become soft and wrinkly.

CAULIFLOWER

Availability: all year round.

Cauliflowers are a variety of brassica with little firm white flower heads known as curds. Both winter and summer varieties are grown. During the winter milder coastal areas such as Cornwall or Brittany produce magnificent heads, firmly packed and representing great value for money. Cut the curds from the thick inner stalk and boil for 3–5 minutes, then dress with a well-flavoured cheese sauce and hard-boiled eggs for a really good cheap meal. Cut cauliflowers discolour within a day or so, but you simply just need to trim off any grey bits. Do turn the cauli over and check for any maggot holes, especially in summer. If you suspect there might be live matter hidden within the heads, then simply soak them for 15 minutes in cold salted water. The little critters will float to the top. Cauliflowers go limp as they go stale so avoid these.

CELERIAC

Availability: autumn through to spring.

Many chefs appreciate this sweet, aniseed-flavoured root but not, it seems, home cooks. Maybe the large size and warty looking skin are somewhat daunting. A shame because it is good as a hot vegetable (especially mashed with creamy potato) or raw, sliced into thin discs then cut into thin sticks to be blanched and tossed in dressing for a salad. However, uncooked celeriac does brown rather quickly once peeled, so drop the prepared slices or chunks into cold water containing fresh lemon juice or wine vinegar. The French have a popular shredded celeriac salad with a sweet mustardy remoulade dressing, good with shellfish.

Treat it hot as you would a large turnip, although it is not a root crop in the botanical sense but a relative of celery. It also makes good soup. Celeriac can be shaved into thin discs and deep-fried as vegetable chips and is traditionally served with game.

ROOT VEGETABLE CHIPS

Use a selection of root vegetables – parsnip, beetroot, turnip, celeriac, etc. You don't need a large amount of each. Peel the vegetables thinly, then shave them into long, thin strips. The best tool to use for this is a swivel vegetable peeler. Heat vegetable (not olive) oil in a deep-fat fryer to a temperature of 180°C. (If you don't have a deep fryer, fill a deep heavy-based pan a third full of oil and heat until a cube of white bread browns in around 30 seconds.) Put a small handful of vegetable shavings into the chip basket and lower into the hot oil. You will find they take 2–3 minutes to soften and crisp. Drain the shavings on kitchen paper and shake over some fine sea salt. Repeat with the remaining shavings, reheating the oil in between.

CELERY

Availability: all year round.

Celery is sold white or green, but both are treated in the same way. In supermarkets, the tops are generally trimmed and the bunched stalks are cleaned, ready to be broken off or sliced. If you find celery in a more natural state, i.e. complete with leaves and roots, then wash it carefully in case dirt is trapped within the stalks. The leaves can be eaten but they do tend to be a bit bitter. However, I like to open up the bunch and pinch out the tender, pale yellowy-green leaves and use these as a garnish. A pack of celery lasts and lasts in the base of a fridge so long as it stays in the plastic bag, opened at one end to allow it to breathe. You can tell when it is past its best when the stalks start to dehydrate and go limp. Snap off stalks as and when you need them and slice thinly on the diagonal for a pretty effect. Older celery may have tough woody ribs and need to be stringed with your fingers.

Use celery in stir-fries, salads and homemade celery soup, which is just heaven, or try the old-fashioned way of braising it. Celery is excellent eaten with good farmhouse cheese, where the crisp texture and aniseed flavour cuts through the creamy dairy flavour. Chinese celery is thinner than our European plant but can be used in the same way. Celery is one of the three vegetables (the other two are green pepper and onion) known in Creole cookery as the 'holy trinity'.

BRAISED CELERY IN TOMATO SAUCE

Trim whole stems and halve them if a little long. Blanch them in boiling salted water for about 5 minutes then drain. Return them to the saucepan and cover with a homemade tomato sauce, or canned chopped tomatoes with garlic and Italian-style herbs. Simmer gently for about 15 minutes until softened.

CHAYOTE AND CHRISTOPHENE

These are 'exotic' squashes with many uses from purées and salads to tarts and puddings or stuffing whole. They can simply be cut up, seeded and steamed, then dressed with a little butter and seasoning and served as a side vegetable or popped into spicy, aromatic stews. Smooth- and ridged-skinned varieties are on sale. Treat them in the same way.

CHICORY

Availability: all year round.

What's in a name? When it comes to chicory – possible confusion! I refer to oval-shaped crisp heads of a salad vegetable that in Britain is called chicory, but endive elsewhere. However, what we call endive lettuce, the French call *chicoree*. They now come in a variety of colours, from pale yellowy-white (known as *witloof*) to pale green and more recently a burgundy red. Most chicory is grown in hothouses and imported from Holland. It has a crisp, clean slightly bittersweet flavour. The bulbs are good value as they have a number of uses and you can use as few or as many as you like.

The leaves can be stripped from the base and served either in a mixed salad (whole or sliced) or filled with a chopped ratatouille-style mixture as a starter. Halved lengthways, chicory can be char-grilled, then dressed with a basalmic vinegar dressing and served with plump raisins, pine nuts and tomatoes. Whole heads of white chicory can be blanched for 3–5 minutes in boiling water, then served wrapped in ham and topped with a cheesy béchamel sauce to be browned with garlicky crumbs under a hot grill.

Red chicory (also known as *radicchio*) confusingly looks either like an elongated chicory head, only streaked red, or like a cross between a chicory and a small splayed-out round red lettuce. Its torn leaves can be found in bags of mixed salad. The leaves are quite bittersweet but the texture is crisp. Firm heads can be chargrilled and are particularly good with grilled goats' cheese or chicken. If you peel off the large cup-shaped outer leaves of radicchio they make lovely 'bowls' for serving saffron-flavoured risotto.

CHILLIES

Availability: all year round though some varieties subject to supply; speciality dried varieties available through mail order.

Think of chillies like grapes for wine. Depending on the variety (there are 200 or so), they give not just spicy heat but also particular aromas and flavours. They are one of the New World's wonder foods and are still king of the spices in Mexican and American cooking. Chillies were introduced to the rest of the world by European explorers in the sixteenth and seventeenth centuries and are now indispensable in Indian, Thai and Chinese cuisines, not to mention the new hip 'fusion' food.

It helps to have a basic knowledge of heat levels and where best to use fresh chillies and when to dare with dried. In general, the larger the size, the milder the flavour, and as green chillies ripen so they turn red or yellow and become sweeter and more aromatic.

Small red or green chillies from Thailand are called *birdseye* and pack quite a punch, so don't be deceived by their dainty size. Their heat levels can literally bring tears to your eyes. If a traditional recipe calls for 5–6 small Thai chillies then halve the quantity to begin with. One Mexican chilli is called the *macho*, but the hottest on sale is probably the *habanero*, sometimes sold as *scotch bonnets*. These chillies are popular in Jamaican cooking, especially in jerk sauces. *Jalapenos* are medium-hot and are the most popular chillies in US and Tex-Mex cuisines. You can also buy them pickled in jars as a relish. Confusingly, long red chillies labelled *cayenne* peppers are quite mild, although their dried powder is hot. Large *anaheim* chillies are nice and mild and are often served stuffed and cooked.

Preparing fresh chillies

The stinging sensation of chillies is due to a chemical called capaisin. The higher the capaisin level, the hotter the chilli. The burning feeling in your mouth signals the brain to release endorphins, which give you a pleasantly euphoric feeling – which is why chilli eating can become quite addictive. Don't cut chillies if the skin on your fingers is broken, and don't rub your eyes or mouth after preparing them.

Using chillies

Indian curries often start with a fresh spice mix of large green chillies, garlic and ginger, and extra dried chilli powder is added later in the recipe. Mexicans use a selection of different chillies in their 'moles' for flavour and heat level, again mixing dry and fresh chillies. For a hint of chilli in a sauce (and to save your fingers), halve a fresh chilli lengthways and add it to a simmering pot but remove the two halves just before serving. Beware! – Thai cooks like to garnish their dishes with thin slices of raw red chilli or simply scatter over small whole ones. Chilli aficionados say the last thing you should drink with chilli-laced food is a cold beer. Indians drink tepid water or a thin yogurt drink called lassi; Mexicans top their fiery dishes with soured cream or cheese, because dairy products lessen the afterburn. Chillies also feature prominently in some European cuisines. Basque cooks (French and Spanish) grow large amounts of espelette peppers, which they dry over balconies and use instead of black pepper. And Hungarian goulash owes its colour and flavour to a very aromatic chilli.

Dried chillies

Drying intensifies the aroma of a chilli. Dried chillies are frequently sold by heat level, mild or hot, so check the label. Some upmarket delis or larger supermarkets sell speciality dried chillies, from the mildish *pimento* graduating up to the hot, hot, hot *habanero*. You can buy them as a ground powder, as flakes with little white seeds, or whole. Whole dried chillies need to be soaked in just boiled water for 20 minutes before chopping or mincing. Sometimes a chilli seasoning will contain other spices or herbs.

A good way of giving a dish a chilli flavour, but without the risk of fiery fingers, is to shake a few drops of hot pepper sauce into the simmering pot. Tabasco, the best known, uses chillies of the same name, while West Indian pepper sauces contain juices of the Scotch bonnet. I find dried chilli has a shorter shelf life than bottled, though if you use it often, this may not be an issue.

TIP: DRYING YOUR OWN CHILLIES

Chillies dry very well and it's easy to do it yourself. Simply leave fresh

chillies dry and uncovered at room temperature for at least a week, or

string them together and hang them up in your kitchen.

SCOVILLE HEAT SCALE

Chilli lovers are guided in their choice of chilli by a heat scale developed by the scientist Wilbur Scoville in 1912. He measured the level of a natural chemical compound in peppers called capsaicin that stimulates nerve endings in the body. Scoville Heat Units (HSU) range from under 100 (sweet peppers) to over a million plus for pepper spray. For general eating purposes, the most common varieties in ascending order of heat are:

Pimento
Anaheim, Pepperdew
Jalapeño, Chipolte, Tabasco sauce, Espelette
Serrano
Cayenne, Tabasco peppers
Bird's-eye chillies, Piri
Habanero, Scotch bonnet

You have been warned!

COURGETTES

Courgettes (also known as zucchini) are small marrows that can be eaten sliced raw, lightly cooked and dressed in butter, as a soup, in classic ratatouille or in stir-fries. Courgette flowers are served dipped in a light batter and fried as fritters or stuffed with a light chicken mousse with a tiny baby courgette attached. Late summer and early autumn is the best time for buying courgettes as they are plentiful and in prime condition with tender skins, but supplies now come from all over the world or are grown in hothouses in cold climates. And, of course, they are easy to grow in a garden.

ROASTED COURGETTES

Whether you do these in a hot oven or on a griddle pan, the end result gives a tasty, roasted flavour and slightly softened flesh.

Heat the oven to 200°C/gas 6 or a griddle pan on top of the stove to a high heat. Meanwhile, cut courgettes lengthways into 4 to 6 slices; for baby courgettes, just cut in half lengthways. If using the oven, place in a roasting pan and brush with, or drizzle over, some oil (olive or vegetable). Season and roast uncovered for about 20 minutes until the slices soften and look lightly translucent. For griddling, do not oil up, just place the slices directly onto the pan surface and cook until deep brown ridges form. Flip over and do the other side, then remove to a shallow dish, season lightly and cover with a clean tea towel so the slices soften in their own steam. Then you can drizzle with some oil and maybe a squeeze of lemon juice.

CUCUMBERS

Natives of south-east Asia, cucumbers have been grown in Europe since well before the Romans. Nearly every country eats them, chiefly raw or in pickles, though they are occasionally cooked. Cucumbers are around 95% water and have a mild but distinctive flavour. Gherkin cucumbers are short and fat with smooth pale green skins and large seeds. Varieties sold in Mediterranean stores are short and their slightly bitter skins are best peeled away. Long, green cucumbers can be eaten with the skin, in fact it is said to aid digestion. These cucumbers have a slightly sweet flavour.

Cucumbers just need simple slicing to serve. They can be seeded if halved lengthways then the seeds scooped out with a spoon. Some recipes call for cucumbers to be degorged – thinly sliced and salted in a colander for about 30 minutes – to draw out the excess water and although the flesh becomes limp the texture firms up. This makes them ideal for adding to mixed salads. Very few people bother to degorge thin cucumber slices for the classic English cucumber sandwich. It's a shame as it makes a real difference in flavour and texture. To make good cucumber raita-style salads, mix chopped cucumber at the last minute with thick Greek-style strained yogurt, seasoning, lots of fresh chopped mint and a hint of dill or cumin. The ubiquitous Greek salad of cucumber, tomato, olives and feta cheese is found in several parts of the Mediterranean – very refreshing on a hot day drizzled with a little oil.

FENNEL

Availability: all year round.

Bulb or Florence fennel is the bulbous pale green vegetable with a sweet aniseed flavour that resembles celery. Apparently, squat bulbs of fennel are the female form and the longer, thinner ones are the male. It keeps for a good week or so in the bottom of the fridge, but the centre can start to turn brown if kept too long. The herb fennel grows wild in many parts of Britain and Europe: you can easily spot the yellow seeds like clusters of fairy showerheads.

Fennel has a number of delicious uses. Small bulbs are best sliced for salads or braised whole to be served with tomato sauces and olives or cooked in a wine-flavoured chicken casserole. Medium-sized heads can be quartered lengthways and chargrilled until softened, then dressed with lemon and olive oil. In Italy, fennel is eaten with cheese as a dessert.

GARLIC

Legends abound about this plant although, strangely considering how valuable it is to cooks everywhere, most of them seem to be of a Satanic nature. 'From his left foot sprang garlic, his right foot onions.' It is also considered medicinal, antibiotic and antiseptic (some would add antisocial, too). There are several varieties, especially European and not to mention Asian strains which crop at different times of the year thus ensuring cooks are never short of a clove or two. Generally speaking, the fatter the clove, the easier to peel and nicer to use. Never use less than two plump cloves at a time!

TIP: CRUSHING GARLIC

To crush fresh garlic, break off two or three cloves and lay them on a board. Place a wide-bladed cook's knife flat on top and smash a clenched fist down heavily on the blade. The clove will split and the skin should slip neatly off. Foodie cooks and chefs like to crush cloves on a board with the tip of a cook's knife, working in a little sea salt: it takes just seconds. Otherwise you can use a garlic press, but that makes for washing up, or you can simply chop the garlic finely on a board. Garlic can turn rancid quite quickly, so use it quickly once peeled and crushed. To get rid of the smell of garlic on the chopping board, scrub it with detergent and cold (not hot) water.

Buying and using garlic

Always buy the largest bulbs you can find. If you use a lot of garlic then an elaborate plait makes economic sense, but if you use garlic slowly, you may find the cloves dry to a grey, musty powder before you use them up so better to stick to one head at a time. Smoked garlic is quite delicious; in the UK supplies come from the Isle of Wight. In summer, when fresh and juicy French and Italian large purple garlics hit the shops, buy several heads and peel away just the outside leaves (no need to separate the garlic into cloves) and then cut the head up like an onion, and mash them in a food processor with a little olive oil and sea salt. Transfer the purée to a small jar, cover with a thin layer of oil and store in the fridge to use within a week.

The pungency of fresh garlic is reduced if you either boil or roast whole cloves in their skins, then just squeeze them from the root end and out they pop, smooth and creamy. For a gentle garlic flavour, pop unpeeled cloves into a stew or stock and fish them out before serving the dish. For a real punch, however, add crushed raw garlic at the end of cooking. To cook garlic, keep the heat gentle and don't let the flesh burn or it will taste bitter. On the other hand, some Thai-style dishes call for browned garlic slices, which you can buy crisp and dried from Asian food stores, or make your own, slow-frying and turning often.

Ready-made garlic purée in a toothpaste-style tube or a jar is OK for occasional use when you just want a hint of garlic but it does tend to have a pasteurised blandness to it. Dried garlic powder or granules have a burnt whiff but are not bad if you are cooking Texan or Mexican style food with spices that blend in accordingly.

GLOBE ARTICHOKES

Availability: all year round, but best during mid-summer.

The edible thistle beloved of keen garden cooks and imported for sale throughout the year from various countries. Big supplies, with large, pale green succulent heads, come in from Brittany. Other countries of origin include Egypt, Cyprus, Holland and the UK. Baby heads, just 5cm long, can be eaten raw, before the spiky chokes develop inside. Otherwise, small whole heads can be halved, fried and served with rich tomato sauce.

Cooking and eating large heads of artichokes requires guidance and varies depending on whether you intend serving the whole of the head, or trimming all the leaves and choke away for the fleshy bottom.

To cook, first break off the stalk, pulling it sharply downwards. If you're skilled, you will be able to pull out some long strings. Have a large bowl of cold water at the ready mixed with 1tbsp of lemon juice. Place the head sideways down on a board and slice off the top quarter, cutting through the tough leaves. Drop the head into the lemon water. When ready to cook, boil in plenty of salted water for about 20–30 minutes or until one of the base leaves pulls away easily. Drain upside-down in a colander and serve either hot with melted butter or hollandaise sauce or cold with a vinaigrette dressing or mayonnaise.

If you're in a loving and giving mood, de-choke the heads. Pull aside the tops of the heads to reveal a cluster of purple-pointed leaves. Clutch these firmly and pull up and out sharply. Using a teaspoon, gently scrape away the spiky choke, making sure none escapes. Discard and replace the purple-pointed leaves in the centre. To eat, pull off the leaves from the outside and dip the base of each in dressing, then clamp the base between your teeth and suck off the flesh. Repeat until all the leaves are sucked and form a neat discarded pile on the side of the plate. Eat the bottom flesh with a knife and fork.

Chefs like to cook raw peeled artichoke bottoms in oil or blanch them and toss in dressing for salads. Either way, artichoke slices are very much part of the fusion food scene. It is increasingly possible to buy baby chargrilled artichokes preserved in oil as an antipasto starter, dressed with fresh lemon. An artichoke liqueur, Cynar is called after its botanical name – Cynara.

HORSERADISH

Availability: late summer.

Horseradish is a truly rural vegetable with a very mustardy hot spiciness that can bring tears to the eyes. But gosh, is it worth it! It's a root and, given half a chance, grows with gay abandon in gardens. Flex your biceps when you try to pull it up because it's a toughie. (Botantically, when the prefix 'horse' is added to a name, it means it's very near the natural state – a wild child.) If you find it fresh (or if you wrench it from the ground), then peel it at arm's length to cut down on tears. I have seen fresh horseradish on sale in supermarkets on rare occasions but most of the time it's to be found sanitised in bottled relish or 'sauces', with much of the punchiness knocked out. Still – better than nothing.

Grate it coarsely and mix with whipped cream or crème fraîche and salt and ground black pepper. It's marvellous with rare roasted beef, or try it (in very small amounts) in a mayonnaise with smoked or oily rich fish. Or you can bring it (grated) to boiling point covered with a little dry white wine or dry sherry, then bottle it in a sterilised jar and store in the fridge ready to spoon out for sauces and relishes. I like to add horseradish in cautious amounts to lots of creamy dishes – for all its ferocity of flavour, it becomes a purring pussycat as a background flavour.

JERUSALEM ARTICHOKES

Availability: winter months.

These are neither artichokes in the true sense (they are related to sunflowers and daisies), nor do they come from Jerusalem. The yellow-fleshed tubers with pinky-beige knobbly skins are actually native to North America. They were described by the first European settlers in Massachusetts as tasting like globe artichokes, but there the similarity ends. 'Jerusalem' is probably a corruption of the term *girasol*, Italian for a sunflower.

Try to buy ones that are as smooth as possible so you don't lose too much in peeling. Treat them as you would chopped-up turnips in that they can be boiled until just tender then mashed and used as a purée in dishes such as soufflés. During the Second World War, the Ministry of Food encouraged people to try them in a cheese sauce and topped with crispy crumbs. As a soup they are superb but they can also be blanched and dressed in vinaigrette or tossed with other vegetables for a salad.

On a more delicate subject – Jerusalem artichokes do have a reputation for causing 'wind' during digestion, which seems to afflict some but not all who eat them. So eat them in moderation!

JICAMA

Availability: all year round.

This less common vegetable looks like the biggest turnip in the world. It has a leathery skin and sweetish, crisp flesh that stays firm even when cooked. You can eat jicama raw or cooked and cut it into slices or sticks. It's popular in Chinese cooking or used in Mexican cooking as a crudité for dipping in lime juice and chilli powder – ouch.

KOHLRABI

Availability: traditionally March–November.

Kohlrabi is also known as the cabbage turnip, because botanically it is more of a cabbage then a turnip. It is pale green in colour. Once peeled treat it as you would a turnip. Some find the flavour more delicate and prefer it. Buy small- or medium-sized kohlrabis because if they are too large the texture is tough and fibrous. It makes good soup.

LEEKS

Availability: generally winter and spring, but increasingly imported in our summer months.

Until recently, leeks were firmly categorised as a winter vegetable, their mild onion flavour enhancing many warming winter dishes. As summer approached, so leeks grew hard woody cores, but now, through modern techniques, growing seasons are extended and we are able to find uses for them in summer cuisines too. Supermarkets sell well-washed plants, either *au naturel*, complete with full stems and roots, or ready trimmed and bagged. Chefs like to use the tender white lower stems in cooking, leaving the thicker greener tops for the stock pot: home cooks use all the plant. If you buy whole untrimmed leeks, cut off the root end and trim the very tough tops but leave a good amount of green on – no need to waste this. Slash the green tops right down to the white a few times like a brush and wash well in cold running water to remove any earth. Then slice or chop.

I find nearly everyone loves leeks, from children to the 'I hate vegetables' brigade. Treat them like onions, cooking them slowly until tender. Finely shredded leeks can be dried in a very low oven for an hour or so until crisp and wrinkled for a pretty pale green garnish for grilled salmon or chicken. Tender young baby leeks are best blanched in boiling water then cooled and tossed in a vinaigrette dressing for a light starter or salad.

EASY LEEK AND POTATO SOUP
Serves 4–6

2tbsp olive or sunflower oil
25g (1oz) butter
2 large fat leeks, washed and roughly chopped
500g (1lb 2oz) floury potatoes, peeled and chopped
500ml (18fl oz) milk
1 litre vegetable stock (made with vegetarian stock cubes) or
water 1tsp sea salt
freshly ground black pepper
a good squeeze of fresh lemon juice
a little half-fat crème fraîche and some parsley or chives,
to serve

Heat the oil and butter gently in a large heavy-based saucepan,
then stir in the leeks and potatoes. Stir well and heat until
sizzling, then cover and lower the heat right down. Cook for
about 12–15 minutes without lifting the lid until the vegetables
have softened and wilted (chefs call this sweating).

Stir again and pour in the milk and stock. Add the salt and lots
of pepper. Bring to the boil, then lower the heat again. Cook
uncovered for about 20 minutes.

For a smooth soup, carefully strain the vegetables and stock,
reserving both. Whiz the vegetables in a blender until creamy,
then return to the pan with the reserved stock.
Check the seasoning, add the lemon juice and reheat gently.
Serve with a dollop or two of crème fraîche and the chives.
You could also add an exotic Middle Eastern touch to this soup.
Heat 2tbsp of olive oil with 2tsp of paprika or mild chilli powder
and trickle this in a swirl into each serving.

LETTUCES AND LEAVES

Availability: all year round.

Goodness, have we seen a renaissance in lettuces and green salad leaves in recent years! Chilled food cabinets seem to sprout a new variety, in a glorious array of colours either whole or ready washed and bagged, every season, from winter to summer. The latest is *Japanese salad greens (Mizuna)* with their craggy leaves and red stalks. Next year, who knows?

Each variety of raw salad leaves has its own flavour, which you have to judge for yourself. In addition, certain leaves can be torn or shredded without too much after-bruising.

The sweet and juicy *iceberg lettuces* are perhaps the most resilient. They can be bought whole or bagged. Whole, I like to keep them in their wrapping, tearing off outside leaves and working my way towards the firm heart over a period of days. The larger outside leaves also make good serving dishes for stir-fried vegetables or rice pilaffs. One nice serving idea is a dish of stir-fried pork mince flavoured with soy sauce, ginger and garlic, all spooned into iceberg-leaf 'cups' and topped with a trickle of hoisin sauce.

Similar large-leaf lettuces available according to season are *Webb's wonder, butterhead* or just called *'crisp'*. Fading out of sight, fortunately, are the old-fashioned, floppy, cabbage-style lettuces we used to see clinging to the side of salad plates topped with tomato slices, cucumber and salad cress.

Cos are long and dark green with a mildly bitter, slightly aniseed flavour. Again, good storers, but if they are very big, the outside leaves tend to be tough, although these can be simmered for soup with fresh or frozen peas. Better to buy small baby Cos hearts or try the American-style *romaine* lettuces which look like Cos but are paler in colour and slightly sweeter – the classic lettuces for a Caesar's salad.

On the frilly side, more and more varieties are emerging on our supermarket shelves. They make a pretty sight as you sweep in with your basket or trolley, a little like a florist's shop. *Lollo biondo* and *lollo rosso* are the tightly crinkly ones (rumour has it these were named in honour of the curvaceous Italian film star, Gina Lollobrigida). These are the leaves favoured by catering establishments as part of their salad garnishes. I find them tasteless and watery and I don't even like their curves. No – my favourite curly leaf is the *oak leaf lettuce* or *feuille de chêne*. The red-tinged leaves look more natural and have more texture and flavour. Similar red leaves in my favour are *quattro stagioni* and *red escarole (green escarole* is also available). However, sometimes they suffer from limpness due to poor storage. If this is the case, simply submerge them in a big bowl of ice cold water, drain, shake dry in a salad spinner and place them in a loose food bag. (Supermarket bags are ideal for storing lettuces because they are roomy yet light enough not to crush the leaves.)

A lettuce you can rarely find whole except in speciality greengrocers is the *frisee*, partly I suspect because it's too large to handle and many of the outside leaves start to decay, making the rest of it look unappetising. It seems frisee leaves are used extensively in ready-bagged salads but a fully grown frisee takes a lot of working through. The leaves are refreshingly bitter and particularly nice as a salad on its own dressed with a hot bacon and basalmic vinegar dressing, with maybe a handful of garlic-flavoured croutons.

The *little gem* lettuce, another of my favourites, looks like a cross between a small Webb's wonder and a baby Cos. They are ideal for shredding, slicing or simply tearing apart to use as crudités. Good, too, for children's lunch boxes. They also last longer bagged loosely in the salad drawer.

Preparing lettuce leaves

Now to the great debate: whether one tears or slices lettuce leaves. Tearing is the gourmets' preferred method because lettuce leaves do bruise easily. However, when no one is looking, I will happily slice leaves into thin shreds because shredded leaves are easier to eat than large pieces. And if you eat lettuce within a few minutes of dressing it, there's no time for bruising. Sometimes chefs do shred lettuce leaves finely: they call it chiffonade and use the matchstick-thin shreds as a garnish.

HOT BACON DRESSING

Snip about 3 rashers of lean smoked streaky bacon or pancetta and fry in a little olive oil until lightly crisp. Remove from the heat and stir in 2tbsp of balsamic vinegar and 2tbsp of water. Toss immediately into a bowl of torn frisee leaves.

COOKING WITH LETTUCE

Lettuce does have a great flavour and cooks nicely. The classic dish is Pois St Germain – peas cooked briefly with shredded lettuce, salad onions and butter. It's ideal for using wilted outside leaves with a pack of frozen peas. Cut up large lettuce leaves, chop 3 or more salad onions, mix with 3–4 portions of frozen peas, a good knob of butter, seasoning and a little freshly grated nutmeg. Cook all together in a saucepan with no added water for 5 minutes or for 3–5 minutes on full in the microwave.

Cresses

These are the little seeds we scattered on wet blotting paper as children and watched as the mysteries of germination unfurled before our very eyes. Salad cress is the mildest: true mustard and cress is more peppery. Just snip the little seedlings off above the rooting mass. If you are frugal, you can continue to water the pot and grow a second batch in a few days. I've seen large salad cress leaves, sold as Japanese cress, which you treat in the same way.

Corn salad, lamb's leaves and mache/rapunsel

These small round leaves are sold in tiny clumps with thin roots attached, and are excellent in winter salads and easy to grow at home. They're good served on their own, just lightly dressed. Pick the leaves from the roots. These leaves are also added to bagged salad mixes.

Rocket, arugula, American land cress

Basically, these oak-leaf-shaped leaves on spindly stalks all have the same peppery, pungent flavour. Wild rocket (a variety not necessarily grown in the wild) has thinner leaves and is easier to eat. Rocket can be bought as a growing herb, but it is expensive. They are a particular favourite with Italian cooks, who wilt them with hot olive oil to serve with grilled meats, cheese and pasta. Great used instead of basil in a pesto sauce. They are used in salads a lot, generally topped with thin shavings of Parmesan cheese.

You can grow rocket easily in a garden: simply scatter the seeds in a patch of bare under-utilised earth, water it occasionally and watch those seedlings grow. A very good winter salad vegetable, but do pick the leaves often or the stalks can go a bit woody.

Watercress

Watercress is the best known and grows in watery fields with a gently flowing current. Sometimes you may spy wild watercress, which tastes wonderfully pungent but may contain liver fluke, so beware. Best to simply admire wild cress from afar. Buy watercress bunched or in bags. If the leaves look wilted, give them the cold-water treatment, drain and store bagged in the fridge until they perk up again. I find bunches more useful as you can chop them more finely or pick off the thicker stalks should you not wish to use them. The stalks are, however, full of flavour so do find a use for them. Watercress is a good source of iron, calcium and vitamins B and C.

There are lots of different recipe ideas for watercress. Try it chopped and mixed into soft cheese, in a creamy sauce for fish or chicken and, of course, as a delicious soup.

WATERCRESS SOUP

Chop two big bunches of watercress and sweat in a saucepan with a chopped onion and two chopped medium-sized potatoes for 10 minutes. Cover with a light stock or water and simmer for 15 minutes. Whiz to a purée in a blender and, for a final silky flourish, rub through a sieve. Return to the saucepan and reheat. Serve hot.

MARROWS

Marrows are dark green overgrown courgettes with a tough outer skin that needs cutting away if you intend serving the flesh alone. They are really nice cooked with onion, tomato and herbs. Older marrows are good served halved, seeded and stuffed with a mixture of minced meat and other vegetables or cooked pulses, tomatoes and herbs. A winter marrow, suspended in a string bag in a cool, airy place, will keep for months.

OKRA

Okra (lady's fingers) is classed as a squash but treated as a green vegetable or bean. It is used extensively in Indian and West Indian cooking: legend has it that this was one of the vegetables West African slaves smuggled out of their native lands and grew in their new enforced homelands, where it retained the old African name of gumbo. Choose firm, bright green and unblemished okra. I've seen many pathetically flabby specimens languishing on supermarket shelves. In fact, the best place to buy really good okra is from ethnic stores, such as halal butchers. Okra oozes a sticky liquid when cut which helps to thicken sauces and soups so, unless you cook it whole, chop it at the last minute. It is delicious cooked in spicy sauces or with tomato. Chinese okra is larger and coarser: you prepare it by peeling the long ridges then slicing it like courgettes to add to stir-fries and braised dishes.

ONIONS

Availability: all year round – there is always an onion harvest somewhere in the world and, as they're easy to transport, supplies rarely run short.

Allium is the botanical name for onions, shallots, leeks, chives and garlic and we'll look at each of these in turn later. It's a rare cook who doesn't use onions – so many of the world's great dishes rely on this most indispensable vegetable that can be used in a wholesome peasant soup or a dish fit for kings. For centuries onions have featured in folklore and folk medicine, treating ailments from colds to baldness. It was the Romans who were responsible for introducing them wherever their armies tramped through Europe. Small or plump, juicy and mild or pungent and hot, there's an onion in almost every kind of dish.

Buying and storing onions

Onions, shallots and garlic are sold lightly dried until the skins are paper-thin and easy to peel off. In the main, the larger the bulb, the milder the flavour. Onions should be pressed lightly before buying. Avoid soft or mouldy onions – they smell awful when you peel them. If an onion starts to sprout, then it is still fine to use provided it is firm. Don't waste the green sprouts – they can be snipped off and used as for spring onions or a garnish.

Spring onions and leeks are sold complete with green stems and fleshy juicy bulbs. The plants we refer to as spring onions are sometimes called scallions or salad onions, presumably because modern growing methods mean they are no longer available only in spring but all year round. Green onions (fatter bulb spring onions) are easier to use, just requiring a little peeling, if necessary, then slicing or chopping. The white bulbs are milder and green tops more pungent. Spring onions are sold young and straight or allowed to grow on until they develop plumb little oval bulbs, ideal for slicing into leafy salads or over tomatoes with dressing and chopped fresh herbs. You can also slash the white bulb end a few times and soak the onion in very cold water until the flesh curls into a brush shape to make an attractive garnish.

Store onions in a cool, dark, dry place.

COOKING ONIONS

Do take the time to sauté onions thoroughly when you cook them. A good 10 minutes over a moderate heat in oil and/or butter helps to caramelise them and lessen the raw, almost tannic flavour. Some Indian dishes require you to cook onions until they turn a deep, dark brown colour – not to be confused with burning onions. Once they are a rich brown colour, they can be drained and as they dry and cool will crisp to a deliciously sweet caramelised garnish.

Onion varieties

There are hundreds of varieties of onions, but the most popular are the golden *Spanish onions* (not necessarily grown only in Spain), also called *Bermuda onions*. The smaller, brown-skinned onion is a favourite with home gardeners and allotment owners but is also imported from Egypt, Hungary and several countries of the southern hemisphere.

Then there are varieties of *red onions*, originally from Italy and varying in size from large and plump to small and dainty. Red onions are ideal for eating raw because of their sweetness but if you still wish to lessen 'onion breath' then soak slices in cold water for an hour or more and rinse again. The distinctive purple-red concentric skin makes them the darling garnish of fusion food joints, as much at home atop a bruschetta as adorning a golden-hued curry sauce or rich and mellow used in a sweet-sour onion 'marmalade'.

White-fleshed onions are also mild and sweet – not that one would actually use them in desserts but their sweet flavour balanced with spices, vinegars and citrus juices is nicely enhanced in salads, relishes and sauces. Sliced raw they are ideal in salads or layered with cheese and/or tomatoes in sandwiches.

Peeling onions

The big question is: how can you peel onions without crying? When you cut into an onion you release enzymes, which take part in complex biochemical reactions. One of these substances is propenyl sulphuric acid, a volatile irritant. So either work quickly, wear swimming goggles, cut the onion under water or resign yourself to having a good cry. My daughter suggests clasping a metal spoon in one's mouth: I suppose it does make her inhale the offending sulphuric acid before it wafts up into her eyes but it does make her look rather silly. I do find, however, that when I blanch whole onions for a minute or so in boiling water, they are less vindictive. Milder onions have less of the offending irritant.

Button onions

These are the baby silvery, white bulbs usually sold pickled but if you can buy them fresh add them to stews and casseroles for the last half hour of cooking as a garnish. They are particularly nice gently fried in olive oil and butter with a few pinches of sugar until they turn an appetising, glossy caramel to serve with lemon butter chicken or scattered over pan-fried liver or gammon. To peel baby onions reasonably effortlessly, blanch them in boiling water for a minute then plunge them into cold water. The skins will loosen sufficiently for you to just pop the little bulbs out.

Pickling onions are slightly larger but stronger and able to stand up to vinegar and spices.

If you can find them, try the French *grelots* or Italian *boretane*, squashed-flat pale brown onions used sliced and deep-fried or whole as garnishes. *Welsh onions* (also known as green onions, cibol onions, Japanese or Chinese onions) look like a cross between shallots and spring onions. They are best served cooked and have quite a distinctive oniony flavour. *Tree onions* (also known as Egyptian onions), clusters of bulbs that grow on a small tree, are undoubtedly ornamental curios but they are good to eat as well.

Shallots

Shallots (French échalote, supposedly named after the town Askalone now in Israel) can be small and fiddly or plump, purple and long. These are widely used in high cuisine circles by chefs and hobby gourmet cooks alike. The mild, sweet flesh dissolves nicely in the pan, making it ideal for delicate sauces as well as a chopped garnish or in dressings. Mixed with wine vinegar shallots are sensational with fresh oysters on the shell. The larger *French* (or *banana*) shallots are worth tracking down in speciality greengrocers or you might like to buy them by the small sackload if you see them on Continental travels. Shallots are also quite easy to grow in vegetable gardens or allotments. They're a popular ingredient in Far Eastern kitchens, and look like little pink bulbs, called *Thai shallots* or *Chinese red onions*.

SHALLOT CONFIT

A very useful homemade purée to store in the fridge and add by the teaspoonful to sauces, pan-fries and dressings for a fine, subtle flavor. Pre-cooking a batch of shallots makes good ergonomic sense. Ideally choose the larger French shallots.

Finely chop 6 large peeled shallots. Heat 5tbsp of olive oil in a small, heavy-based saucepan and when hot stir in the shallots. Add a sprig of fresh thyme and a small bay leaf then turn the heat right down. Cook very gently for up to half an hour stirring occasionally, until the shallots melt into a golden purée. Cool and store in a sterilised jam jar covered with a layer of oil.

PARSNIPS

Availability: mostly winter and spring.

Native to Britain and enjoyed by patrician (i.e. posh) Romans, parsnips
have a longer history than both carrots and potatoes and early recipes have
them as the traditional accompaniment to roast beef and salt cod. Even
today, there's little to beat a sweet, slightly caramelised roasted parsnip
or a smoked fish and parsnip soup. They still remain a singularly British
vegetable – the French remain mystified as to why we like them so much.
The curse of culinary chauvinism! Before the easy availability of sugar,
parsnips were used in cakes and jams, so modern fusion food recipes in this
vein ain't so hip after all.

Parsnips are damaged if they are tossed around too much so when buying,
do check them over for bruises, visible as softer, darker flesh. Store parsnips
like carrots – in a cool, dark and dry place.

Young parsnips are really nice lightly roasted with oil, a light sprinkling of
soft brown sugar and the juice of an orange. Aniseed-flavoured spices such as
cumin, coriander and caraway complement both parsnips and carrots.

ROAST PARSNIPS

A particular favourite in my family. Peel the parsnips thinly and
top and tail them. Cut off the tapering tail as one piece, then
cut the thicker end either in half or into long quarters so that
you have pieces of about the same dimension to ensure even
roasting. Heat about 4tbsp of olive oil (or a little animal fat such
as beef or lamb dripping) in a preheated oven at 190°C/gas
mark 5 until good and hot. There is no need to parboil parsnips,
simply stir them into the hot oil, season lightly with salt and
freshly ground black pepper, sprinkle with a pinch or two of
curry powder if you wish, and roast for about 20–30 minutes,
stirring once or twice.

PEAS

As a junior working for a frozen food company several years ago, I was privileged to witness the drama of a fresh pea harvest. When a machine called a tenderometer measured the right degree of ripeness in a sample of fresh peas, an army of harvesters swung into action, just like in the movies. Within 90 minutes the pea vines were stripped and the peas blanched and frozen so the ultimate texture and flavour would be preserved. All very reassuring, but it does illustrate just how delicate legumes can be and how freezing is the best method of preserving certain vegetables. The fresh peas I nibbled during the harvest were very similar to the frozen peas from a pack.

Garden peas are very delicate vegetables with a limited shelf life because enzyme activity starts within an hour or so of picking, affecting the flavour. It is therefore not a good idea to buy 'fresh' peas unless you really are sure they are very fresh. However, because they freeze so well, peas have become one of our most popular vegetables. A fresh pea on sale may well be two to three days old and staler than a frozen pea. Not worth the premium price, not to mention the effort of shelling them and discarding the pods. For the best flavour, I simply thaw frozen peas and reheat them for just a minute until piping hot. After all, they have already been cooked by blanching.

Petits pois are a small tender variety of garden pea, not simply baby peas. They are considered to be the finest-tasting pea and are readily available frozen or canned.

Dried peas are special varieties that are freeze-dried and have a different texture and flavour. The traditional *marrowfat* pea for mushy peas was originally developed for the Japanese market, maro being the variety name.

Mangetouts (French for 'eat all'), *sugar snap* and *snow peas* are peas still attached to their tender edible pods. They may need topping and tailing first – simply snap the top stalk and pull down to string the one side, then snap the bottom of the pod and pull up the string on the other side. These need just light cooking by boiling, steaming or stir-frying.

CRUSHED PEAS WITH CRÈME FRAÎCHE AND MINT

Or how to turn frozen peas into an *haute cuisine* side dish.

Cook your usual amount of frozen peas (or petits pois, for a sweeter flavour), then drain, return to the pan and lightly mash or crush with a fork – it should be lightly lumpy. Season and mix in dollops of crème fraîche to taste and some chopped fresh mint or flat leaf parsley.

PEPPERS AND PIMENTOS

Availability: all year round.

While we're in the chilli mood, let's look at their milder cousins – peppers and pimentos. Holland is a major supplier of peppers in a glorious selection of colours and shapes, from cute baby-sized in the UK to long, thin elegants. Again, green peppers ripen and sweeten into red but other colours range from yellow and orange through to purple and black. Other than the colour there is very little to distinguish them from each other.

Pimento peppers, on the other hand, are a speciality of Hungary and Spain where they are used in a great variety of ways. Wonderfully aromatic, pimento peppers can be roasted and canned, or dried and ground to make paprika. Hungary boasts several types of paprika, which are used widely in cooking. The Spanish and Basques also love paprika and sell it in a sweet (*dulce*) or stronger roasted (*picante*) form.

TO ROAST PEPPERS

Roasting or grilling at a high heat not only gives the pepper flesh a delicious smoky flavour but also helps the skin to peel away more easily. Cut each pepper in quarters and remove the stalk and core. You can grill peppers but it's better to use the oven if you're preparing a lot. Preheat the oven to 225°C/gas mark 7. Lay the pepper quarters skin-side up on a baking tray and cook for 10–12 minutes until the skins blacken or blister or both. Remove the tray and cover with a clean tea towel to retain the steam, which helps to loosen the skin. When cool enough to handle, peel the peppers and store them in the fridge until required. Or slice them, pack into a clean jar and cover with olive oil. Keep chilled and use slices in cooking or salads within ten days. For small quantities, place the quarters skin-side up under a very hot grill until the skins blacken and blister. Cover and peel as above.

POTATOES

Availability: earlies from May; main crop from September.

It's hard to imagine a day going by that doesn't include some form of potato in our diet, be it a side dish, a takeaway snack or even for breakfast. Along with bread, potatoes are a main staple in our diet and yet their European debut (from central and South America) was only some four hundred years ago in the late 16th century. Within sixty years potatoes had become the staple food of the Irish, having been introduced into County Cork by Sir Walter Raleigh. But the French thought they were poisonous. It took an 18th-century French chemist, Antoine-Auguste Parmentier, to popularise them and apply what would now amount to modern marketing techniques to make potatoes 'hip', including surrounding a field of potatoes with guards so people would think they were a precious gourmet food and persuading the doomed queen Marie-Antoinette to wear potato flowers in her hair. The rest, as they say, is history.

Victorian kitchen gardeners perfected this most versatile of root vegetables, propagating an almost bewildering selection of tubers, many of which are still around a century later. Shapes, colours, sizes and textures abound and yet most of us end up buying bags labelled simply 'reds' or 'whites', with little idea of what is beneath the skin. Some supermarkets are now labelling potatoes by their suitability for cooking – mashing, chipping, roasting, for salads and so on.

Potatoes are defined by their textures from waxy to floury. The Potato Council hosts a good cooking website – www.lovepotatoes.co.uk – and categorises varieties as Fluffy, Salad and Smooth. This can help you decide which variety to choose if remembering names is not your forte. So, if you want a nice firm boiler or one that slices easily and thinly for Dauphinoise, choose a smooth variety. For creamy, fluffy mash or crispy roasties aim for King Edward or Maris Piper, although if the variety is too floury you might find most of it boils away to pulp (great for soup, though).

Salad spuds hold their shape and texture well and are nicest served unpeeled and simply tossed in a little butter or a light salad dressing. (Always toss potatoes while they are still hot and let them cool in the dressing for the nicest-flavoured potato salad.) Varieties to look out for are (lots of girls names it seems!) – *Charlotte, Anya, Nicola, Belle de Fontenay, Roseval, La Ratte* (a delicious French variety), *Francine* (another good French potato), *Scottish Shelagh* and the curiously named *Pink Fir Apple* (with an almost nutty flavour). *Jersey Royals*, with their distinctive kidney shape, are in a class of their own, well worth the premium price but do make sure they are genuine Jerseys, sold in distinctive wooden crates and best around mid-summer. *Cyprus new potatoes* are also a delicious treat. *Black* or *purple* potatoes are something of a designer curiosity – fun but not a lot else going for them.

Buying and storing potatoes

Potatoes keep well when stored out of daylight in a cool, dry place. With our modern, well-lit kitchens without stone-floored larders or outhouses, this may mean the salad drawer of the fridge is the only option. This is fine, so long as the potatoes are lightly wrapped in a bag and the temperature is not so cold that they might freeze. What you have to avoid is greening skin due to poor storage and exposure to light. A little green can be cut out, but a lot of green means the potato should be thrown out. Most potatoes are now sold ready washed, though they actually store better if coated in lovely wholesome soil. If you buy muddy potatoes, let them soak for a few minutes in tepid water to loosen the dirt before scrubbing.

Boiling potatoes

Potato purists (and top chefs) boil potatoes in their skins then peel them, wearing rubber gloves to protect their hands – honest! This retains the vitamins and flavour, which lie just below the skin, and also ensures that floury potatoes do not boil away to a sludge.

Roasting

If you intend to roast potatoes, choose a floury variety and peel them thinly using a swivel peeler. Cut the spuds into even-sized pieces, say 4–5cm (1½–2in) cubes, and parboil them for about 3 minutes. Meanwhile, heat 4–6tbsp of sunflower or olive oil in a roasting tin at the top of an oven set at 200°C/gas mark 6. Drain the still firm potatoes well and shake them a little in the colander to rough up the outside so they cook to a craggy crispness. When the oil is hot and very runny, carefully add the potatoes, spooning hot oil over the top. Shake over some fine sea salt, plus a little black pepper and maybe a pinch or two or dried thyme or rosemary. Return to the oven for 20 minutes without moving the potatoes to let the undersides turn a golden brown. Then turn each potato piece over using a fish slice or palette knife. Season again and return to the oven for another 20–30 minutes or until golden brown and crisp. Drain on kitchen paper and serve as soon as possible lightly sprinkled with a little more salt.

PATATAS BRAVAS

Roast and serve your potatoes Spanish style. Sprinkle lightly with sweet paprika and serve drizzled with slightly runny mayonnaise (thinned, if necessary, with dribbles of cold milk or water) and more dribbles of a mild or spicy tomato sauce or ketchup. Great for tapas or to serve with roast chicken or burgers.

Mashing

For perfect mash, choose a floury potato. Peel thinly and cut into even sizes then boil in lightly salted water for about 15 minutes until they are just tender, but not too soft. Drain well and return to the pan, which can be set back on the heat for a minute or so to let the potato dry out. To mash: if possible press the cooked potato through a potato ricer (this makes the most wonderfully light potato), otherwise use a masher or a fork, but never an electric beater or food processor or the mixture will turn gluey. Beat in a good knob of butter or olive oil spread, then beat in about 150ml (5fl oz) of hot milk. Season well and add a little freshly grated nutmeg or a pinch of ground mace.

MEDITERRANEAN CRUSHED POTATOES (ÉCRASÉ DE POMMES DE TERRES)

French chefs like to crush boiled potatoes with a fork, adding extra-virgin olive oil, chopped fresh tomatoes, chopped black olives and chopped fresh tarragon and basil for pommes écrasées. Other flavourings to add to creamy mash are pesto, crushed garlic, finely chopped spring onions (to make champ), shredded boiled cabbage or kale (to make colcannon), horseradish sauce, coarsegrain mustard or grated Cheddar. Serve topped with another big knob of lovely butter!

PUMPKINS

Pumpkins are beautiful! And luckily we are seeing them more than just around Halloween time. There are many varieties of pumpkin and a great many ways of cooking and eating them. Not only the Americans but also the French, Italians, West Indians and Arabs have lots of recipes that use them. You will find large 4 kilo sizes right down to small 1 kilo Jack-be-Little pumpkins. West Indian pumpkins are ridged and the skins all shades of green.

For cooking, buy wedges as you need them, that way you can check to see if the flesh is fibrous and if it is don't buy – it should be smooth. You may find the skin hard to peel, so chop up the flesh first and peel it in smaller sections. Cook pumpkin flesh in hardly any water at all, because although it is not actually watery it makes its own juice. Once cooked to a firm chunky pulp, use it as required. Stir it into risottos, or make it into soups. Of course, there's American pumpkin pie where cooked and puréed flesh is mixed with beaten eggs, soft brown sugar, melted butter and spices, then baked in a sweet flan case until just firm. The seeds can be spread on a baking tray, roasted until crisp and seasoned with salt to be nibbled with drinks.

PUMPKIN AND HAM PASTA
My favourite recipe

500–600g (1lb 2oz–1lb 5oz) pumpkin flesh (or one small
pumpkin), peeled and cubed
2 slices of white bread, crusts removed
1 fat garlic clove, crushed
sea salt and freshly ground black pepper
3tbsp olive or sunflower oil
250g (9oz) pasta shapes
125g (4½oz) ham, cut into strips
25g (1oz) butter
1 red onion, thinly sliced
1tsp grated fresh ginger or ginger purée
150ml (5fl oz) carton single cream
50g (1¾oz) fresh Parmesan cheese, grated
a little chopped fresh parsley

Place the pumpkin in a saucepan with just enough water to
cover bring to the boil, then cover and cook for about 10 minutes
until tender. Drain well.

Meanwhile, place the bread slices in a food processor and
run the machine to make breadcrumbs. Add the garlic and
seasoning. Heat the oil in a frying pan and stir-fry the crumbs
until lightly browned. Set aside and wipe out the pan.

Cook the pasta according to the pack instructions in a saucepan,
drain and return to the pan. Add the ham.

Melt the butter in the frying pan and fry the onion and ginger for
about 5 minutes until softened, then mix in the cooked pumpkin
and the cream.

Heat until bubbling, then mix in the Parmesan and parsley.
Stir into the pasta, reheat and serve topped with the garlicky
crumbs.

RADISHES

Availability: most of the year.

Nearly all the great cultures and civilisations of the world enjoy radishes it seems, in one way or another throughout Europe, the Middle East, Greece, the Americas and the Far East, chiefly as appetisers or in salads. You generally buy them ready trimmed and bagged or bunched and leafy, though sometimes they look a sorry wilted and bedraggled sight. Not to worry, a good soak in ice-cold water and they soon spring back to life.

We seem to assign radishes only to salads, which is to underrate them. The French enjoy their radishes – oval-shaped with white with pink tips and a peppery flavour – for breakfast. They dip them in sea salt and eat them with crusty bread and unsalted butter. Or try them in the North African way, sliced with fresh orange slices, salt and lemon juice. Ideally buy red or pinky-white radishes with leaves and prepare them by pinching out the larger leaves, leaving the smaller edible ones still attached. The fresher the radishes, the more flavour they have.

Mooli or *daikon* is a long white radish used in Japanese dishes but ideal in Western salads too. Try it coarsely grated with grated carrot tossed in a light rice wine vinaigrette topped with chopped fresh mint and chives. Or shave into long thin wafers using a swivel vegetable peeler and soak for half an hour in cold water to crisp up, then toss into a salad of mixed leaves with shavings of carrot. Alternatively, cut wafer-thin rounds from a fat mooli and dress in a basalmic-flavoured vinaigrette mixed with a little soy sauce and sesame oil and sprinkled with sesame seeds. Fantastic with smoked salmon and a little salad of lamb's lettuce.

Store radishes either in a food container or bagged in the fridge to stop them going limp in the drying cold. Moolis, I find, don't last too long before they lose their crispness.

SALSIFY AND SCORZONERA

Availability: autumn through to spring.

When you find these two vegetables in a greengrocer's or supermarket they look quite similar. Their long, thin roots are like carrots in shape but salsify is a pale sandy colour, and scorzonera charcoal/black. They taste similar too – some say a little like oyster, others vaguely like a parsnip – but the texture is closer and slightly waxy. Scrubbed clean or thinly peeled and blanched, then dressed in butter both salsify and scorzonera are popular with French and Italian chefs who like to serve it as a bed for fish or chicken. They make good soup and I've eaten them in a chicken pie with mushrooms. They are nice, blanched and tossed in dressing, in salad with other vegetables, particularly artichoke bottoms. And scorzonera leaves are supposed to be good eaten in salads, but I've never found any with leaves still attached.

SEA VEGETABLES

Two movements in the food world are contributing towards an increasing awareness of seaweeds, or sea vegetables to give them their proper title, as they are hardly weeds: vegetarianism and Japanese cooking. Many sea vegetables are now cultivated: most are sold dried, which makes them a true convenience food; others are sold 'fresh' but, because they come from the sea and are coated in salt, they have a relatively long life for a fresh food. Sea vegetables are a very rich source of proteins and minerals such as potassium and iodine, vital in the maintenance of a healthy metabolism. Some are flavourless but useful as thickening or setting agents. Sanchi is a good Japanese brand name on packs of dried sea vegetables.

Dulse

Red or green dulse is not particularly exciting as a flavouring apart from its sea-salt tang. In Ireland, it is added to mashed potatoes for a form of champ. Rinsed, lightly boiled and refreshed in cold water it can be used in salads. It can also be dipped in batter and fried as fritters. It is eaten in France, where it is called sea lettuce.

Kelp

The health foodies' mineral supplement – I take one little green kelp pill every day. There are many types of kelp but perhaps the best known is *kombu*, used in Japanese cooking to add flavour and nutrients. It is the sea flavouring for the classic Japanese dish Dashi – a broth-cum-stock (see page 270).

It is sold dried in packs and is very expensive, but a small section is all you need at one time. I add about a 3cm length to a pan of cooking rice. It is also good added to stews and soups for flavour. If cooked briefly, it can be patted dry with kitchen paper and re-used.

Laver

The classic accompaniment to roasted Welsh lamb, eaten like mint sauce. This seaweed needs lengthy soaking and cooking to make it into a silky mixture called laverbread, sometimes flavoured with a little orange juice. Laver can be stirred into other dishes as a flavouring. It is available canned, which is far more convenient to use.

Nori

Nori is a form of laver processed by the Japanese into sheets of various thickness, sometimes gossamer-thin. I have found it in colours from a bright 'hunters' green to dark purple. Its chief use is as a wrapping for sushi but nori sheets can also be waved over a high gas flame until crisp and then snipped into strips to serve over soups, noodle pots and salads. Larger supermarkets now sell nori sheets in their speciality sections. Yaki nori is ready-toasted nori, so no need to do the flaming. Do try making your own sushi: it's easy and tastes much fresher than the very expensive sushi selections sold in chill cabinets. Although you will need a sushi mat, it will cost very little.

Samphire

In late May you might see baskets of bright green samphire (also known as sea asparagus), a sea marsh plant which looks like a thin, stringy cactus. Buy a couple of big handfuls and boil it for about 5 minutes until just tender. Drain and dress with a little melted butter to serve with poached or grilled salmon. Or, drain then rinse in cold water and toss into a green salad or new potatoes.

Wakame

Wakame (also known as *dabberlocks*) is not very 'seaweedy' so it is a good mild sea vegetable to experiment with. It is sold dried in sheets and can be chopped to add to stews or shredded to add to clear broths, traditionally the Japanese instant miso soup. It can also be made into a tea or deep-fried as a garnish.

Sea vegetables for setting

These include *carragheen, agar-agar* and other varieties that glory in such names such as *knotted wrack* and *oarweed*. The last two are well and truly processed beyond all recognition and used in the food industry as alginates for ice creams, soft drinks, jellies etc. They are like the seaweeds you see washed up on British beaches with little pouches you can pop with a stick. Carragheen, or Irish moss, and agar-agar are sold in health food shops and used by vegetarians as a substitute for gelatine. They need to be boiled with milk or juice, rather like cornflour, to make set jelly puddings. For a firm set you will need to use less liquid in the ratio to setting agent than for gelatine.

SPINACH

Availability: originally spring and summer, but now all year round.

There are many types, but much of what we buy is actually spinach beet, whose leaves have long tender stems and are easier to pick with less earth clinging to them. Traditional spinach as found in gardens is a denser, low-lying crop and the leaves are a little more bitter. Sales of leaf spinach rocketed after modern farming methods grew them cleaner than before and they were sold ready washed and bagged.

Seakale beet or (Swiss) *chard* is closer to the bags of spinach beet leaves but with thicker stems and heavier leaves, both of which are delicious. Cook chard in two parts, the stems sliced and placed in the pot first, then the leaves shredded and popped on top of the stems after a few minutes. (*Sea kale* per se is a British coastal leaf plant rarely on sale, but if you do find it on the beach, the leaves should be blanched by boiling. The slightly nutty flavour suggests you eat it like asparagus.)

Collard greens and *callaloo* are popular greens in soul food cooking and are available fresh in West Indian markets. Callaloo is even more delicious than spinach, if that's possible. It's the leafy tops of the taro tuber. Chop roughly and cook briefly as for spinach. As a child I ate this vegetable in a soup of crab and coconut and I've never forgotten the wonderful flavour, though the slightly slimy texture took a bit of hard gulping.

SQUASHES

Squashes come in beautiful colours, generally yellows, golds and stippled greens. They can be divided into two main groups: summer and winter. Summer squashes have thinner skins and are eaten unpeeled (e.g. courgettes) while winter squashes have tougher skins and are best peeled (e.g. pumpkin). We associate squashes with American cooking and certainly it has a great array of recipes and dishes. Squash varieties do differ in taste and the best advice is to buy small individual ones and try them, boiled in chunks and dressed with a little butter and seasoning. Some are good as vegetables, some as relishes and some are best pulped to use in baking or soups.

Popular varieties on sale in the autumn and winter months are *butternut, acorn, kabocha* (from New Zealand) *vegetable spaghetti* and *custard marrow*. These all need to be quartered, peeled and seeded, if necessary, then chopped up before cooking the flesh. Small *pattypan squashes* can be eaten just trimmed top and bottom then cooked like courgettes to be served whole. Other squashes include the *turban* or *buttercup squash* (very delicious), *summer crookneck* and even the *snake gourd*. Indian *tindoori gourds* are used in pickles, and *kerala* (bitter melon) is sliced and cooked with spices. *Chinese winter melon* is served cooked as a savoury in soups or stir-fries: it grows to quite a size and is often sold cut into wedges.

SWEDES

Availability: usually all year round.

Swede (or to give it its proper title, Swedish turnip) is particularly popular in northern Britain and over the border in Scotland, where they are known as 'neeps' and are served with haggis. Swede is called rutabaga in the USA. It has a reputation of being watery and bland. I beg to differ: if they are not overcooked, swedes crushed with a fork (not mashed with a potato masher) and mixed with tangy fromage frais, a knob of butter and lots of fragrant grated nutmeg make a side dish that approaches the sublime. You can prepare carrots and parsnips in the same style of mixture. As yet, we haven't been treated to baby versions of this root crop, chiefly I suspect because it is still regarded as a fodder crop for sheep and hasn't quite the same culinary cachet as other roots.

Although they are available most of the year they are most popular in wintry weather. I tend to buy small swedes because they are easier to peel and handle but large ones can be cut with a large-bladed knife to get through the tough skin and dense flesh.

Store swedes like other roots – in the cool, dark and dry.

TOMATOES

Availability: all year round from both hemispheres depending on seasons; home-grown season is mid-summer.

Tomatoes are sub-tropical berries, which makes them technically a fruit. The last decade has seen quite an explosion in varieties grown, but then the tomato has a way of popping up in all manner of ways. It was the Aztecs who first cultivated what was then a golden-coloured wild Andean fruit, not dissimilar from today's cherry tomatoes, which the European conquerors called 'golden apples' – hence the Italian name *pomodoro*. So the yellow and orange varieties now appearing in our stores are reverting to type.

Grown as botanical curiosities from their European debut in the mid-16th century, tomatoes began to be cultivated commercially in mid-19th century sunny Mediterranean Italy and Spain and further north under glass in hothouses. Consistent quality and supply gave rise to a flourishing canning and preserving industry, especially in Italy where outdoor sun-ripened tomatoes developed the best flavour, a principle that still holds true today. Food lovers find it slightly amusing when growers now claim to sell tomatoes 'for flavour'. What did they have before, one wonders?

Fresh tomatoes

Fresh tomatoes are classified by growers into four groups. The supply of specific varieties depends on demands by retailers, distributors and finally, one hopes, the customer.

The classic size and shape for general use still accounts for over three-quarters of the crop – a good all-purpose tomato. Baby-sized *cherry* or *cocktail tomatoes* are for eating whole and they do tend to taste sweeter.

They are sometimes used whole, cooked and sieved, in sauces and soups. *Plum tomatoes* have less moisture and more flavour. They are favourites with chefs and gourmet cooks and they also can and sun-dry well. *Beef/beefsteak tomatoes* are large, firm and good for stuffing or slicing – a favourite in Mediterranean salads. Most highly prized are the *Marmande* variety, originally from the pretty town of the same name in Aquitaine, France. Having said that, tomato varieties are all interchangeable in recipes so you can use any for a sauce, tossed into casseroles, for roasting or simply for nibbling on their own.

Gardeners may like to experiment cooking with green tomato varieties, or least tomatoes that never seem to turn colour. They will still have a wonderful sharp flavour, ideal for using in relishes or raw fruit salsas. Have you seen the film *Fried Green Tomatoes at the Whistle Stop Cafe?* You can make your own fried green tomatoes by dipping slices of under-ripe beefsteak tomatoes in coarse cornmeal or polenta and frying the slices in a mixture of oil and butter. It's wonderful for breakfast with rashers of bacon.

Tomatoes develop flavour if allowed to ripen naturally, so if you buy under-ripe fruits, leave them at room temperature for a few days in the fruit bowl. Fruits sold 'on the vine' have more flavour. Keep them still attached until ready to eat and give them a good smell to tell when they are ready for eating. A well-ripened tomato will have a heavenly scent, slightly minty with hints of aniseed.

PANZANELLA (Italian tomato salad)

Panzanella is really easy and ideal as a starter or a light meal, if served with slices of mozzarella cheese. You need full-flavoured, slightly over-ripe large plum or Marmande tomatoes and some slightly stale country-style bread. Slice the bread thickly and use to cover the base of a salad bowl. Slice two to three large tomatoes and arrange on the bread, sprinkling between the layers with sea salt, ground black pepper and good extra-virgin olive oil. Tuck in some torn leaves of fresh basil. Cover and leave in a cool place for about two hours. Chill lightly before serving. The sliced tomatoes give off a juice that trickles into the bread below and the dish tastes like a savoury summer pudding.

TO SKIN FRESH TOMATOES

There are two ways to do this. If you have a gas stove and need to skin only one or two tomatoes, skewer a firm tomato on a fork from the stalk end and hold over a full flame until the skin pops and starts to blister. Turn the tomato a few times until most of the skin has burst, then remove from the flame, allow to cool and peel. To skin a batch of tomatoes, first cut out the stalk end in a small cone with a small sharp knife, then slash a cross in the skin at the other end of the tomato. Place in a big bowl. Pour over boiling water to cover wait a minute, then drain. (Don't leave for longer or the flesh will soften.) The skins should have loosened and be easy to slip off. If a recipe calls for tomato concassé, this is simply skinned tomatoes that have been halved, seeded, cut into long thin strips then finely chopped.

Canned tomatoes

The best come from Italy where outdoor production ensures supreme flavour and less moisture, so do check the can labels or tube for country of origin. Well over half the canned tomato market is controlled by own-label supermarket brands. Otherwise brand names are Napolina (Naples was one of first centres of the Italian processed tomato industry), Cirio and Bianca. Canned plum tomatoes come whole (beloved of boarding-house landladies), chopped, crushed or creamed. After skinning, the tomatoes are covered in juice made from round tomatoes, then pasteurised and sealed in a can. Out of season, when a recipe calls for cooked tomatoes in a central role, use good-quality canned tomatoes – from Italy, Mexico, Provence or Spain – instead of indifferent fresh. Creamed tomatoes are sold as sugocasa or passata and have a texture similar to thickened tomato juice. They are ideal in sauces, Gazpacho or soups.

Sun-dried tomatoes

You can always tell when a new food has really caught on because supermarkets start to market their own brands. This is certainly the case with sun-dried tomatoes. But, be warned, qualities do vary greatly. I've eaten some exquisitely flavoured, tender, sweet Italian tomatoes with a slightly salty backbite from my local deli that were almost too good for cooking but wonderful for eating like a fruit. Then I've also had very poor specimens in indifferent oil and others hard as old shoe leather.

Good sun-dried tomatoes are spread out on polythene sheets and simply left to dry in the hot summer sun until they take on a lovely caramelised flavour. I tend to buy good 'dried' sun-dried tomatoes out of oil as they are more versatile and easier to snip. Oily ones are messy to cut up but fine for using in pasta and it has to be said that the oil can be used to make nice salad dressings.

Tomatoe purée or paste

Tomato purée is a concentrate of cooked tomato pulp with the water extracted. Look for the double-concentrated purée for the best flavour – again Italian brands have most flavour.

TURNIPS

Availability: mainly winter; baby French turnips in the early summer.

Another 'one for the pot' root vegetable creeping back into our popularity stakes, presumably because of the penchant for chefs to use baby turnips complete with tops as a dainty garnish. However, baby anything has little going for it save looks. Turnips allowed to grow a little more to 'toddler' size will reward you with more flavour! In the early spring, purple-white turnips are best topped and tailed but left unpeeled, boiled until just tender, then dressed with a little melted butter or nut oil – hazelnut or walnut is worth trying. Older turnips may need peeling thinly, then cut them into chunks to be dropped into casseroles or mashed into potatoes with butter and nutmeg. A turnip past its best will become soft and smell strangely peppery.

WILD LEAVES AND EDIBLE FLOWERS

These include many you can grow easily in your garden but which we are also beginning to see in shops.

Purslane, an old Tudor salad herb, is quite astringent with fleshy, succulent leaves. It's often found in Middle Eastern food stores. *Salad Burnet* leaves look like smaller versions of rocket – well at least from a distance. They're excellent as a garnish but good too tossed into a mixed green salad. The leaves are set on long thin stalks, which are eaten too. Not widely available but an edible curiosity. *Sorrel* has a sharp, acidic taste. It can be used as a salad herb or chopped and stirred into a buttery sauce for an accompaniment to fish (especially salmon) and chicken and in omelettes. It goes greyish when heated so it's often used with spinach to keep an attractive colour. It's sold in little supermarket packs by enlightened retailers but it's also a good herb to grow as you need only a few leaves at a time.

Dandelion leaves are used in salads, particularly in France where they're called *pissenlit*. They're on sale in small greengrocer's and, of course, there is always a plentiful free supply of dandelion leaves – just look outside in the garden or on wastelands. Use the younger leaves.

Good *King Henry, red orach* (red spinach), *nasturtiums* and *mizuno* are just a few of the leaves (and in some cases flowers) salad herbs growers are experimenting with. Some are oriental in origin, some old cottage-garden varieties. They are all variations on the sour or bitter theme but look so pretty tossed into bowls of mixed green and russet leaves. In spring you will find the tips of *young green nettles* good cooked in soup – wear rubber gloves when you pick them and rest assured that the sting disappears on heating.

On the flower front, *nasturtium flowers* are the best known – like the leaves, they taste peppery. *Pot marigolds* look like orange daisies: you pick the petals off and scatter them over green leaves as you would grated carrot. They were popular in Tudor cooking as a colouring. *Pansies* and the smaller *heartsease* add blue and purple colours. *Chive flowers* are very pungent and oniony. *Rose petals* are best scattered over fruit salads. *Borage* flowers make a pretty garnish for sliced strawberries and are stunning frozen in ice cubes for Pimm's cocktails.

YAMS AND EXOTIC ROOTS

Availability: all year round.

One of the great staple foods of the world, yams and their associated starchy root vegetables are cooked in many tropical countries as an accompaniment for spicy stews or simply eaten as smooth porridge-like dishes. Yam skins vary from rough and hairy to smooth and the flesh comes in colours ranging from yellow and creamy right through to purple. Boil and mash with a knob of butter or scrub, wrap in foil and bake. In the southern American states they bake yams in a butter and brown sugar glaze to serve with hams.

Cassava is a similar vegetable, treated in the same way. Some varieties of cassava are poisonous until cooked, so don't try any raw unless you're absolutely sure they're safe. Tapioca is a flour by-product of cassava as is cassareep, a syrup used in Caribbean cookery.

Taro, dasheen and *eddoes* are varieties of the same root vegetable with a slightly sweet, nutty flavour. They are popular in West Indian and African cookery. Peel with rubber gloves because the flesh can irritate. The Chinese like to cut taro into shreds and deep-fry them shaped into baskets.

Sweet potatoes were originally from South America but are now popular all over the world. These roots are eaten as a staple in the southern American states where they are called potatoes, while our white potatoes are called Irish potatoes. Skin colours vary from yellow to pink. Peel and mash them with lots of butter, as you would potatoes, or roast them in butter and brown sugar, or mix half and half with potatoes. My family likes them cut into thick slices, parboiled and chargrilled on the barbie – especially my vegetarian daughter who used to bemoan the fact there was little for her to eat when I held barbecue parties. Sweet potato pie is similar to pecan or pumpkin pie – but some may find it an acquired taste.

Water chestnuts are small and crunchy Chinese tubers that retain their unique texture even when cooked. If using fresh water chestnuts (should you find any), peel thinly, cut into slices and keep in acidulated water (that is with a little lemon juice) until ready to cook as they can discolour. They are mostly found canned, which is a good substitute for fresh.

Kudzu are starchy roots from South-East Asia with a sweet, white flesh. Choose young roots as older ones can be tough. Fresh *lotus roots* look like a string of pale cream sausages but when sliced and cooked they have such a pretty lacy form. They are mostly bought canned to be used in stir-fries or steamed. The Chinese preserve them in syrup for sweet treats at their New Year celebrations.

GROWING YOUR OWN

The downturn in the economy and the upturn in a desire to eat truly fresh vegetables in season, combined with a host of home gardening books and TV shows, has led to a huge rise in the popularity of growing your own. After all, the Cubans have been doing it for decades because of a ban on the import of fertilisers, and they eat some of the best organic vegetables in the world.

So if you have a barren backyard or an overgrown brambly corner in your garden and feel energetic, then now may be the time to turn the turf with a fork, buy a few packets of seeds and a watering can, and take pride in growing your own vegetables. Waiting lists for allotments have grown in many city and towns but some garden centres are now renting out allotment space, complete with little sheds and water taps on their scrub patches. Alternatively, you may like to ask neighbours if they have some garden to spare or a redundant veg patch to share. Some people like to grow common and garden veg like onions, spuds, cabbages and carrots; others prefer to try their hand at exotics, while ethnic communities form groups to grow exotic greens and squashes and herbs that remind them of home.

FRUIT

Storage and transport considerations are now the deciding factors when it comes to the availability of fruits. All fruits are natural storehouses for young seedlings and so are designed to last for at least a while. Many fruits can be grown in several parts of the world, depending on the variety, hemisphere and time of year. So there is increasingly a supply of most fruits most of the time, albeit it at a higher price when supplies are limited. And while fruits do taste their best when allowed to ripen naturally on the plant, ripe fruits do not travel well and can be easily damaged. So they are frequently under-ripe when transported and though they may technically ripen, in that they soften and change colour, the flavour might not be as good. It is difficult therefore to pinpoint exact seasons with many fruits. Cold storage means it is possible to keep fruits from one season to another but the quality may be variable.

AKEES

Availability: all year round. Also available canned.

A fruit originally from West Africa and taken to the West Indies during the dark days of slavery, akees are now a popular staple there where they are eaten in several ways but chiefly with salt fish as a vegetable. Fresh you have to avoid the seeds, which are poisonous. The fruit is red and shiny with a creamy yellowy flesh. A little tricky to prepare, it's best bought ready canned. Soak the canned flesh in cold water for an hour. The cooked flesh is said to resemble scrambled eggs.

APPLES

Availability: all year round, but home-grown best in early autumn.

It was the Romans who first introduced the cultivated apple into Britain. In the 15th century Henry VII, alarmed at the amount of imported fruit (even in those days), sent the Royal Fruiterer to France learn about commercialising the recently acquired monastic orchards. England soon grew to become a great apple producer although the French imports still kept on coming. During the years of great colonisation, European settlers started up orchards in North America, Australasia and South Africa. Now varieties come to us from all over the world at all times of the year. But sadly, instead of a delightful range of the thousands of fruits developed by dedicated breeders, varieties are becoming standardised to meet the rigours of the distribution systems.

Apples were the subject of one of the most interesting tastings I have ever attended. We munched our way through 25 varieties, using descriptions such as 'wet leaves', 'melon', 'elderflower' and 'lemon' for the flavours that tickled our palettes. The fact that the tasting was organised by a major supermarket launching a campaign of traditional regional fruits was encouraging, but it still seems the chief quality of apples has to be an ability to store for several months and transport without bruising. It also helps if they have perfect shape and colour. And, as an afterthought, flavour would be an asset too.

If you are interested in learning more about apples and experiencing their great variety, contact The Brogdale Trust (www.brogdale.org) for genuine speciality growers. Many farm shops are quite a disappointment now – they just seem to mirror supermarket supplies – but the genuine ones still survive and thrive.

A good-tasting apple should have a nice balance of sweetness, acidity and juiciness. The colour of the skin is matter of personal preference – green, russet, pink, auburn, burgundy red, golden or a combination of any or all of these. Texture, too, depends on variety and length of storage. As an apple ages so it loses water and crispness. It needs careful handling too: an apple can easily bruise, which is a waste of fruit. Store assistants who shake boxes of perfect fruit on to shelves can spoil an otherwise perfect batch of well-stored apples because tell-tale signs of bruising will appear a couple of days later. Although apples store well at room temperature in the fruit bowl, they keep longer if loosely stored in a food bag at the base of a fridge. I think they also taste better when lightly chilled.

Apple varieties

Apple varieties abound. Most of the fruits we buy are dessert apples, but there are specific cookers and some that can be used for both purposes.

Our home-grown fruit starts appearing in late August, with green and red *Discovery* and *Worcester Pearmains* – a delightfully perfumed apple but unfortunately its limited shelf life means it soon softens. When the new season's Cox's (Cox's Orange Pippins, to give them their full title) appear, treat yourself to the largest you can find and bite into what many consider to be the perfect example of an apple. A really fresh one plucked straight from the tree will have a mouth-puckering feel – crisp and juicy with a lovely floral bouquet and the right balance of sweetness and acidity. Maybe this is due to the fact that they are home-grown, allowed to tree ripen for longer and are not subject to the rigours of international distribution, because any freshly picked apple will be in the peak of perfection. Similar to Cox's are *Sturmer, Laxton, Tydeman's, Starking, Fiesta* and the New Zealand *Fuji* apples. A speciality apple with a truly rural look is the *Egremont Russet*. It has a firm, slightly rough olive-green skin and a sweet but palette-rasping flavour. It's a personal favourite and wonderful with cheese.

One of the commercial successes of recent years is the *Braeburn*, with hints of Cox's in its appearance, texture and flavour but sweeter. Look forward to early summer imports from New Zealand for prime fruit, but now they are also grown in France and are almost as good.

Golden Delicious may be regarded as the plebeian of the apple world, but imports from South Africa are quite delicious with a delightfully golden apricot-blushed skin and crisp, perfumed flesh.

North American apples, such as the *Mackintosh Red* and *Pink Lady*, are big, shiny good lookers but some people consider their flavour bland. The skins can have a bitter afterbite, and some varieties are so highly polished I do wonder if they've been given a silicone-style treatment. No doubt back in their own country there are many delicious specimens: indeed, there were many significant American apple growers in the 19th century during the glorious days of fruit breeding.

A few apples are rated solely as good cookers, in particular the *British Bramley Seedling*, a plump jolly green giant of a fruit. It has fruity, sharp flavour and fluffy texture when cooked in pies and crumbles and it is still the best apple for baking. As it does not hold its shape in cooking keep it for these traditional puddings. To my mind it is also one of the nicest apples for apple sauce to accompany roast pork or to cook with red cabbage.

Two apples rated highly by chefs as good all-rounders are *Granny Smiths* and *Jonagolds*. They both have good flavour balance and hold up well when poached, cooked in tarts and sliced in syrup. The Jonagold has a limited season – mid-autumn for northern hemisphere countries and early summer for the southern hemisphere – but do try it when you can. It is popular in Germany.

BAKED APPLES WITH SAUTERNES AND MARMALADE

Here is a recipe idea for baking apples in the style of Jane Austen, the early 19th-century novelist. They're best served at room temperature so are ideal for baking ahead.

4–6 large Bramley Seedlings
4–6tbsp bitter marmalade
300ml (10fl oz) sweet dessert wine, preferably a Sauternes
300ml (10fl oz) water
small knobs of unsalted butter
single cream or custard, to serve

Core the unpeeled apples, making sure the holes are large enough to spoon in the marmalade. Score round the belly of each apple and stand them in a roasting pan. Spoon the marmalade into the core holes (you may need to chop chunky peel to fit). Pour the wine and water into the pan, then top each core hole with a small knob of butter. Bake in a preheated oven set at 160°C/gas mark 3 for about an hour, basting the fruits with the syrup two or three times, until the apples are tender and the flesh fluffy. Allow to cool and serve with pouring cream or homemade custard.

APRICOTS

Availability: South African at New Year; French and Italian at mid-summer.

January is a month keen cooks look forward to. Strange but true, for when our weather is wintry many wonderful fruits come in from the southern hemisphere, albeit at a slightly premium price, but the quality is superb. To my mind, one of the most eagerly awaited is South African apricots. There is little to beat their sweet, firm yet juicy flesh and I rarely have a chance to cook them, so quickly are they devoured in my kitchen. Early to mid-summer sees the next influx from France, Turkey and Italy, with their pretty apricot-pink speckled skin.

The honey-scented *hunza* apricots are a gourmet's delight, but don't get too greedy – they do have an extraordinary laxative effect! Dried apricots are a well-known source of dietary fibre but they are also good sources of beta-carotene, one of the anti-oxidants nutritionists advise we eat more of. A purée of cooked dried apricots flavoured with honey and cinnamon and folded into thickened whipped crème fraîche or Greek-style yogurt makes a delicious fool. Whenever you can, top apricot desserts with crushed almond-flavoured amaretti biscuits – apricots and almonds are culinary kissing cousins. In Middle Eastern stores you may come across sheets of dried apricot paste called armadine, which are ideal for cutting into squares to eat as sweet treats or for adding to stews and spiced lamb casseroles. These sheets can also be heated with a little water and turned back into a purée.

Of course, apricots make the best jam and it is perfectly possible to use the semi-dried, no-need-to-cook variety, adding the juice of a lemon for sharpness. If you buy apricot jam, look for a good brand such as the English Tiptree, the French Bonne Maman or Hungarian Hero – or my own homemade with vanilla!

QUICK APRICOT TARTS

Preheat the oven to 200°C/gas mark 6. Use a sheet of ready-rolled puff pastry and cut out four rounds using a small saucer as a template. Prick the base well and place on a non-stick baking sheet. Halve and stone 12–16 ripe apricots, then slice roughly. Pile these on top of the pastry round. Sprinkle fairly liberally with light soft brown sugar and grate over some nutmeg. Dot with small knobs of butter and bake for 10–12 minutes or until the edges have browned and crisped and the fruit starts to soften. Remove and brush over some runny apricot jam, then leave to cool to room temperature. These are wonderful served with dollops of crème fraîche and are one of the nicest ways of serving cooked apricots.

BANANAS

Wild bananas grow from India through to New Guinea from a plant that is botanically a giant herb not a tree. There are many varieties of bananas: the dessert variety that we eat have a higher level of sugar than cooking bananas, also known as plantains, which have higher levels of starch. For a tropical and sub-tropical fruit, it's amazing how essential bananas have become to Europeans and Americans – one has only to read how enthusiastically the war-rationed British greeted the first imported bananas after many years of deprivation. For many children it was their first taste. Nowadays athletes favour bananas for their high carbohydrate levels and rich source of potassium.

Central America, Ecuador, West Africa and the West Indies all grow bananas for export, as do the Canary Islands with a smaller, thinner skinned variety. A banana ripened naturally on a tree is exquisite, believe me, but the fruit we see in our stores has ripened during storage. We are now seeing more exotic varieties and colours – *apple bananas, lady's fingers* and *red bananas*, all generally small and sweet with a creamier texture. Try to buy Fairtrade fruits – the few pence more helps give plantation workers a better future.

Fresh bananas

Bananas should be left to ripen out of the fridge as their aroma will penetrate even the toughest of plastic packaging, not to mention the fridge lining. They give off mild gases that will ripen any other fruit nearby, an effect that can be put to good use. If I have hard pears in my fruit bowl, a couple of ripe bananas will soon bring them to ripeness. The metal banana 'trees' sold in kitchen catalogues make sense if you eat a lot of bananas.

We use sweet ripe bananas as desserts, in cakes and trifles and for that modern classic of the condensed milk can – banoffee pie. For savoury dishes, use under-ripe bananas sliced and fried to serve with spicy fried chicken or for breakfast with grilled bacon and pancakes.

For baking, look for bananas with spotted skins as they have a lot more flavour. Otherwise buy with a pale green tinge and ripen at home to your taste.

Dried bananas

Dried bananas chips are a good nibbling food and a healthy alternative to sweets. Chefs use under-ripe bananas to make into banana crisps. They slice them wafer thin, dip the slices in a lemony sugar syrup, then dry them in a low oven.

Plantains

The banana-like plantain is eaten as a vegetable and is one of the main food crops of East Africa and some West Indian islands. When green they are under-ripe, when yellow mid-ripe and if the fruit is black they are very ripe. However, they all need to be cooked before eating – either fried, baked in their skins, roasted or added to stews.

BLUEBERRIES

Availability: generally all year, better in summer months.

These are a North American fruit, some imported and some UK-grown, sold in small punnets at a premium price. They do have a delicious sweet, creamy flavour and are particularly nice mixed with sharper fruits such as strawberries or apples in pies, breakfast muffins, cheesecakes, ice creams and fruit salads and make a good jam, mixed with the higher-pectin apples. The commercial varieties we buy are from lowbush shrubs, but you can sometimes find highbush shrubs grown in the UK. You can buy semi-dried blueberries, with a quite divine concentrated flavour for nibbling straight from the pack, or stir into cake or biscuit mixes before baking. But don't get too carried away as they are quite pricey.

Bilberries/whortleberries are wild versions of native blueberries, and can occasionally be found on British moorlands.

BREADFRUIT

Availability: all year round.

Another tropical staple fruit eaten as a vegetable. Captain Bligh is credited with having introduced the breadfruit to the West Indies as a cheap food for African slaves and the quest for it sparked off the most famous mutiny of all, that of the *Bounty* in 1787. The fruit can be boiled, baked, roasted or fried. The flavour is slightly reminiscent of chestnuts. Breadfruit is good used in chowders, dipped in batter and fried and made into a pudding.

CHERRIES

Availability: summer months and occasionally mid-winter as a speciality.

The quality of this popular fruit has certainly improved in the last few years and supplies are becoming more prolific. Cherry colours range from deep (cherry) red and almost black to pale yellow and pink. The ones we tend to eat fresh are dessert fruits, either home-grown in June and July or imported from the United States, Spain, France, Turkey and Italy. America is the home of the *Bing* cherry, and the Spanish have started to export a large, deliciously sweet and juicy cherry called *Picota* from the Valle del Jerte. Some supermarkets and up-market food halls sell semi-dried cherries.

Dessert cherries are best eaten from a bowl just as they are. There are also many dessert classics such as cherry clafoutis, which is a sweet batter poured over stoned, ripe red cherries then baked like an oven omelette. Or try a Russian kissel – stoned and lightly chopped fresh cherries cooked with other red berries such as raspberries and redcurrants served chilled and thickened with arrowroot (see page 217). Fresh cherries are one of the must-have fruits for the British summer pudding, a lightly crushed mixture of sweetened red berry fruits served in a bread-lined mould.

Cherry varieties are also grown as cooking varieties. Sour and with a full, fruity flavour, they are ideal for bottling in syrup or making into jam. One of the classic cooking cherries is the *morello*, another the white *Napoleon Biggarreau*, used in the glace fruits of Provence for luscious French glacé cherries. Rich poultry is traditionally served with a cherry dressing or sauce, at one time made with the French variety *Montmorency*.

HOW TO STONE FRESH CHERRIES

If you use cherries a lot, it is well worth investing in a proper stoner. They are frequently combined with a garlic press, having a small cup with a tiny hole in one arm of the press and a blunt spike on the other. Place the cherry in the cup and bring down the spike on top. Out pops the stone into the little hole, although sometimes it does need a little extra manual assistance.

COCONUT

Availability: all year round.

Coconuts are so widespread in the tropics that no one country can claim to be their indigenous home. They fall naturally on to beaches and can float for months on the sea so they've spread themselves all round the world. To harvest, they are either left to fall and then gathered by nimble-footed youths or they can even be harvested by specially trained monkeys. Honest! Until recently, in the UK we seemed to use coconut only desiccated, sweetened and grated in cakes and biscuits and whole coconuts could be found at fairgrounds and occasionally as fun items in greengrocer's.

But as the popularity of Indian and Thai food grew so we came to realise the potential of this delicious ingredient. There are just so many different culinary uses. Now they are readily sold in ethnic food shops. Fresh straight from the tree, you can slice off the top and drink the delicious pearly juice, then scoop out the jelly-like flesh. (This is assuming you are holidaying on some exotic tropical paradise as it is difficult to get truly fresh coconuts outside the tropics.)

To tackle a whole coconut, you first need to pierce two of the three sunken hollows with a sharp spike and drain out any liquid. Then place the pointed end of the coconut on a stone surface and hit it. The shell should crack into chunks to reveal the fibrous white flesh inside. Lever out the flesh in chunks using a firm table knife and peel off any dark skin with a vegetable peeler or small sharp knife and eat.

If you want to make your own coconut cream: grate the flesh coarsely, then place in a saucepan and cover with boiling water. You should find a thick cream forms on the top which you scoop off. Cover the grated flesh in boiling water again, steep and scoop off the thinner layer. And so on. Or, you could buy ready-made coconut products which are very acceptable and now very easy to obtain: some supermarkets even make their own brands.

COCONUT PRODUCTS

Creamed coconut is very thick, like butter and sold in boxes wrapped in plastic. Keep it chilled so it is easy to cut off a block whenever you need to add a coconut flavour.

• Coconut cream is the thickness of double cream.

• Coconut milk is like single cream.

• Coconut juice is similar to the thin liquid you drink from the inside of a fresh coconut.

If you wish to make you own coconut liquid from desiccated coconut, cover about 50g (1¾oz) of unsweetened desiccated coconut with 400ml (14fl oz) of boiling water. Leave until completely cold. Drain, reserving the juice.

CRANBERRIES

Availability: fresh mid-winter in time for Christmas; frozen all year.

A truly all-American fruit grown in wet fields in New England, Wisconsin, the Canadian borders and out west in Oregon. A fruit popular with native Americans and introduced by them to the Puritan settlers, when they were on good speaking terms over three hundred years ago. Thence it became a popular preserve to serve with roasted meats, especially turkey at Thanksgiving, and now we use cranberries in many puddings and pies. Originally called bounceberries – because a ripe cranberry bounces – you'll find these hard, deep burgundy-red berries on sale fresh from November onwards. Cranberries are the one fruit that is as good frozen as it is fresh, so buy more packs than you need in November/December and pop them straight into the freezer.

I like to throw in handfuls of fresh berries when making apple pies, but perhaps my favourite is the semi-dried cranberry sold all year round as a speciality baking item. They are divine for snacking. For home baking, toss them into biscuit mixtures, muffins or fruit cakes instead of the sweeter glacé cherries. Cranberry juice is a healthy drink, particularly recommended to help with kidney and bladder problems, and slightly less tart mixed with raspberry or apple juices.

CRANBERRY PARTY PUNCH, LOW-ALCOHOL

A simple idea that looks and tastes like grown-up wine but with a third of the alcohol. Simply mix a litre (1¾pt) each of light cranberry juice, dry white wine and sparkling mineral water If you like, you can steep some semi-dried cranberries and blueberries in a little juice until plump to serve at the bottom of the punch bowl. Serve well chilled with a few thin fresh orange slices. Or fill a tall Tom Collins glass with ice cubes, top up with the punch and finish with a snazzy straw for a low-alcohol cocktail.

CUSTARD APPLES, CHERIMOYA AND SOURSOPS

Availability: late autumn–early winter.

Natives of tropical America but now grown in West Africa and South-East Asia. The skins are pale green which go a waxy grey when ripe. Soursop skins are a darker green and harder and the fruit is more oval in shape. The flesh is a creamy colour and texture and the flavour sweet with a hint of sourness. These fruits are high in vitamin C.

These fruits are picked under-ripe because they don't travel well when ripe but then, as usual, the flavour is not as Nature intended. Let them get quite ripe, but not so the skin turns black. The hand-cupping technique should work. When made into ice creams their creamy sour-sweet flavour comes into its own. But you will need about 8–10 of the fruits to get enough pulp. Their shiny black seeds should be picked out and discarded.

DATES

Availability: preserved all year round; fresh late autumn to mid-winter.

Fresh dates come from three main sources – Israel, Egypt and California. If you drive along highways in the Middle East, you will find the roads lined with date palm trees. They are a very prolific crop with many commercial uses. Much research is currently being undertaken in many Arab countries to make this ancient food a highly efficient ingredient in modern food processing.

Dates are very nutritious but, above all, they taste delicious and have many uses apart from just nibbling on at Christmas from a paper-doily lined box. No doubt some of us remember the sticky square packs of dates, which would be chopped and added to cakes and tarts. In fact, that still remains a good way of cooking with them: simmer chunks of 'squashed' dates in a little water until you get a smooth purée.

Fresh dates, however, are more exciting and found in supermarkets in the exotic fruit section. For all their abundance in the Middle East they are sadly expensive, but still worth the indulgence. Israel supplies smooth but slightly tough-skinned fresh dates, sold in boxes, with a stone that is easy to pinch out. These dates are ideal for stuffing with almond paste or maybe a cream cheese or silky blue cheese. The more wrinkled *Medjool* dates originate from Egypt but are now grown in California. They have a slightly softer texture, a wrinkled skin and fragrant, sweet flesh. A really good alternative to chocolates as an after-dinner treat with coffee. If you live in a city with Arab stores, keep a lookout for fresh dates still on their stems – they are worth chewing but don't eat them under-ripe as they taste a little sour.

DURIAN

Availability: late summer.

I'm including this fruit only on a need-to-know basis, because I haven't yet plucked up the courage to try one. Their price in Western ethnic stores (if and when they're in stock) is unbelievable. The durian is a big fruit that looks like a giant spiky hand grenade and has a smell like putrid garlic. Some airlines won't allow them as hand luggage and who can blame them?

So why bother at all? Because once you have braved the skin and the outside stench, inside it is supposed to taste divine. The ultimate in tropical fruits, durians are natives to tropical South-East Asia but are now grown in Zanzibar. It is said that elephants and tigers in the wild will travel great distances to get at one when they pick up the scent. The flesh has been described as tasting like honey that melts like smooth butter. You can make a cake with the creamy pulp, if you ever get that far.

ELDERBERRIES AND ELDERFLOWERS

Availability: flowers in June; berries in September.

You can't as yet buy either of these two great foods in shops but, even better, they are available completely free all over the countryside and on some inner city wastelands. June and September are two eagerly awaited months in the culinary calendar because of the unique flavours these foods give. Don't pick elderflowers or elderberries by a busy roadside because of possible lead contamination from petrol fumes.

Elderflowers hang off these shrubby trees in clusters, like flowery flying saucers. Just pick the clusters whole, then when you get home pull off the delicate fairylike flowers. The only effective way of preserving their heavenly scent is in a syrup: I have tried freezing and drying them with no success. Make a sugar syrup (see page 307) and add good fistfuls of elderflowers until they wilt. Then remove from the heat and allow to cool while the flowers steep and give off their fragrance. Strain the syrup and discard the flowers. To store the syrup for a good few months you will need to use glass bottles sterilised in a low oven for an hour or so or the syrup might start to ferment. Return the syrup to a rolling boil and pour into the sterilised bottles through a funnel, then seal, cool and store.

Elderberries come into harvest in September and those flowers that escaped picking turn into small dark-purple berries with a rich sweetness and flavour not dissimilar to blueberries. Strip them from the heads with the prongs of a fork and stew them with a little sugar as you would blackcurrants. Use them like blackcurrants, too, mixed with chopped apple in crumbles, pies etc.

FEIJOA

Availability: mid-winter.

Relatives of guava from the same myrtle family, feijoas are grown now in
New Zealand and have a slightly gritty texture with a fragrance described as
pineapple mixed with gooseberry. Indeed, their alternative name is pineapple
guava. Their shape is long and oval and their skin colour green, turning to a
reddish-green as the fruit ripens. Feijoas are in season around Christmas time.
Use them like guava.

FIGS

Availability: late summer months.

Another fruit of the Ancients, but I fear many people associate figs, swimming
in sickly syrup, with dreary hotel breakfasts. How wrong they are! Fresh,
they are a revelation and completely different, at their best plucked ripe from
a tree. Fresh figs are very fragile and are picked unripe so they travel well.
Consequently, they do not have the advantage of tree ripeness, which gives
them so much of their unique character. To eat a fresh fig, you should cut it
into quarters. The skin is thin and tender and quite edible and inside is the
rose pink flesh containing lots of tiny seeds. The only part of the fruit you
can't eat is the hard stalk. An under-ripe fig will leak a light milky fluid, still
edible but not as flavourful. Figs over-ripen quickly, often in the shops, so
check them carefully before you buy. In fact, it is best to buy them under-ripe
and leave them for a day or so at room temperature until the flesh gives when
gently squeezed.

There are several varieties and skin colours of figs. The gourmet's choice
is the *Italian Kadota*, which is the classic fig to serve with Parma ham.
Otherwise, figs are good teamed with juicy melon or a tangy, salty cheese such
as Roquefort or Stilton. Figs dry very well, and there are now packs of semi-
dried soft figs which make fine eating. A Greek friend once presented me with
her mother's home-dried figs – split, sandwiched with almonds and packed
with dried sage leaves. But be warned: don't get carried away with figgy
gluttony – they are good natural laxatives.

FRESH CURRANTS

Availability: mid-summer.

Another of the eagerly awaited fruits of the summer, currants come in shades of red, black and white, each variety with a distinctive flavour and different levels of tartness. All fresh currants are enhanced by fresh mint: just add a few sprigs to a gently simmering compote.

Redcurrants have many uses for cooks in both savoury and sweet dishes. The luminescent red berries hang on their bushes in clusters and are sold in punnets still as little bunches, sometimes at quite a price. They are often served stripped from their stalks (the easiest way to do this is with the prongs of a fork) and lightly stewed with a little sugar to drizzle over sliced peaches. Or mix them with raspberries and sliced strawberries in a light, summery fruit salad. Commercially, redcurrants are used to make a jam or preserve to serve with lamb or game such as venison. A more spiced version of the preserve is known as Cumberland sauce – wonderful with goose.

Blackcurrants are sometimes sold fresh in small punnets but they are the fruit I associate more with home gardeners and jam making and for the virtue of their high vitamin C content. Blackcurrants make excellent jam because their full, tart flavour is enhanced by sugar and they are naturally high in pectin, so have good setting properties with a short cooking time, thus preserving much of the natural flavour. They make a wonderful addition to a homemade crumble or fruit salad. Out of season, canned blackcurrants are a good substitute for fresh, so it's worth having a can or two in store for a quick sauce to heat and pour over fresh ice cream.

White currants are actually a very pretty translucent pale pink that can be used in the same way as redcurrants. Small clusters of both red- and white currants make dainty decorations in summery desserts. For special occasions, dip clusters first in a little beaten egg white then into caster sugar to give them a frosting. Lay these sparkling frosted clusters on baking parchment to dry.

GOOSEBERRIES

Availability: May–June.

Gooseberries come into our shops around the end of May (like that other summer favourite, home-grown asparagus) and can be found for up to six weeks thereafter. Their short season coincides with the blooming of elderflowers and gooseberries cooked with a few of these flower heads deliver a muscatel flavour that says 'summer'. (In fact, 'gooseberry' is one of the flavour descriptions used by wine tasters for sauvignon blancs.) A few spikes of fresh lavender, another summer flower, also cook well with gooseberries.

You can buy small, firm and quite tart gooseberries that are delicious when cooked with sugar or larger dessert gooseberries, which are sweeter and juicier but lack the distinctive lemony sharpness. Gooseberries are high in water, so cook them with the barest amount, even just the water clinging to their skins after washing. They will need topping and tailing, with your fingernails or a small pair of sharp scissors. This may account for their lack of popular appeal – too much like hard work!

Cook gooseberries until the berries just burst open, or layer them uncooked in a pie dish, sprinkle sugar over (and elderflowers if you have them) then cover with pastry or a fudgy soft brown sugar and butter crumble mixture and cook.

Unsweetened gooseberry purée makes a good sauce to serve with mackerel. Cold sweetened purées can be mixed with equal amounts of whipped cream for a classic gooseberry fool. Gooseberry jam is well worth making and the fruit turns a pretty pink on cooking.

GRAPEFRUIT

Availability: all year round.

At one time in my life, when my father lived and worked in Jamaica, he had shipped to us each Christmas the most perfect grapefruit we had ever tasted – sweet, thin-skinned and virtually seedless. I can't remember the colour but they were so good we ate them like oranges, peeling the skin and pulling off segments. After a few years the quality started to deteriorate and eventually the boxes stopped coming but I still rate grapefruit according to those fine specimens.

Now, in addition to yellow-skinned, white-fleshed fruits, we find green-skinned sweeties and pink grapefruit, which are both good for eating as segments. Variations on grapefruits are *pomelo* (also known as the shaddock), with bittersweet flesh and large segments, and the unfortunately named *ugli*. This fruit looks unprepossessing, with thick peel and pith: however, as a cross of grapefruit, Seville orange and tangerine developed in Jamaica, the fruit segments are juicy, virtually seedless and rated highly on the flavour stakes. So, make an ugli's day and give it a try.

GRAPES

Availability: all year round depending on variety.

Most grapes grown for eating are quite different from those grown for wine. The few exceptions include the flower-scented Muscatel grape, which is also used in certain dessert wines. We import grapes from all over the world so there are always some available although quality and flavour will vary. Green and red grapes are different varieties.

When you get grapes home, place them in a colander and wash off any pesticide or storage residue under tepid water, then allow to drain. Grapes can ripen quickly so store in the fridge or eat them up quickly.

You can cook with grapes. They're nice in tarts, set in a fresh lemon and wine jelly, or mixed into fruit salads. To serve grapes as part of a fruit bowl, it is good etiquette to snip them into little bunches of about dozen grapes each.

Grape varieties
Current favourites are *Thompson Seedless*, which are grown in different countries but chiefly imported from Israel, South Africa and Greece. During the autumn you can bite into plump *Italia* grapes – their sweet, lightly scented succulent flesh is worth crunching into a few hard seeds. *Red Flame Seedless* is a small, light red, round sweet grape with a light powdery skin and a slight tannic finish. Dark red/black grapes could be *Alphonse* or *Colmar* varieties. In America, the slightly spicy Concorde grape is popular, particularly in grape juice such as Welch's.

Dried vine fruits
Dried fruits have been with us for centuries, long before sugar was used for sweetening. When you dry fruits, their natural sugars concentrate, which helps

to preserve them. They take on different qualities from the fresh fruit while retaining most of the nutrients, though not the fragile vitamin C. Dried vine fruits are good sources of dietary fibre and trace elements such as iron and are a good source of easily absorbed energy, popular with sportsmen and women.

Greece is one of the homelands for dried vine fruits of an excellent quality and flavour and has an export history that stretches back centuries. Australia is another good supplier, especially of *sultanas*, and California is now synonymous with plump, juicy *raisins*, generally seedless and promoted not just for baking but for everyday eating. Indeed, they are so good you can eat them by the fistful. Christmas is a good time to stock up on quality dried fruits and a visit to a leading food hall or speciality deli should see many varieties on display – an edible Aladdin's cave.

The three main vine fruits are *currants*, sultanas and raisins. Currants (the name derives from 'Corinth') are small dried red grapes; sultanas (sometimes called 'golden raisins' in America, and in Middle Eastern and Indian recipes) are seedless green grapes; and raisins vary according to the original grape. Raisin purists insist on using the scented Muscatel raisins from Malaga, which are just fantastic in steamed puddings, but you have to take time to slit each one open and scrape out the pips unless you don't mind the crunch.

Many dried vine fruits are coated with sulphur dioxide or castor oil to give them a longer storage life. Generally in minute doses this is harmless but you might find fruit imported from countries with less stringent controls may have more, resulting in uncomfortable stomach pains. Dried fruits bought overseas from colourful folksy markets as tourist mementoes may carry this risk, so give the fruits a good rinse in tepid water when you come to use them and leave to dry spread out on kitchen paper towel. Branded dried fruits sold as 'washed and ready to use' should pose no such problem: you can eat them straight from the pack.

Although dried fruits are associated with baking, they make valuable contributions to savoury dishes (a touch of sweetness makes a savoury dish more tasty). The old school-dinner curried mince with handfuls of poor-quality sultanas bore only a passing resemblance to a classic Indian curry. Native chefs would use a much smaller amount of better-quality golden sultanas, in a true korma for example. I like to soak dried fruits briefly in hot brandy or rum for topping ice cream. Or for an unusual salad dressing heat a handful of raisins in 3–4tbsp of balsamic vinegar. This is excellent mixed with sliced roasted peppers and a trickle of olive oil to serve with a smoked cured ham such as Parma or Serrano.

GUAVAS

Availability: late summer.

A native of Brazil and a member of the myrtle family, guavas were introduced into India and the rest of the Pacific area by Portuguese and Spanish colonists. In fact in some areas the guava thrives too well and has to be controlled. Guavas look like small, hard, pale golden plums. There are many species, but it is the *strawberry guava*, with a creamy pink flesh, that is the most highly prized.

Guavas are mostly used for delicious juice, jam or fruit jelly. The flavour is very intense, acidic and fragrant, quite distinctive. The juice is also five times higher in vitamin C than orange juice, so it's very healthy. Fresh guavas on sale in European countries can be a bit of a disappointment, especially if you have eaten them in their natural tropical habitat where they are sweet and juicy, so make sure they are nicely ripened before you cut into them. The big problem with guavas is their seeds, which are hard to crunch and best spat (delicately) out. So peel and quarter them, remove the seeds if possible and chop the flesh. Or blend the juice with other juices.

JACKFRUIT

Availability: all year round.

An Indian fruit related to breadfruit introduced into the New World by Europeans. It is very large and the whole fruit looks like a hedgehog on the defensive. It has quite a strong odour and juicy yellow flesh. It is eaten, raw or cooked, with savoury dishes. The seeds are edible too, and can be ground into flour.

KIWI FRUIT

Availability: all year round.

Maybe I shouldn't confess to remembering when the first kiwi fruits hit our shops many years ago. I adored them from the start. Not for me the kiwi snobbery that disdains the fruit as a victim of its own success and culinary overkill. A ripe kiwi has the right balance of acidity, sweetness and juiciness. It is a stunning colour and easy to eat either on its own, from the skin as you would a boiled egg, or sliced in fruit mixtures. They are also one of the best possible sources of vitamin C – a kiwi a day should certainly help keep colds away. Kiwis are so acidic that they break down the animal-based gelatine, so jellies are not possible.

Kiwis are the great marketing success story of enterprising New Zealand farmers but they are also grown in many other countries – France, Brazil and Italy for example. To maintain their quality edge, New Zealand farmers now use the brand name Zespri on their fruit labels.

One of the nicest kiwi dishes is a bowl of fresh kiwi slices lightly dressed with a sprinkling of caster sugar and a little kirsch (served in France to accompany a perfect *tarte au citron*). However, do check them for ripeness before cutting open: cupping the fruit in your hand with gentle pressure should give you the tell-tale signs. A shrivelled kiwi will be past it best and beginning to turn pasty (but still suitable for whizzing to a purée in a food processor for a light fruit sauce): an under-ripe kiwi will be too tart and astringent.

KUMQUATS

Availability: mid-winter, occasionally all year round.

Food writers often lump these fruits into citrus fruit sections because they look like baby oranges, but in fact they are from a quite different family. Kumquats are natives of China and are associated with the Chinese New Year. Their golden colour is said to bring good fortune: their bittersweet flavour certainly brings good opportunities to cooks.

The whole of a kumquat can be eaten. While you can eat well-ripened kumquats without cooking, many people find them a little too astringent to pop straight into their mouths. So, to use raw, pick off the tiny green stalks, slice the flesh thinly (you may need to scoop out bigger pips) and toss into winter leaf salads. Or cook the whole or halved fruit gently in a sugar syrup until just tender. Kumquats can be bottled in a thick syrup to be scooped out and eaten as a special after-dinner dessert. I have also removed preserved kumquats from their syrup and topped the jar up with gin for a particularly zesty G&T.

Should you come across any, *limequats* are a cross between kumquats and limes, with characteristics of both.

KUMQUAT PARFAIT

Cook the kumquats, as above, and blend them into a purée, mix with rich whipped double cream and crushed meringue. Spoon into a loaf tin and freeze, then when frozen turn out for a delicious kumquat parfait to slice and serve.

LEMONS AND LIMES

Availability: all year round.

It was an 18th-century British ship's doctor who discovered the cure for the seafarers' curse, scurvy, by getting his sailors to sip the juice of limes (henceforth saddling Britons with the nickname Limeys). It was well over a hundred years later before scientists found the reason – their high concentration of vitamin C.

Lemons, limes and the Mediterranean fruit *citron* are chiefly used in cooking or as a part of recipes and dishes. We rarely eat them alone unless they are sweetened or, in the case of North African cuisine, salted and pickled. But there are few fruit bowls that do not have at least one lemon nestling among the other fruit. Cooks utilise their sharp acidity to accentuate sweetness or saltiness. When top chefs taste a sauce for flavour they often add not just salt and pepper but also a squeeze of lemon. Asian chefs use the more fragrant lime in the same way. Green-skinned citrons are used chiefly for their skins, which are candied or crystallised.

Limes are harder to squeeze than lemons but a few seconds microwaving makes the process easier. A simply way of obtaining the essential oil from lemons and limes for use in a sweet dish is to rub the skins with a sugar cube which is then added to the recipe – no grater to wash afterwards. Lemons and limes that have been kept until they become very small and soft have a heavenly scent. Asian cooks often use wizened whole dried limes in cooking. Limes from Thailand, like the knobbly-skinned Kaffir, have a more fragrant bouquet than your average lime.

TIP: GRATING CITRUS PEEL

Coating citrus fruits, especially lemons and limes, with a wax spray helps

to stop the skin drying out and shrivelling for the long haul to the stores.

If you wish to grate the peel, it is best if you buy unwaxed fruit and store

them in the fridge to help them keep a little longer. Otherwise, scrub the

waxed skins in warm water before using them.

LOQUATS

Availability: late spring.

Loquats are the Japanese medlar. They look like a cross between a small yellow pear and an apricot and are harvested in the spring. They are native Chinese and Japanese fruits that have found their way into Western stores and are now frequently grown in sunny Mediterranean countries. But they aren't seasoned travellers and bruise easily: any we find in our stores will have been packed under-ripe and may be a disappointment when sliced into. Cut open, they look like a yellow plum with two centre seeds that should be discarded. Fragrant and slightly sharp, they are generally halved and stoned and cooked in a sugar syrup or pulped and made into an ice cream.

LYCHEES AND RAMBUTANS

Availability: all year round but best in mid-winter.

Once the exclusive fruits of the Empresses of China, lychees are now widely on sale for most of the year for us more ordinary mortals, and aren't we grateful. The rough, knobbly skin is simple to peel off in one fell swoop, then inside the soft, pearly white sweet fragrant fruit is easily separated from the shiny mahogany-brown stone.

For many of us, our first introduction to this luscious Imperial fruit has been in Chinese restaurants. Canned lychees are a good substitute for fresh and are stoned, as befits a royal fruit now available to the greedy masses, but fresh they are less sickly and particularly nice to bring out, still in their pink jackets at the end of a casual supper party. My children used to enjoy three or four lychees with a few physalis (see page 172) slipped into their school lunch boxes until they realised they got more playground 'cred' with a small apple (but they continued to eat them happily at home).

Rambutans look more alien, almost like small red sea urchins. They are favourites of the Malays and Thais, their flavour even more exotic but still fragrant. They crop twice a year and so are readily available most of the time.

I never seem to have a problem judging the ripeness of either of these fruits. When a nice blushing pink, lychees are ripe, and I haven't yet come across an over-ripe one. Both rambutans and lychees can be used in the same ways – elegant in fruit salads or purée and delicious for sorbets, ice creams or even, if you have a surfeit, for jam. One of my popular easy entertaining desserts is to pile prepared mixed Oriental fruits on a bed of crushed ice and sprinkle rose water lightly over. Place the dish in the centre of the table with chopsticks. Guests then help themselves and have some fun at the same time.

MANGO

Availability: all year round, according to variety.

When I was a child in the West Indies, the mangoes were so juicy my father would make my brother and I eat them in the bath, then our mother would come in and hose us down with the shower head. But we never did find a way of picking the tiny fibres from our front teeth. I've yet to find anyone who doesn't enjoy a ripe, juicy mango and now they are on sale all year round.

Mangoes originated in the Indo-Burmese region of Asia and there are thought to be over a thousand varieties in India alone. The Tamil name for mango is *manga*, as is the Portuguese name used in Brazil, now one of the world's biggest exporters of the fruit. It was the Portuguese who took the fruit from India to Brazil.

Mangoes vary enormously in size from tiny baby ones right up to the size of a rugby ball. Skin colours range from green through to red and yellow. It is difficult to describe the flavour of a mango to someone who has never had one before – the taste is so unique that it is often used as a description by wine-tasters. But the taste is sweet with a gentle sharpness, an exotic fragrance and a creamy texture.

Check the ripeness of a mango not by its colour as it can vary, but by the feel. It should give slightly when squeezed gently in your cupped hand. Wrapping the fruit in newspaper makes them ripen more quickly. Mangoes are slippery little fellows and tricky to peel and serve. I once saw a woman at a Thai food festival deal with several fruits in a flash. She held a fruit flat in one hand and peeled the top thinly with a small sharp knife. Then she made several straight cuts down to the long, flat central stone at right angles, simply slipped the knife under the cuts and – hey presto! – off slipped perfect neat slices. She then turned the fruit over and dealt with the other side in the same manner. You may find it easier at first to cut two thick chunks off each side of the stone, then peel and slice. Flesh still clinging to the stone can be sliced off in a more ad hoc manner. There are many descriptions of cutting mangoes that involve turning the 'halves' inside out, but I've never managed to do that neatly. Alternatively, just buy them ready-cubed from a chill cabinet.

The *Alphonso mango* from India, occasionally on sale in June/July is regarded as the best in the world. It has an ethereal floweriness and no fibrous tissue. I've seen Indian friends pummel small ripe fruits in their hands then suck out the juice like a drink through a hole in their fists. Under-ripe mangoes are quite astringent – ideal for a spicy, sweet chutney but also good in Thai salads when grated coarsely and tossed in a chilli and lime dressing with fish or tiger prawns. There are hundreds of wonderful mango recipes: you can make a delicious speedy mango ice cream by mixing a purée of mango (fresh or canned) with whipped cream and extra sugar, adding a spoonful of tangy mango chutney to accentuate the flavour; they are good served with a quick sweet Thai rice and coconut pudding; and on a chilly day you may like to heat mango slices gently in a butterscotch mixture of butter and light soft brown sugar.

MANGOES WITH SWEET THAI COCONUT RICE

Put 250g (9oz) of Thai Jasmine rice into a pan with 600ml (20fl oz) of water and ½tsp of salt. Bring to the boil then stir cover and lower the heat right down. Cook for about 10 minutes without lifting the lid. Remove from the heat, stand for 5 minutes, then uncover and stir in 4–6tbsp of caster sugar and 2 x 200ml (7fl oz) cartons of coconut cream. Allow this to be absorbed by the rice for another 10 minutes while you peel and slice about 3 large ripe mangoes. Serve the sweet rice in a mound on a flat dish (in Thailand this would be on a clean banana leaf) with the mango slices by the side.

MANGOSTEENS

Availability: irregular.

Their hard reddish-brown skin is not very inviting, I admit, but many Asians rate mangosteens the most delicious fruit in the world, along with the unattractive durian. It does make you wonder which brave soul ever had the bright idea to try them in the first place. The mangosteen is something of a rambutan in the way you peel it, with a hint of mango in its flavour. It is not an easy fruit to grow outside South-East Asia as the fruiting season is short and rather irregular.

To prepare, you break open the thick, slightly brittle skin – scoring first with a short sharp knife helps. Inside you will find five white fleshy segments which you chew. If you come across a stone, then spit it delicately out. Not all segments have one. Sometimes I have been disappointed and found mangosteens past their best: if this happens to you take them back to the store, although you may just get an indifferent shrug from small store owners.

MELONS

Availability: all year round. European varieties in summer.

Melons are from the same botanical family as cucumbers, squashes and courgettes, which is not surprising as the skins look similar, and they grow by trailing along the ground. They are thought to have originated in Africa. In warm sub-tropical countries they can be grown out of doors but it is also possible to grow melons indoors under glass, which is evident from the number of melon houses found in old kitchen gardens, heated ingeniously by decaying compost packed into tunnels under the walls. The seeds of melons are edible but can also be crushed to give oil.

Melons have a very distinctive bouquet, more pronounced in some varieties than others. Nearly everyone loves a good, juicy wedge of melon but making sure they are ripe before they are cut open can be a bit of a hit-and-miss affair. Two tips may help: the first is to press the base (the opposite end to the stalk) of a melon and if it gives slightly it is just about ready; the second is to smell it – a ripe melon should smell of ripe melon! Some melons have particularly tough skins so, of course, the smell will be tricky to detect. Certainly, don't buy a rock-hard fruit – it will take for ever to reach any ripeness. I never buy melons cut into wedges apart from watermelon from ethnic stores.

Melon varieties

Varieties abound but here are some names to help you choose.

Some desert armies issue their soldiers with *watermelons* as part of their water rations. They vary in size and shape from long and pale green to buxom, round and dark green. I don't think the sniffing technique works with these so buy your watermelon from a Greek or Middle Eastern store and ask an experienced shopkeeper about its ripeness. You'll need only a big chunk at a time so don't feel you have to have to buy in kilos. When you get that watermelon home, you'll find the inner section is quite floury and contains all the black seeds. Experienced eaters can sink their teeth into the juicy flesh and spit out the seeds elegantly: first-timers may prefer to pick them out with a table knife. If the melon wedge is small, simply cut it out the seed section, then cut the chunks into wedges and serve the wedges piled high on a plate. One of the nicest ways of serving watermelon is as a simple starter: cut the fruit into chunks and toss with cubed feta cheese and a little olive oil dressing.

Honeydew – the most widely available though not the most exciting flavour, so make sure a honeydew is well-ripened before you cut into it.

Galia, from Israel and Spain, are very nice when ripe. Their distinctly 'netted' skin turns from dark green to golden as they ripen.

Cantaloupe melons are the gourmet's favourite so long as they are ripe. The skin is an irregular shaped, marked out in wedges in either green or a golden colour. Inside, the flesh is either orange or grccn.

Charentais is a form of cantaloupe with a pale green skin with darker green markings, sometimes slightly oval in shape. They are quite small compared to other melons. The peachy-orange flesh smells divine and the flavour is just as good. Charentais melon makes a good summer soup blended with olive oil, vinegar, basil and – amazingly – chunks of lobster.

Ogen is another yellow-flecked green-skinned melon with nicely flavoured green flesh.

Piel de Sapo – the name means 'toad's skin'. A Spanish melon akin to the honeydew, not too flavoursome unless really ripe.

ORANGES

Availability: all year round.

The best time for oranges, to my mind, still remains the winter despite all the advertising for summer oranges. Maybe it's psychological, because of a need for vitamin C to combat winter colds, but I'm sure there is a better selection of varieties in December, January and February.

Orange varieties

The *Valencia* is about the most important variety in the world. *Shamoutis* come from the Mediterranean, chiefly Spain, Morocco, Israel and Cyprus. *Tangerine* types of oranges include mandarins, minoelas (from Jamaica) and the smaller clementines, which are excellent for making juices and marmalade or popping into children's lunch boxes). Outspan and Jaffa are brand names of fruits from South Africa and Israel.

The limited season of the *Seville* orange is, of course, one of the highlights of the cook's calendar. It might seem to possess every possible disadvantage in terms of appearance, juiciness, number of pips and bitterness. But all those minuses are insignificant in the face of its one very big plus: it is supreme champion when it comes to homemade marmalade and, if you are a student of haute cuisine, a classic Sauce Bigarade. It is also the orange of choice in Spanish and North African meat casseroles.

Blood oranges have become fashionable in recent years. I find the flavour deeper and slightly sharper but maybe this is the psychological effect of the dark sanguine colour. The juice is stunning used in homemade jellies.

Using oranges

Oranges are mostly eaten fresh either in segments or, increasingly as the juicing craze gathers momentum, as home-pressed juices. Other than this, there's little to discuss in depth about using oranges except that, if you enjoy cooking, don't waste the peel. Remove as much as possible in large strips, and slice off the bitter pith with a small, sharp knife. (Alternatively, peel the skin thinly first with a swivel vegetable peeler so the pith is exposed to peel off as normal). Place these thin strips of peel on baking parchment paper on a tray and dry them out in either a very low oven or the airing cupboard. All citrus peels contain highly flavoured essential oils and you can use the dried peel strips in many recipes. Once dried, they can be ground in a food processor with some caster sugar and used to sprinkle over fresh fruits, cereals etc.

PAPAYA

Availability: all year round.

Originally from the Panama region of Central America, the papaya (also known as paw paw) spread rapidly round the world and is particularly popular in West Africa. Because they are grown in so many parts of the world they are generally available most of the year. There are many other names for this beautiful fruit, but where the name 'Mummy's Apple' comes from is a mystery to me.

The skin turns from green to yellow as it ripens, with the ripe flesh inside softening into a fragrant, sweet, creamy orange with a very slightly bitter afterbite. The little black seeds in the centre are easily scooped out with a teaspoon, then you might like to squeeze a little lime juice over, although I prefer to eat them neat. They are very refreshing for breakfast and can be eaten like an avocado pear straight from the skin. Under-ripe papaya is grated and tossed into a shredded vegetable salad in Thailand. I've also used finely chopped under-ripe papaya in a spicy salsa and it makes a good chutney.

The papaya has another virtue, though. Latex drained from the under-ripe fruit contains the enzyme papain, which, like pepsin from pineapples, tenderises meat. African cooks sometimes wrap tough meat in papaya skins when baking, and papaya can be cooked with meat in stews and casseroles.

PASSION FRUIT

Availability: all year round.

So called because this fruit comes from the same family as the flowering vine Passiflora, not because it arouses great passion (well, it may for some). A native of Brazil, it is also grown in many other sub-tropical countries such as Kenya, Columbia and parts of Asia.

We mostly see the purple-skinned variety in our shops; these can be eaten as soon as the fruit starts to wrinkle, but not so wrinkled that they have become over-ripe. Purple passion fruit have an intense sweet acidity and unique flowery fragrance that it is impossible to link to other flavours. The pulp inside is jelly-like and juicy, with small black crunchy seeds that are edible if a little crunchy. You can sieve them out, after mixing the pulp with a little hot water, but for small amounts this isn't worth it. The flavour is very intense so two or three fruits are sufficient. The Australian dessert pavlova has passion fruit juice mixed into the whipped cream centre and little puddles of seedy pulp dotted around on top of the billowing meringue case.

There is also a yellow-skinned variety called *granadilla* which never seems to wrinkle, so cut these open soon after purchase. The granadilla has a pleasant flavour, though not as intense or exciting as its passionate cousin's.

The two varieties can be used in the same way. Both make nice sorbets and jellies and are good bases for layered fruit terrines and mousses when mixed with other fruit juices.

PEACHES AND NECTARINES

Availability: chiefly in mid-summer but some out-of-season supplies.

Originally grown in China over two thousand years ago, peaches and their smooth-skinned cousins, nectarines, have changed little since then. Peaches and nectarines are imported fruits grown in Mediterranean climates such as Italy (a main supplier of some of the best fruit), France, Spain, South Africa and parts of America. They need great care in handling because they bruise so easily. Check the fruits carefully if you can (which is difficult if they are sold in boxes). I advise buying these fruits hard and allowing them to ripen at room temperature to lessen the waste of bruising. White peaches are sold as variations of yellow peaches.

Fresh peaches oxidise and turn brown when sliced so if preparing ahead for, say, a fruit salad, cover the slices in a little sugar syrup (see page 307) flavoured with a few shakes of Angostura bitters (see page 276). Or you can sprinkle the cut surfaces of halved peaches with icing sugar. Canned peaches in natural juice are excellent value, especially the *Cling* variety. Good semi-dried, no-need-to-soak varieties make good sweet treats.

QUICK AND LUSCIOUS PEACHY PUDDING

Press a small nugget of marzipan into a peach or nectarine (hollowed out after stoning), sprinkle with caster sugar and grill until browned and bubbling. Drizzle over some rum or brandy and serve with ice cream.

PEARS

Availability: best in the autumn for home-grown fruit.

Another naturally late-summer/autumnal fruit. The main European centres for pear growing have been France, Belgium and Germany but now we also have a number of British varieties and you will see fruits from Italy, South Africa, New Zealand and even further afield, depending on the season.

A truly ripe, sweet juicy pear is one of the great delights of the fruit bowl but pears are contrary and their peak of ripeness occurs in only a short space of time: you can wait a number of days for rock-hard fruits to ripen only for them suddenly to appear over-ripe. This is why I advise buying pears a few at a time, not in a big bag unless, there are a lot of pear-eaters in your household. I would also suggest buying pears marked 'ripe for eating' a day or so before you intend to bite into them – invariably they are too hard on the day you buy them but fine for eating a day or two later. Colour is not an indication of ripeness, but texture is. Cradle a pear in the palm of your hand and gently squeeze; if there is a slight tenderness, then bite into it and enjoy. Leave it longer and the flesh becomes floury.

Canned pears in natural juice are of an excellent quality, and naturally sun-ripened dried pears make a delicious chewy alternative to sweet snacks. Or if you want to use them cooked, then simply stew them lightly in a little water with a couple of strips of lemon peel and maybe a cinnamon stick.

PEARS IN RED PEPPERCORN SYRUP

Hard pears are the best for cooking as their ripeness can
be a bit of a guessing game. I use the old English variety of
Conference, allowing one large fruit per person and generally
cooking at least six at a time.

Peel each pear neatly using a swivel vegetable peeler then
poach in a sugar syrup solution (see page 307) with a little
cinnamon bark, 1tsp of black peppercorns, two star anise
and a little freshly grated nutmeg. For special occasions you
could add red wine to the syrup. Simmer for 10–15 minutes
then leave to cool in the syrup before eating. The syrup can be
strained and re-used two or three times more. Wonderful with
dollops of mascarpone.

Pear varieties

Like apples, the quality of the modern-day pear owes much to the painstaking
research of enthusiastic breeders from two hundred years ago. Three main
varieties still in popular demand can be traced back to this time – the
Conference, Cornice (from France) and the *Williams*. The Conference pear
was a top award-winning variety submitted by one of the leading Victorian
horticulturists to an 1885 international conference and accorded the name in
honour of the occasion.

The South African *Packham Pear* is a neatly contained rounded shape
much favoured by chefs. A fragrantly sweet, golden-skinned pear from Portugal
called *Rocha* is making regular appearances in our stores. Pears with 'beurre'
in their name indicate a buttery flavour. The Cornice is largely used as a dessert
pear, while the *Barlett* pear is the most popular variety in America and one
frequently used in canning.

Asian pears

Most chefs regard exotic fruits with professional detachment, but the Asian
pear (also known as the oriental pear, nashi and tientsin) could rightly become
a regular favourite. It looks like a fat, rough, golden-skinned apple and has the
crisp texture associated with apples. But the flavour and juiciness are those
of a pear and well worth trying. Quarter the fruit, remove the core and slice as
you would a dessert fruit, or serve the Chinese way, sliced horizontally.

PERSIMMONS AND SHARON FRUIT

Availability: late autumn.

The bright orange, squarish, tomato-sized fruit you may find in late
autumn are likely to be the Israeli Sharon fruit, a highly bred version of
the perfume-rich persimmon found in Italy and the South of France and
a favourite of the Japanese.

   True persimmons may be deliciously sweet but, unless eaten at the right
stage of ripeness, have a mouth-puckering side-effect that can be quite
unpleasant. The trick is to know when to peel a persimmon – the fruit has
to appear almost over-ripe before you cut into it. The enterprising Israelis
developed a fruit without this puckering effect, but some gourmets claim this
was at the cost of much of the delicate fragrance (the flesh itself is sweet and
good looking but not exciting). Slice the flesh to make a good topping for tarts
or combine the flesh in mousse or ice-cream mixtures. A beautifully ripe
persimmon, however, needs only to be opened up and eaten with a teaspoon.

PHYSALIS

Availability: all year round.

Possibly one of the most popular of the so-called exotic fruits because they are
easy to eat and need little preparation, except to pop each one out of its sandy-
coloured lantern-shaped skin (or, to give it the true name, calyx). Their slight
gooseberry flavour is responsible for their alternative name of Cape gooseberry.

   Children love physalis and they make good decorations on cheesecakes
and mousses. Chefs also like to make them into petits fours, dipped into
a thick fondant syrup then left to drain and dry on baking parchment. At
home, we like to dunk them into a runny dark chocolate dipping sauce made
in the microwave. To prepare, just peel back the skin in sections and give
the skins a good twist – then they look like fairy parachutes. Or if you want
to be more serious you can just pull them from their skins. Halve them if you
want to add them to fruit salads.

PINEAPPLES

Availability: all year round; good supplies in autumn.

The name, pineapple comes from the Spanish word for pine cone, *pina*, whose shape it resembles. It is a New World plant from the plains of Brazil, distributed around the world by Old World colonists. Columbus first set eyes on a pineapple on the island of Guadeloupe during his second voyage to the New World, and its sweet, fragrant juicy flesh gained popularity very quickly. By 1548 it was being grown in India, having being planted there by the Portuguese. During the 18th century the pineapple became a symbol of hospitality and people in the mood for entertaining would stick a fresh pineapple on the gatepost to welcome visitors. We still do this, only now the pineapples are carved in stone and stuck on garden walls.

The most important pineapple-producing countries are Hawaii, Malaysia, South Africa and increasingly West Africa. Pineapple production is one of the most technologically advanced industries of all commercially grown fruits and modern transport means we can now enjoy these fresh, juicy fruits almost as nature intended.

Pineapples are very nutritious, high in vitamins and also a pepsin enzyme used in tenderising tough meat, which is why it is impossible to make a fresh pineapple jelly using a meat-extracted setting agent such as gelatine. To peel a pineapple, either practise the technique of cutting down in spiral strips or just peel thinly, then use the tip of a potato peeler to cut out the 'eyes'. To serve in slices, cut horizontally to the size you want, then use a small plain scone cutter to cut out the core, or quarter the fruit lengthways and slice off the core. (Personally, I like the core and regard it as a 'cook's treat'.)

Pineapples are rarely sold by variety names, but if you find a small *Natal Queen* then enjoy its sweet, crisp texture. West Africa exports baby-size pineapples that may look wonderful in a fruit bowl or flower arrangement but should be eaten before they get too ripe. You can tell the ripeness of a pineapple by the smell and by pulling out one or two of the central leaves: a ripe fruit will give up its leaves easily. Under-ripe pineapple is used in exotic spicy cooking such as Thai food and Cantonese-style sweet and sour dishes. Sprinkle fresh pineapple with fresh orange or lime juice and a few jiggers of Kirsch or white rum. Pineapples in natural juice are a good substitute for fresh.

PITAHAYA/DRAGON FRUIT

Availability: all year round.

These look like disfigured pineapples but are actually a cactus fruit from Columbia. Cut the fruit in half and you'll find white spongy flesh flecked with tiny black seeds. The flavour is quite pleasant although it benefits from extra sweetening with icing sugar and sharpening with a little fresh lime juice. It's good as a speciality sorbet. There is also a very vibrant bright pink pitahaya with pretty pink flesh inside. Scoop this out and use it as a dayglo decoration.

PLUMS

Availability: home-grown fruit, around late summer and autumn.

To my mind, these are essentially fruits to grow in a garden because commercially grown plums can be such a disappointment – all looks and no flavour. Home-grown English plums have such a wonderful flavour and sweet, juicy texture that I suspect they are difficult to grow in a consistent, modern, marketable way. So many delightful old-fashioned trees have been scrubbed out and our main source of supply is imports from Italy, Spain, the United States and France. Imported plums tend to lack the flavour of home-grown plums and if they feel hard on sale should be left to ripen at room temperature. Under-ripe plums do, however, make good, spicy Mexican-style fruit, onion and tomato salsas.

Plum varieties
France is the home of fine plums, planted by royalty in châteaux gardens. *Reine Claude*, is one variety, taken by Sir George Gage to Britain where it became the *greengage*. Another well-loved variety, *Victoria*, is also named after royalty and is a favourite dessert or cooking plum. Plums are natives across much of the northern hemisphere, from Europe to the Americas and Japan, which produce rounder shapes. Small French golden *mirabelles* sometimes find their way to our markets and, like gages, make delicious honey-sweet jam. Yellow plums include the prolific *Peshore Egg* plum often found canned in syrup. Also on sale in late summer are *Czars* and *Marjorie Seedlings*.

Damsons were originally called the Damescene plum because they were brought to England from Damascus by Crusaders. Now they are associated very much with British puddings, in particular crumbles, and the purée is used to make a bittersweet, deep purple fool blended with whipped cream. Damsons have a low ratio of fruit to stone and, as they are small fruits at the best of times, this means an awful lot of stones to deal with. Don't even attempt to stone damsons fresh: cook them first in a little water with a fair amount of sugar and when the fruit is cooked you will find that the stones are floating on the top and can be easily spooned off.

Prunes

Two chief suppliers of prunes, the dried fruit of plums, are the dimpled stoned *Californian prune* (various varieties but *Sunsweet* is the best known) and the juicy, fragrant French *pruneaux d'Agen*, wonderful without soaking or cooking eaten for dessert. Other speciality prunes to watch for are *Portuguese Elvas* and *Carlsbad plums* (really prunes). In fact, most prunes now can be cooked without pre-soaking.

POMEGRANATES

Availability: winter months.

Pomegranates are the ancient fruit of all wisdom. Christian rulers from the Holy Roman Emperors onwards liked to be painted holding a cut pomegranate to show that they possessed great wisdom. Pomegranates were found in ancient Egyptian tombs. They are also associated with fertility because, when you cut one open, there is a host of plump pink seeds cushioned within papery membranes. On Greek islands pomegranates are pinned to the front door of a newly married couple by the hopeful in-laws as a big hint.

We think of pomegranates stuffed down the toe of a Christmas stocking but they are very versatile eating with many uses for both savoury and sweet dishes. Now they are sold prepared in pots, ready to cook with, or sprinkle over, salads or desserts. Just learn to love crunching all those seeds. Iranian and Turkish cooks use pomegranate juice liberally. Its astringent, slightly tannic sweet juice goes well with rice and aromatic meat stews, especially with duck and pheasant. Or one can mix the juicy seeds with fresh chopped walnuts in salads. The juice makes refreshing drinks: a sweet cordial called Grenadine is made from pomegranate juice. At Christmas time, scoop out the seeds of several fruits and pile them high in pretty glass dishes to hand round as a refreshing dessert after a heavy meal. Turkish and Iranian cooks also use a thick, dark red pomegranate syrup, *nar eksisi*, or molasses to sharpen sauces in the same way as Indian cooks use tamarind. Fresh pomegranate juice can be used like lemon juice, great with olive oil for marinating rich meats such as duck or lamb. To extract the juice, halve the fruit widthways like a lemon, then press the seeds and flesh on to a lemon squeezer. But don't press too hard: the bitter membrane affects the sweet-sour juice.

PRICKLY PEAR

Availability: July–February.

Also known as the Barbary fig. My Greek schoolfriend loved these and picked them from roadside cacti near her home in Rhodes then handed them to me to peel. You need to slice off the two ends and peel back the prickly skin with a sharp knife as if you were peeling an orange, or slide your knife under the skin and release the flesh in one go. Handle the fruit with rubber gloves unless the grower has obligingly rubbed off the prickles before putting it on sale. The flesh is quite sweet and can be eaten as it is whole or cut into pieces, but it is probably more inviting puréed and sharpened with a squeeze of lemon juice. It makes a nice jelly.

QUINCES AND MEDLARS

Availability: autumn and early winter.

Quinces are the lovely, downy, golden-yellow and ethereally scented fruits of ancient legends. They are related to apples and pears but sadly they are rarely sold in stores except in Greek and Middle Eastern shops. If you do find them, buy some and give them a try. They freeze well.

They have a very hard texture and will need cooking: quarter, core and peel if the skins look unattractive. Chop the flesh and place in a saucepan with sugar to taste and cover with a little water. Simmer with a stick of cinnamon and strip of lemon zest until soft and a pretty translucent pink, then taste their fragrant and exquisite flavour. You can, of course, make them into jams and jellies.

The quince is popular in hot Mediterranean countries such as Spain and Portugal where it is made into a thick fruit paste (or, as British cooks would call it, a 'fruit cheese'). The Spanish paste is called *membrillo*, the Portuguese *marmelo* – from which we derive our favourite breakfast conserve, marmalade. Both the Spanish and Portuguese eat quince paste with cheese, especially sharp ewe's milk cheeses, but I have served it with roasted pork and duck. Quinces are used in Middle Eastern meat stews and stuffed with a spicy minced lamb mixture.

Medlars are related to quinces but are found more in colder climates and old kitchen gardens. They have a tough light tan skin and are characterised by five large seeds which stick out at the base of each fruit. Discard the seeds and peel and chop the flesh. They are best cooked when over-ripe, when they are described as 'bletted'. They make a fine jelly and unusual ice cream.

RASPBERRIES, BLACKBERRIES, TAYBERRIES AND SIMILAR

Availability: mid-summer; out-of-season imports at a price.

These berries are all from the genus *Rubus*. Their seeds are contained inside little 'drupelets' shaped around a central core, unlike the strawberry where the seeds are sunk into the main fruit. (The drupelets are the reason why such berries freeze better than strawberries; there is less volume of water and the cell structure is smaller.) Cultivated berries are derived from wild bushes. Wild picked berries need to be checked carefully for insects. Don't wash any soft berry because you will affect the flavour: simply brush lightly.

Raspberries are associated with the lowlands of Scotland where the best-flavoured fruit is grown, harvested around the end of July and, like home-grown strawberries, eagerly awaited. Out of our summer season, good-flavoured supplies reach us from Chile and New Zealand but their price means they are mainly used for special occasions. *Loganberries* are thought to be natural hybrids of raspberries and blackberries but are now cultivated on a commercial scale. Tayberries are a further development of loganberries, as are *boysenberries*. All these soft red berry fruits are best eaten as they are with little else except some sugar. If you have a surfeit of any of these red berries, cook them lightly as a jam, adding equal amounts of granulated sugar, for just a few minutes to a soft set so as not to lessen the flavour.

Blackberries (also known as brambles) make excellent cooking combined with apples or, more unusually, with pears in crumbles and pies. Blackberries also make good ice cream and fools, and you can use them as a sauce for serving with duck. Cultivated blackberries are large and inviting but lack the country flavour of the wild bramble.

Mulberries are a wonderful old cottage-garden fruit. They are rarely on sale commercially because they grow on trees that take many years to mature. The fruit tastes fragrant but doesn't last long so eat them the day you pick or buy them.

RHUBARB

Availability: forced rhubarb early spring; main crop early summer onwards.

When my children were small I deliberately made them lots of fresh rhubarb puddings because I wanted them to grow up enjoying this wonderful old cottage-garden fruit. It worked and they enjoy the fools, crumbles and squashy cakes as much as I do. Rhubarb is available from supermarkets and greengrocers in two forms – forced and main crop – depending on the season.

In early spring you will the find long, dayglo-pink stems with small yellow-green leaves of forced rhubarb. In other words, the plant has been grown in long tubes to make it reach for the daylight – an old-fashioned gardeners' trick which gives tender, well-flavoured stems. They need the simplest of cooking with a little sugar (I always use unrefined soft brown sugar, such as Billingtons, with rhubarb because its mildly caramel flavour goes so well with the tartness). Or you can copy top chefs and 'roast' young forced rhubarb: cook short lengths in a mixture of clear honey and butter in a shallow pan over a medium heat, stirring gently for about 5 minutes until the stems are just tender but still whole and the pan syrup has almost evaporated away.

Later in the summer you will find main crop rhubarb, with thicker, greener stalks. Good for making into puddings as crumbles, pies or my favourite, cakes. Main crop rhubarb does need to be cooked in a little water with sugar, but even the gentlest poaching does not prevent it from breaking up into a sludge – not that it matters: rhubarb is often served mixed into whipped cream for fools or under pie crusts so no one will notice. The classic flavourings that enhance rhubarb are ginger and grated orange, but once cooked and chilled you will find strawberries are good mixed in. You can make a lightly sweetened rhubarb sauce to serve with pork chops or pan-fried duck.

SQUASHY RHUBARB UPSIDE-DOWN CAKE

450g (1lb) washed and chopped rhubarb
3–4tbsp unrefined soft brown sugar
150g (5½oz) butter or baking margarine, softened
150g (5½oz) soft brown sugar
150g (5½oz) self-raising flour
½tsp ground mixed spice
1tsp baking powder
3 free-range eggs
Crème fraîche, whipped cream or ice cream, to serve

Preheat the oven to 180°C/gas mark 4 and lightly grease a
20cm (8in) round cake tin about 4cm (1½in) high. Lightly
cook the rhubarb with the unrefined sugar until just tender but
not too broken up or runny. If a lot of juice has seeped out,
tip much of it away (or mix with fizzy water for a refreshing
drink). Spoon into the base of the cake tin and spread around.
Put butter or margarine, soft brown sugar, flour, spice, baking
powder and eggs in a food processor and run the machine until
smooth, scraping down the sides once or twice. Spoon on top
of the rhubarb, spread it evenly to the sides then bake for about
35 minutes until the top is golden-brown and springy when
you press it with your finger. Leave for about 5 minutes before
turning out on to a serving plate. Allow to cool and serve warm
with crème fraîche, whipped cream or ice cream.

STAR FRUIT

Availability: all year round.

A native fruit of Indonesia, star fruits (or carambolas) are fast becoming indispensable as an instant garnish but do serve them ripe because they taste of almost nothing otherwise. However, I do not advise you buy them ripe because they bruise so easily, even just carrying them home. I buy pale green star fruit and find by the next day the ridges are tinged with brown, a sign that they are ripe enough to slice. Don't peel, just slice thinly. Inside the sour-sweet flesh is juicy and very refreshing, a nice addition to fruit salad mixtures. Or slice three or four, sprinkle lightly with icing sugar and a little white rum and serve for a nice dessert. They look stunning mixed with kiwi slices on their own or atop a meringue pavlova. You can make a jam with them if you find yourself with a lot of fruit.

STRAWBERRIES

Availability: all year round; home-grown season is June and September.

The cultivated strawberry, popular throughout the world, is of American origin and was introduced into Europe at the beginning of the 17th century. It took its name from the fact that the early plants were grown on straw. The advent of railway transport helped popularise strawberries because they could be sent for sale into towns and cities while still in the peak of perfection. Now, it seems, we can have too much of a good thing, and there are many cooks and gourmets who will not eat strawberries unless home-grown and in season.

Strawberries can be cropped twice in a year, in early summer and late summer, which in Europe occurs around June and September. Strawberries are best left to ripen naturally on the plant, then eaten shortly after picking – only possible for fruit eaten close to where it is grown. Certainly, naturally ripened fruit has a greater depth of fragrant bouquet and flavour. Ideally, if you've time, hull the fruits by twisting off the green stalks and at the same time pulling up the central core (a ripe strawberry will hull easily).

The English June strawberries are eagerly awaited and greedily devoured, mostly on their own with maybe just a dip of caster sugar. Strawberries, suit a number of flavourings – vanilla is one, or they can be lightly sprinkled with rose water (the strawberry and the rose are botantically from the same plant species). Italians like to sprinkle sliced strawberries with well-aged balsamic vinegar, the French with a light red wine. There are also people who grind some freshly ground black pepper over a dish of strawberries, and in America strawberries are combined in a salad of sliced avocado and chicken. A useful tip: if you find some strawberries in the punnet that are squashy and past their best, don't waste them. Crush them with a fork and a little sugar, then mix back into the whole fresh fruit.

Occasionally, extra-large American strawberries complete with stalks appear in stores. Many people find they lack favour, possibly because they are picked before ripening. They are nice, though, held by the stalk and dipped into hot melted chocolate.

Strawberry varieties

Varieties depend on the country of origin. *Elsanta* is a variety we see often in shops – a bit dull but it keeps well. Then there's *Driscoll Jubilee* plus *Ava* and *English Rose*. *Little Scarlett* is an early variety still used in jam-making for a fine flavour. Much research around Cambridge gives us names such as *Cambridge Favourite* and the long-standing *Royal Favourite*.

Alpine or *wild strawberries* are smaller fruit with prominent seeds that stick out of the fruit rather than sink in. You may have noticed how prolific they can be in gardens and they are a popular container-grown plant. Often it is a race for who can reach them first – wild birds or the gardener. In June speciality greengrocers will sell small punnets of Alpine berries, but you may find them a disappointment when compared to sweet, juicy cultivated fruits. It's far better to grow your own for free.

ETON MESS

A favourite tuckshop pud for past Eton schoolboys was to mix ice cream with crushed strawberries and meringues. Instead of ice cream and to embellish the recipe a little, try whipped double cream or the tangier crème fraîche with ½tsp of vanilla essence. Lightly crush a large punnet of hulled fine-flavoured home-grown strawberries and about four meringue shells. Fold everything together just before serving in a pretty glass serving bowl. The mixture should look gently swirled.

TAMARILLOS

Availability: late autumn.

New Zealanders call this beauty of a fruit the tree tomato. Well, it certainly looks like a pointed plum tomato with a shiny, smooth skin flashed with orange streaks and a long curved stalk. When you cut it open the sections and pips inside look even more like a tomato. It even tastes tomatoish, with overtones of a sharp orange, a true cross between sweet and savoury.

It was originally a native of the hills of Peru but it is now grown elsewhere and supplies come to us from other sub-tropical countries. Tamarillos are best thinly peeled, cooked and sweetened but they can be served unsweetened as a purée to accompany fish or light meats. Tamarillos also make excellent chutneys, as you would expect from a colourful sour fruit.

FUNGI

MUSHROOMS

Of the 100,000 species of fungi throughout the world only a few are edible, though increasing numbers of these few are becoming available on sale or for picking. A wild mushroom that we see above the earth or on a living or decaying tree, known as the fruiting body, is only the visible part of a much larger network of underground hyphae or filaments, like roots. They come in a variety of cap shapes – shallow or deep convex, pointed, wart-like, depressed in the centre and bell-shaped.

Edible wild mushrooms 'fruit' at different times of the year, though autumn is generally accepted as offering the most plentiful supply for picking. Mushrooms grow throughout the world and many more are now imported from overseas to supplement home-grown crops. The most widely available is still *Agaricus bisporous*, the one sold as *button* or *close-cap mushrooms*.

Until a hundred years ago or so, mushrooms were picked wild – if at all, it must be said, because although wild mushroom hunting has been popular in Europe for centuries, the British developed something of a phobia about it.

Grown in sterilised compost in dark sheds all year round, our common *Agaricus bisporous* mushrooms are picked at different stages of growth. So, a large, flat grilling mushroom is the same species as a baby button mushroom, just more grown up. You will also find variations are on sale such as the *Portabellini, Champignon de Paris* or *Brown Chestnut* – all still the same *Agaricus bisporous* but with a more developed flavour and darker colour. Organic mushrooms are often of the brown chestnut type.

But it is the cultivated 'wild' mushrooms, about which we know so little, that should be of more interest to us. At certain times of the year it is possible to buy genuine wild edible mushrooms on sale in certain delis (chiefly Italian ones), speciality greengrocers and, increasingly, supermarkets, albeit those in metropolitan areas with a more discerning clientele.

'Wild' mushroom varieties
Oyster mushrooms are mostly pale grey but sometimes pink and yellow, both natural colours, and with inverted caps and well-developed gills. They come in all sizes: slice larger oysters but leave baby ones whole, they look so pretty. Give them only a light cooking because they quickly become a bit slimy and

soft. Their flavour is more delicate than *Agaricus bisporous*. Oysters grow naturally on trees in clusters – you may spot them during autumnal walks, but most in shops are cultivated.

Shiitakes are oriental in origin but now grown under cultivation. They have a mid-tan colour and slightly leathery skin. Their chief characteristic is the shape of cap which when sliced looks like an upturned moustache. Dark and almost meaty in flavour, these suit rich stews or oriental stir-fries and braises. Pinch out the woody stalks or, if you have a lot save them for the stockpot. Shiitakes are also sold dried, either sliced or whole, in Chinese food stores. All you need do is soak what you need in warm water for 15 minutes, then drain and pat dry with kitchen paper (save the soaking liquor to use as a light stock) and treat as fresh.

The other main cooking mushroom is the *cep Boletus edulis*, also called *Porcini* in Italy or, as so charmingly dubbed by the Victorians, *'The Penny Bun'*. They range from tiny fairy size right up to saucer size and, like shiitakes, they have a mid-tan skin. They are dumpier in shape than the *Agaricus bisporous*. They can be found fresh on wild mushroom rambles or in delis and some food halls and stores. Treat fresh ceps as you would the common *Agaricus bisporous* in everyday cooking, though you will find they have a richer flavour, which is why the French and Italians love them so much. Trim the base of the stalks, which you can discard should you wish to present a dish with neat caps, but from a flavour point of view they make good eating. You can also find ceps sliced and dried: if they seem expensive in their small packs, remember they have a lot of flavour and swell on soaking, plus the soaking liquor is most useful.

Other chefs' favourites are *morels* and *chanterelles*. Morels are in the same category as truffles and with their honeycomb texture look like small deep-sea sponges. They are a spring mushroom, which you can buy fresh or dried, and they're popular with gourmets everywhere and, increasingly, in the UK. Morels have a distinctive fragrance (a word much used by mushroom aficionados) that chefs love to exploit in soups and sauces. Serve them whole with fish or meat dishes or finely chopped in soups and sauces. Cappuccino soups will frequently have a delicate cluster of baby morels at the bottom of the cups or bowls they are served in. I like to serve morels with monkfish, brill or light-flavoured game birds such as guinea fowl or pheasant, even with a full-flavoured, free-range, corn-fed chicken. If you are out picking wild mushrooms, a little tip about morels: beware the false morel, which looks more like a brain than a sponge. Best to leave picking to the experts.

And now chanterelles, also known as *girolles*. They have centrally depressed caps and distinctive irregularly shaped gills and their warm, autumnal apricot colour makes them a lovely garnish. They're particularly nice as an omelette filling. Chanterelles are in season for home-based picking or fresh in shops from late summer to early autumn. The delicious dark charcoal-grey mushroom called horn of plenty is related to the chanterelle. They are wonderful simply sautéed on their own or added to rich stews and sauces where their dark colour blends in.

Other great edible mushrooms include *giant puff balls, parasols, shaggy parasols, saffron milkcaps, chicken of the woods, blewits* (literally pale blue, and one of my favourites), and *hedgehog fungus*. Sometimes you may see these on sale in delis and occasionally packed in boxes labelled 'gourmet selection' in flagship supermarkets. I often pick these up as a mixture towards the end of the day at a ridiculously low price, due, I suspect, to produce managers panicking that they might 'go off' and poison unsuspecting customers. They have subtly different flavours and the best way to deal with them is to lightly sauté and eat them on toast or tossed into pasta.

WARNING

Don't pick wild mushrooms unless you are sure of their identity. Arm yourself with a well-illustrated guidebook or seek the advice of an expert. In public woods you must contact the forestry authorities for permission and guidance first. Remember, most wild mushrooms aren't edible, so proceed with care.

Storing mushrooms

All mushrooms have a high water content, which affects them in various ways, so avoid washing if possible as it only makes them soggy. Cultivated mushrooms will at the most need only a light brushing with a clean damp cloth: any tenacious dirt can be trimmed off with a sharp knife. Ideally, eat mushrooms within 24 hours of picking if they are genuinely wild, or by the sell-by date on a pack. As mushrooms age they sweat which makes the outsides slimy. If you buy them loose or in pack, when you get home decant them into a paper bag. Fridges draw moisture out of fresh food, so mushrooms begin to dehydrate because of their high water content – you will notice this because they start to go spongy and wrinkled. This is not detrimental to the flavour, indeed it intensifies it. If you find a batch of shrivelled fungi in your fridge, cover with warm water for 15 minutes, then drain, pat dry and cook immediately.

Cooking mushrooms

To cook mushrooms, melt a good knob of best butter in a frying pan with 2tbsp of olive oil and when you can feel the heat rising from the pan toss in the sliced or whole mushrooms. Keep the heat high and stir and toss them, keeping them moving over the heat so they cook evenly. That way they should stay plump and juicy without any liquid seeping out. When they feel softened but are nicely browned on the outside, add 2 tbsp of white wine, dry sherry or vermouth. A few shakes of light soy sauce is nice, plus sea salt and freshly ground black pepper. A crushed garlic clove and maybe a dollop or more of half-fat crème fraîche add depth of flavour. Finally, top with chopped fresh parsley. For the ultimate quick starter simply serve these on slices of hot fresh granary toast or toss into pasta.

A *duxelle* is a finely chopped 'purée' of cooked mushrooms for which chefs find many uses. It's a good way of dealing with a selection of mushrooms you found in the woods or maybe a pack or more of shop bargains. Top chefs always suggest you hand chop the mushrooms very, very finely, for which you will need a sharp, heavy bladed knife – don't use a food processor or the mushrooms will turn to pulp. Melt some butter and olive oil in a wide shallow pan and when hot add your finely chopped mixture. Keep stirring and tossing until the duxelle softens down to a rich, dark purée. Add wine, sherry or vermouth plus seasoning, and cook until evaporated down. Then remove, allow to cool and use as a topping paste, or a pâté to spoon on to bruschetta, or in a classic Beef Wellington. An alternative use for a selection of mushrooms would be to turn them into a rich and creamy mushroom soup.

TRUFFLES

Availability: generally the autumn from September to January.

Forget gold, silver or diamonds. If I need spoiling then a whole truffle will keep me sweet for many a day, preferably a white one from northern Italy, but a black one will do very nicely too.

Truffles are fungi that seem to defy all attempts at cultivation. Fresh truffles don't freeze, dry or bottle well, either. The nearest I can come to holding on to the heavenly scent is to pop scraps from shavings or choppings into small bottles of fine olive oil, which I then trickle over dishes but even preserved in this way don't let it hang around for too long. Also, don't store a fresh truffle for too long, unwrapped, in the fridge unless you want everything smelling of truffle – the aroma is all-pervading.

You can buy commercial truffle oils and pastes, but check the labels for the varieties used. Oils are best used over cooked pasta or try them on baby new potatoes, in salads or even on wafer-thin raw, cured meats such as Parma ham or bresaola. The paste is divine spread lightly on cocktail-sized bruschetta topped with chopped fresh tomatoes and maybe a little fresh buffala di mozzarella. Or try it spread inside a split chicken breast which is then pan-fried.

Chefs will often stack a few shavings on top of each other, cut them into fine shreds, then finely chop the shreds. This truffle 'dust' is then sprinkled lightly over cream sauces, light soups and vegetables because a little is all you need, the aroma is so distinctive.

Truffle varieties

I give the botanical names of the varieties because it helps to identify them should you come across them in a preserved state.

The best of all are the rare *white truffles*, which glory in the name of *Tuber magnatum*, and grow within the roots of deciduous trees such as oak and beech around the north Italian town of Alba. They look like badly contorted potatoes. The aroma (smell is too lowly a description) is quite simply divine and penetrating. No wonder truffles have been credited with aphrodisiac powers.

They often come wrapped in slightly damp newspaper, otherwise they are best stored in a box of rice, preferably risotto rice, which can subsequently be cooked. Do not wash a white truffle: scrub any dirt off. Check it thoroughly for any maggots or holes that might have been plugged with hard mud to make up the weight. A fresh truffle should feel heavy for its size and keep fresh for about a week.

Black truffles (Tuber melanosporum) are available from late autumn through to the beginning of spring. They are traditionally associated with the Perigord region of France but are also found in Provence and parts of northern Italy. They're cheaper (well, that's probably a relative term) than white truffles and they keep longer, for up to 14 days. The skin is tougher and can be lightly washed and scrubbed but do dry it well and store it in a cool place, ideally a box of risotto rice.

Summer truffles (Tuber aestivum) are English 'cousins'. They are found on chalky English soils, usually nestling between beech trees. Edible but, sadly, not exciting.

PULSES

Ever since Man the Hunter became Man the Farmer, he has harvested the seeds of leguminous plants, some to eat fresh but most to dry for later. There are literally thousands of species in the world, their distribution depending on localised growing conditions. Many species reach our stores, and many we grow for ourselves, to be used in a host of dishes. In addition, some legumes such as soya beans have huge commercial potential beyond their edible use.

All legumes are high in vegetable proteins, starch (carbohydrates), fibre and minerals and some are good sources of mono and unsaturated oil. However, the protein is not as complete as animal proteins in all the essential amino acids, but if they are eaten in combination with other foods, notably grains which contain the missing amino acids, then the protein 'circle' is complete and the meal becomes as nutritious as any containing meat proteins. Subconsciously, Man the Eater has based his staple dishes around this concept – hummus and pitta bread, rice 'n' peas, pease pudding and dumplings, potatoes, lentils and rice, pasta and chickpeas, even baked beans on toast!

We buy pulses and legumes in two forms: they are good canned in water, with little alteration to their structure and flavour, and just need draining before use; or we buy them dried to be soaked and cooked. Dried pulses can be sold skinless and split (what the Indians call dhal: the whole bean they call gram), which makes them quicker to cook. We can also germinate them as seeds and eat the tender, nutritious sprouts within a few days, so varying our diet even more (see page 93).

ADUKI BEANS

At one time these were thought truly exotic beans, but now we are becoming used to their distinctive flavour and slightly meaty texture. They are the bean favoured by Chinese and Japanese cooks. For their small size they seem to take a lot of simmering, but once cooked they are great in many dishes. I like to use them cooked, then partially ground and shaped into vegetarian burgers. In the Orient, the slightly sweet flavour is exploited by using aduki beans in sweet bean pastes, cakes and dipping sauces. And they make good sprouts.

BLACK-EYED PEAS

These peas, also known as cow peas, actually look like small beans with their creamy skin and small black 'eye' where the bean was attached to the pod. Their distinctive, slightly nutty taste blends nicely with spices and coconut and they are popular in several countries with great native cuisines, from Mexico and the United States to West Africa and India. A good soul food ingredient.

BROAD BEANS/FAVA BEANS

Another wide category that includes *butter beans, lima beans* (from Peru) as well as the *dried brown fava bean* and the *fresh green broad bean*. Sizes may vary slightly. Fava beans were used by the ancient Egyptians and were also popular with the Romans – the Italian first name Fabio is a derivative. Lima beans are one of the beans used by native Americans in the stew-soup succotash, later taken up by the colonial settlers. Butter beans may conjure up bad memories of school dinners but, nicely cooked in a creamy parsley sauce, they are one of my favourites. Fresh broad beans, sold very young and tender, are enjoying something of a revival, though broad beans can also be bought frozen. Ideally, you should pop them from their outer skins after cooking, then reheat in a little butter with garlic and herbs. They make good eating with juicy, sweet lamb. Broad beans can be bought fresh or frozen.

CHICKPEAS

Chickpeas are also known as garbanzos in Spain and the United States. They are vital to Middle Eastern, Indian (where they are known as Bengal gram), Spanish and Mexican cooking. They are often used whole in stews or soups but also have their uses pulverised raw then cooked. The chickpea holds its texture well, even if slightly overcooked. It cans well, too, and a couple of cans are useful as a storecupboard standby.

    Chickpeas marry well with many punchy flavours and spices. Hummus is the best-known example of a cooked purée flavoured with tahini, oil and garlic to eat as a dip. Cooked and dressed in olive oil, lemon juice and lots of chopped fresh herbs, they make an excellent salad. Dried chickpeas make a good flour eaten as a flat bread called socca in the South of France. In India the flour is known as besan or gram flour. Roasted chickpeas make good snack nibbling, like peanuts, but much healthier as they don't have anything like as much fat. You'll find uncooked but soaked chickpeas are one of the easiest pulses to sprout (see page 93).

FUL MEDAMES

If you have ever visited Egypt you may have enjoyed the national dish of these small, round, brown beans cooked in a spicy sauce, mixed with rice and tomatoes or served in salads. Outside of Egypt we don't see much of them, but they are worth tracking down in Middle Eastern stores.

HARICOT BEANS

These beans are favoured by chefs because they hold their shape well yet have a good creamy texture inside. The name haricot is actually an old French term for a cut of stewing lamb with which these beans were originally cooked – indeed still are. They are used as a vegetable or mixed with an olive oil dressing for salads. Chefs in the culinary stratosphere like to put a spoonful of dainty, creamy haricots at the bottom of their cappuccino soups flavoured with a shaving of truffle. The green haricot is called *flageolet* and is the bean to serve with a tender garlic-spiked roasted leg of lamb, dressed simply with the meat juices poured from the carving plate. French settlers took their favourite haricot bean to the New World, where they became the *navy bean* used in Boston baked beans, a dish left by god-fearing Puritan cooks to simmer overnight in big pots with onions, tomatoes, molasses and ham hocks for eating on the Sabbath. Nowadays, they are spooned on to millions of plates each day, drenched in tomato sauce as baked beans.

KIDNEY BEANS

Choose your favourite bean colour – red, black, cream, speckled pink, stripy brown – the kidney bean has a colourful palette. They are all varieties of the *Phaseolus vulgaris* or common bean, but they differ not only in colour but also slightly in flavour. Natives of South America, they feature prominently in the cuisine of all the Americas. The Mexicans favour r*ed kidney beans*, for chilli con carne, and *pink pintos*, for refried beans: Brazilians like *black* *kidney beans*, for spicy pork or stuffed into peppers. In Italy they like the *speckled borlotti* bean in soups and the *white kidney bean* (or *cannellini*) mixed with tuna in salads. Kidney beans hold up well in cooking, keeping their shape and texture when gently simmered. All kidney bean varieties are interchangeable in recipes and are widely available dried or canned.

LENTILS

Lentils are thought to be the most ancient of the legumes and are grown in many parts of the world. There are many types of lentil, but the ones we tend to see most are *continental brown* or *green lentils*, good all-purpose pulses that can be used in stews, soups and salads. They are good too for sprouting with lots of natural flavour.

Puy lentils are the gourmet's choice, with a slightly nutty flavour, pretty dark petrol-blue colour, and they remain whole even if slightly overcooked. These are best served as a vegetable, lightly dressed with olive oil and perhaps a hint of roasted garlic. It is the only pulse to have its own AOC in France, a guarantee that the lentil is truly a Puy. *Lentilles vertes* are a similar variety grown in Canada but slightly greener in colour than the true Puy.

Castelluccio lentils are high-grade little lentils from Italy with an equally good flavour. Use in the same way as Puys and try them tossed into a dish of the best pasta – truly a noble peasant's delight.

Red split lentils, from the Indian *masoor lentil*, are a great British staple and a useful pulse always to have in the storecupboard. They can be cooked straight from the pack in under 20 minutes for a creamy sauce or soup. I often use 3–4 tbsp of red lentils as a protein-rich thickener instead of flour, especially when I want to make a quick pasta sauce for children.

MARROWFAT PEAS

Marrowfat peas were developed in the 19th century for the Japanese market – their name is taken from the Japanese word *maro*, meaning round – but they found favour with the hungry British worker. Marrowfat peas are now chiefly bought in cans. A pinch of bicarbonate of soda is frequently added to their cooking water, which makes them appear bright green. They are the pea for chip shop mushy peas and you may well acquire a liking for their distinctive flavour if you eat them with fish and chips.

MUNG BEANS

Originally from India and still tremendously important there. These are small, dark-olive green beans are also known as green gram. Cooked they have a slightly pasty flavour and floury texture – indeed, mung beans can be made into a flour. The Chinese use mung beans chiefly as bean sprouts but also in sweet cakes and fermented to make sauces. Mung bean starch is turned into fine thread noodles. Make your own mung bean sprouts at home (see page 93) and taste the difference.

PIGEON PEAS/GUNGA PEAS

These are the same size and shape as ful mesdames but are a lighter, speckled brown in colour. They are popular in the cooking of some West Indian islands and are widely available canned. Debates about the true bean or pea to use for Caribbean rice 'n' peas seems to come down to which island we are talking about. Jamaicans, for instance, like to use red kidney beans, others insist that gunga peas are the must-have bean. Pigeon peas also feature in Indian cuisine, where they are known as red gram.

SOYA BEANS

Hundreds of years ago, vegetarian Chinese Bhuddists realised the potential of this miraculous but rather dull bean. What foresight! Though the dullest beans to eat plain, they are the most useful and versatile in the plant kingdom. They yield oil for cooking and industrial use; when crushed they make milk and curd; and they can be fermented and salted for pastes, sauces and flavourings.

The Japanese embraced soya beans with their usual thorough enthusiasm and there is a host of soya bean products as a result (see separate entries for tofu, miso, soy sauce, etc.). If you cook with soya beans add a lot of spices, herbs or other flavourings to counter their blandness, which is probably caused by their low starch content. If cooking from fresh, be prepared for them taking up to four hours. They do, however, make good sprouts.

SPLIT PEAS

Yellow or green split peas are the dhals of many Indian dishes and are also ground into flour to make poppadoms. In European cooking, these pulses are used to make thick pea soups and pease puddings. They seem to have an affinity with bacon and smoked pork.

SPROUTING BEANS AND SEEDS

See page 93.

COOKING BEANS AND PULSES

Soaking pulses is simply to help shorten the cooking time and lighten the texture. Lentils need only a short time if any, say 1 hour, whereas kidney bean and chickpeas benefit from a long, slow soak overnight. If you forget to soak beans well beforehand, you can try a shorter method: cover with cold water in a saucepan, bring to the boil, cook for 5 minutes then remove and steep in the same water for at least an hour, preferably more.

Once drained, rinse the beans and put a fresh pot of water on to boil. Add the beans to the boiling water, stir and boil for a good 10 minutes. This is very important because some beans contain a mild toxin which is destroyed by boiling. Lower to a gentle simmer and part-cover the pan to reduce the accumulation of steam in the kitchen. If the beans are to be cooked for a long time then check the water level from time to time and top up with boiling water if necessary.

There is debate in the culinary world about whether one should season beans during cooking. Most cooks say no because it is supposed to toughen the skins, but some scientists point to a lack of evidence about this and certainly I have noticed no difference. However, as we are all encouraged to eat less salt it makes sense to leave the water unsalted. I do, however, add a couple of large bay leaves and maybe a few onion slices, a carrot and a couple of unpeeled garlic cloves, plus any woody herb sprigs to hand.

After cooking, drain the beans, rinse in a little water from the tap if wished, and dress in a little olive oil, sea salt and freshly ground black pepper. Sometimes, the beans are so good this simple they're hard to resist spooned from the colander, my particular favourite being puy lentils.

If cooking beans for a salad, dress them with vinaigrette while they are still warm for the best flavour.

Microwaving and pressure cooking dried pulses

Microwaving beans does not save time but it is less messy and there is no danger of forgetting to check the beans or letting them boil dry. You will need a deep non-metallic bowl with a vented cover (or cover with cling film and fold back a small edge to allow steam to escape). To replace the boiling time at the start, pour in boiling water and cook on Full for a good 10 minutes after you have noticed the water boiling. Then reduce to Medium.

Beans and pulses are brilliant cooked in a pressure cooker, it can cut the cooking time by half to two-thirds, depending on the cooker. Check the instruction book for times.

COOKING DRIED PULSES

After soaking when necessary, then boiling for 10 minutes, turn down the heat to a medium simmer and cook the pulses for these times. And don't forget to check the water level, topping up with boiling water.

Kidney beans, including borlotti and pinto	1 hour
Chickpeas, pigeon peas	1 hour
Haricot, navy and flageolet beans	50 minutes
Mung beans	40 minutes
Aduki beans	40 minutes
Butter, lima and fava beans	1 hour
Ful medames	50 minutes
Black-eyed peas	50 minutes
Split peas	20–30 minutes
Lentils continental	25 minutes
Puy and lentilles vertes	15–20 minutes
Soya beans	up to 4 hours

These times are approximate. I have noticed that some older beans approaching or just past their use-by date take longer to cook than beans brought more recently. To check on the 'doneness' or texture, simply fish out a few beans towards the end of the above cooking time and bite into them.

Microwave times are similar. Pressure cooking takes about two-thirds, depending on the pressure cooker.

NUTS AND SEEDS

All nuts and seeds are potential new life. This means they are packed with nutritious elements to give a new seedling the best possible start in life. They grow on trees, on shrubs, and underground on roots. Some are rare and eaten as delicacies, others so plentiful they have become an industrial crop, but most of them contribute greatly to the human diet. They are suppliers of energy and protein plus additional fat-soluble vitamins and certain minerals. In general they all store well, certainly from one season to the next, but if kept for too long they deteriorate and their natural oils turn rancid, which affects the flavour of the flesh. Nuts and seeds are also suppliers of oils from the brash and plentiful to be used in cooking to the fragrant and delicate for salads and flavouring. Because nuts are high in oil most of them are twice as high in calories as other protein foods – sometimes up to 800 calories per 100g.

NUTS

ALMONDS

Another of the treasured foods of ancient Mediterranean lands – along with milk and honey! Almonds are related to peaches and apricots even though the flesh of fresh almonds is not eaten. They account for a large share of the world trade in nuts; the major almond-producing regions are Italy, Spain, France, Turkey and California.

The nuts are mostly used for eating as they are, though they do make a very fine, delicately scented oil much favoured by bakers and confectioners. There are two varieties of almond: sweet and bitter. The latter is pressed for oil used in skin products, and whole bitter almonds are used in certain confectionery products, chiefly with chocolate, but they do need to be roasted first to destroy a mild toxin.

When fresh, during the early autumn, almond shells can be opened with ease and the nut inside tastes moist and almost juicy. The Jordan almond is highly prized but crops poorly except in Spain, so you will pay more. Many Mediterranean countries have their own delicious almond dishes, generally using ground or finely chopped nuts in sweet pastries – think of the Greek and

Turkish baklavas or Italian amaretti biscuits. Even British macaroons need sweet, ground almonds and, of course, what would Christmas cake be without a layer of delicious almond paste, or marzipan – the medieval 'march pane'. Almonds were used in olden times as a substitute for meat and finely ground to make blancmanges (white meals), which have since evolved into horrible packet puddings: the originals had real class.

Almond praline

One of the most useful homemade ingredients to have to hand and worth making in a batch to sprinkle over ice-cream or fold into whipped cream as a gorgeous topping for trifles, Swiss rolls etc.

Line a baking sheet with baking parchment paper and place on a cooling tray. Put 250g (9oz) each of whole unblanched almonds and granulated sugar into a wide heavy-based saucepan plus about 3tbsp of water. Allow the sugar to dissolve slowly over a very low heat without letting it boil, gently swirling the pan to aid the dissolving but taking care not to get sugar crystals round the sides of the pan. (If you do, wash the sides down with a wet pastry brush.) When the sugar has dissolved completely, turn up the heat to medium and let the mixture turn to a golden-brown caramel, swirling the pan carefully again. When the colour is a mid-caramel, tip out on to the baking sheet. Be careful – it might spit a little. Spread the nutty caramel level and allow it to go cold and hard. Break it up into chunks with a rolling pin and feed the chunks into a food processor, whizzing until you have a fine powder that glistens like glinting sand. Or bash with a rolling pin for chunks of almond brittle. Store in an air-tight container.

TIP: BLANCHING ALMONDS

To blanch whole almonds in their skins, simply cover with boiling water,

wait a minute, drain, cool and pop the nuts from their wet skins.

BRAZIL NUTS

A strange nut indeed. In fact Brazils grow inside large hard fruits containing up to 24 individual nuts, each wrapped again in a hard skin – like pass the parcel! Each of these nuts has to be cracked open to extract the kernels we know as Brazil nuts. Supplies come from wild trees in Brazil and Venezuela. (A similar nut called the *sapucaya* or *paradise nut* is considered by nut connoisseurs to be even finer, should you come across it.) Brazils are the highest in calories, nearly 800 per 100g. They are moist and good dipped in caramel, or chopped for baking, but because of their high oil content they do not keep well and should be eaten before they turn rancid.

CANDLE NUTS

These are similar to macadamia nuts and are used in Thai and Malaysian cookery. They are mildly toxic raw and are always roasted before use. They're good for spicy stews and soups where their creamy richness helps to temper chilli flavours.

CASHEW NUTS

The cashew is a curious plant. The nuts hang down from a small pear-shaped fruit. When ripe they are harvested, roasted and shelled by hand, which probably accounts for their high price. Cashews, originally from the New World, are grown commercially in East Africa and India. They are popular as cocktail snacks and also feature in Chinese and Indian recipes, where their creamy, smooth, slightly sweet texture blends well with spices and soy sauce flavourings. They are particularly good mixed with a spicy Chinese-style dressing then open roasted for party food.

CHESTNUTS

Christmas, open fires, chestnut-roasting pans – and burnt fingers as we try to peel the charred skins before the nutty insides go cold and become unpeelable. That probably sums up chestnuts for most of us, but in fact they are used in a more imaginative way in other parts of Europe, chiefly Italy.

The edible chestnut is from the sweet chestnut tree, also called the Spanish chestnut, introduced to the UK by the Romans, no doubt to remind them of home comforts. They are completely different from the horse chestnut, that great supplier of inedible conkers. Chestnuts take a lot of peeling: you need to blanch them in boiling water or bake them until the skins pop open but before the insides explode – quite a business. Better to buy them ready peeled and vacuum-packed or canned from France. Unusually for nuts, chestnuts contain almost no fat and have instead a higher amount of starch. British sweet chestnuts do not make good eating as they are not bred 'for the pot', which is just as well because the grey squirrels get to them first, unlike chestnuts from Spain and Italy, which are.

The nuts can be ground into flour (*farina di castagne*), which is used to make cakes, porridge and fritters. The nuts are also fed to pigs in Italy, where chestnut-reared pork fetches good prices. In France they steep chestnuts in rich syrup for *marrons glacés*. For stuffings you could use chestnut purée, but check it is unsweetened. The Chinese use chestnuts too: in fact in Chinese food stores you can buy ready peeled dried chestnuts that just need soaking in warm water to rehydrate. They are almost as good as fresh. In Italy, they serve a delicious Christmas dessert called *monte bianco* (white mountain), a sweetened, rum-flavoured chestnut purée extruded into squiggles in a mound on a plate and covered in whipped cream. When I made this one Christmas for an ex-pat Italian, she promptly burst into homesick tears.

GROUNDNUTS/PEANUTS

Groundnuts, also known as monkey nuts, are technically legumes but they are treated and eaten as nuts. They are one of the world's most important crops, supplying us with a top-grade cooking oil that can be taken to high temperatures without burning, so it is popular with oriental cooks who stir-fry over a fierce heat. The French call this oil *arachide*, should you come across the name on a bottle; otherwise it is sold as peanut or groundnut oil. It is one of the oils used in making of margarines.

Groundnuts, as their name suggests, are a root crop because the nuts grow below the soil. They are produced in many countries; most, like India and China, produce them solely for local use and harvest them by hand. Nigeria and the United States are great exporters of groundnuts, sending the nuts to oil extraction plants in Marseilles, Liverpool and Hamburg. After pressing, the residual oil is made into valuable cattle-feed cakes.

The nuts are also a popular human food worldwide. For snacking, they are sold in their pods (shrivelled with a netting effect), or podded but still in skins, or skinned. Then they can be roasted plain, or roasted and salted. Varieties differ in size, too. Peanut butter is made by removing the skin and grinding the nuts into a paste, with or without salt. Peanuts also form the basis of satay sauces for Indonesian and other Far Eastern cuisines.

NUT ALLERGY

The increasing number of young people who are developing allergies to nuts, especially to peanuts, is of growing concern to the medical profession. The reaction of these allergy sufferers can be very serious, even life-threatening. Please remember, if you are feeding young guests any dish you suspect contains peanuts or peanut products, including groundnut oil, to ask if they are allergic. The problem is taken so seriously that many food processing companies isolate their nut products from their non-nut products during processing to protect against cross-contamination. If you suspect nut allergies in your family, check labels on all products, sweet and savoury, for peanut or groundnut ingredients.

HAZELNUTS AND COBNUTS

St Filbert's Day is in mid-August and the time when fresh cobnuts, also known as filberts, can be gathered. Fresh, they are wrapped in a leathery skin that can be peeled off and then the shell easily cracked open. Like wet walnuts, they need to be eaten quickly.

Hazelnuts are closely related to cobnuts and have been with us for thousands of years, judging from the nuts found in Mesolithic tombs and ancient sites. Turkey is one of the world's main producers of this delicious and versatile nut, but Spain, Italy, France and even Armenia are other suppliers. Fresh hazelnuts are sold with their skins. If you need to remove the skins, place the nuts in a moderately hot oven for about 10 minutes, allow them to cool, then rub handfuls between your hands so the skins come off. However, some supermarkets sell ready-roasted hazelnuts and even chopped roasted hazelnuts, which are a good storecupboard ingredient. I like to add a good handful to family pilaffs and stuffing mixtures or sprinkle them over gratins – they add a hint of a crunch and lots of flavour.

Hazelnut oil is another speciality oil useful for salads and trickling for aromatic flavouring. Use as walnut oil (see page 205).

MACADAMIA NUTS

Macadamia nuts are also known as Queensland nuts so, obviously, they are an Australian contribution to nut cookery, though they do also grow in Hawaii, California, Central and South America. With the growing popularity of Pacific Rim cookery, one could be forgiven for thinking we were in the throes of macadamia mania. But they're hard nuts to crack, even commercially, which accounts for their high price. The rounded, creamy-white nuts have a rich buttery taste, and they make good nutty toffee.

PECANS

Pecans belong to the same extended family as walnuts but a different line. Pecans are longer and thinner in shape and have a sweeter, less bitter flavour than walnuts. They are rapidly becoming very popular and are associated with American-style baking and desserts – cookies, muffins and ice cream, for example. Whole, they have a beautiful glossy red shell that is easily cracked. Pecans are certainly easier to tackle than the crumpled walnut.

PECAN PIE

The most famous use for pecans. Don't overcook a pecan pie – the filling needs to be moist and slightly chewy.

Preheat the oven to 200°C/gas mark 6. Line a 20cm (8in) flan tin with shortcrust pastry, bringing the dough well up the sides. Prick lightly, line with foil and fill with baking beans, Bake the flan case for 15 minutes. Remove the foil and beans and reduce the oven temperature to 180°C/gas mark 4. Roughly chop 200g (7oz) of shelled pecans and scatter them over the flan case. In a food processor if possible, beat together 3 large eggs with 250g (9oz) of dark soft brown sugar, 1tsp of vanilla extract, a pinch of salt, 4tbsp of melted butter and 4tbsp of golden syrup. Pour this mixture over the pecans and return to the oven for about 30 minutes or until the mixture is risen and mid-brown, Remove and cool in the tin.

PINE NUTS

The essential nut for pesto. These are the seeds of the stone pine, a hardy Mediterranean tree related to desert pines, though pine nuts are softer and so edible. (In fact, the stone pine is not the only variety with edible seeds: many parts of the world, from the Himalayas to Central and South America, have pines with fruitful cones.) The pine cones in which the seeds are contained open in the heat of the sun to yield their rich pickings, but each tiny nut is contained in a hard casing which has to be crushed to extract it, so not cheap. Remember that the next time you scatter them over a dish with abandon! They are also used in stuffings and fillings in many Italian, Spanish and Arabian dishes. Pine nuts have a high oil content and can turn rancid quickly, so buy in small quantities and eat well within their use-by date.

PISTACHIOS

Pistachios are natives of Mediterranean countries but are now also grown commercially in the southern states of the USA. Pistachio nuts form in long strings on small deciduous trees. Like almonds, they are contained in an outer coat which is peeled to reveal the hard kernel, which is a beautiful green so distinctive it has given its name to a fashion colour.

Pistachios are most often eaten as a snack food or in confectionery. As a snack, they are salted and roasted to be sucked then detached from the shell halves, with or without the use of fingers. There is quite a skill to popping a pistachio into your mouth, extracting the nut and spitting out the shell all without hands.

Unroasted, green pistachios are highly prized by bakers and confectioners. Whole they are used in nougat, layered into terrines and are the 'green bits' you see in Mortadella sausage slices. Finely chopped or ground they are turned into tempting Turkish-style pastries. When mixed to a paste they are essential for many haute cuisine ice creams, petits fours and biscuits.

WALNUTS

My elderly and eccentric aunt had a majestic tree growing in the garden of her newly built sheltered housing. It was all that remained of an old kitchen garden. She complained bitterly at the end of her first summer about small green balls that fell from the tree and covered her tiny lawn. Fortunately we recognised them as *fresh green walnuts* and talked her out of having the tree chopped down. *Wet walnuts* are highly prized in France and countries where walnuts grow in abundance but they do not keep well and need to be dried. Turkey, China, Spain and the United States are producers and exporters.

Walnuts have a lovely sweet, slightly bitter flavour but they are not great keepers so don't buy them in large quantities unless you use them frequently. They should be eaten well within the use-by date on the pack, otherwise they turn rancid. They are also sold chopped or in halves, which are much more expensive – try to extract a walnut half intact and you'll understand why. If you need ground walnuts in a recipe, then grind your own in a food processor.

Walnuts complement so many foods, sweet and savoury. The Iranians and Turks use them in rich meat stews, often combined with pomegranate juice. They are classic with oranges, great mixed into creamy cheese, good Chinese-style with chicken and nice in American breakfast muffins.

Walnut oil is one of the speciality oils sold in small bottles for a high price. Mix with a little of each of sunflower and olive oil and use in salad dressings, or try trickling neat over hot new potatoes or brushing over grilled meats and fish. Walnut oil can go rancid quickly once opened, so store it in the fridge.

SEEDS

LINSEEDS

These tiny, shiny brown seeds have become noteworthy since they were recognised as a good source of linoleic acid, one of the nutrients valuable for women of a 'certain' age. So, health stores promote them for scattering liberally over food. You'll find they are one of the seeds used in the enriched bread branded Burgens originating from Australia. They do taste good – for everyone, not just ladies.

POPPY SEEDS, FENUGREEK, ALFALFA

All these seeds make lovely light, feathery seed sprouts (see page 93) to add a gentle spiciness to salads and stir-fries. Poppy seeds are available either white and black and are good used in baking or just sprinkled over salads. Fenugreek seeds are a little too hard to use 'neat' in salads.

PUMPKIN SEEDS

Dark grey and cream-coloured stripy seeds from the inside of this popular squash. They are dried and roasted, sometimes also salted, and are good for nibbling as snacks or scattering over salads. They can also be roasted and crushed for an aromatic seed oil to be used in little trickles in the same way as sesame oil.

SESAME SEEDS

Where would we be without sesame seeds for burger buns, Greek breads, grissini, candy bars and a sprinkle over garnish? The Arabs love sesames, as do the Chinese, Japanese, Africans and, of course, all burger bar kings. The main producers are India, China, Nigeria and the Sudan.

Sesames give foods good looks, flavour and, when crushed into an oil, aroma. The sesame (also known as *sim-sim* and **benniseed** in Africa) grows on a plant that looks a little like a tall basil bush. It forms small white trumpet-shaped flowers which drop off to reveal seed pods that, when cut and dried in the sun, burst open. They are then turned upside-down and shaken so all the tiny seeds fall out.

Rich in oil, sesame seeds are roasted and pressed to extract oil. Toasted sesame oil is a very potent flavouring. Used in moderate amounts, it is essential to a great deal of Oriental cooking. Sesames are a rich source of calcium – ladies of a certain age take note. In the Middle East and Greece, sesames are ground into a delicious paste called tahini, which makes the most wonderful dressing for dipping and for trickling over roasted vegetables. Buy light-coloured tahini for the best quality. You must stir tahini paste thoroughly in the jar before use as the oil tends to settle on the top, making it a little thick and stiff.

TAHINI DRESSING

Pour half a 400g (14oz) jar of stirred tahini into a food processor and add two crushed fat garlic cloves. Whiz the paste in the machine and, with the blades still running, slowly pour in about a cupful of cold water through the spout. Scrape down the sides then pour in about 6tbsp of good olive oil, plus the juice of half a lemon and lots of sea salt and freshly ground black pepper. Whiz thoroughly again until you have a creamy, smooth beige cream. Taste and adjust the seasoning. Sometimes I add 1tsp of sweet paprika, or pinches of chilli powder. Store in a clean screw-topped jar in the fridge until ready to use.

SUNFLOWER SEEDS

The sunflower plant is a member of the daisy family – no surprises there, given its shape. If you drive through southern Europe in mid-summer you will see field upon field of bright yellow sunflower heads that turn to follow the sun during the day. These are the plants that give us our main cooking oil, are a good fodder crop for cattle. They also yield little seeds that can be roasted and scattered over salads or used in rich seedy breads and savoury crackers. They have a mildly creamy flavour and a pleasant texture. Don't buy too many at one time as they can turn rancid if left too long.

RICE, GRAINS AND BREAD

The main food group of the world. Practically every human being consumes a staple grain of some form or another – wheat for bread, pasta or noodles, rice, millet, corn, rye, barley, and many grains that survive poor soil, little water or extremes of climate in isolated parts of the world. All grains are good sources of carbohydrates, nutrients that give us energy not only for basal metabolism like breathing and blinking but also energy for working and playing. Half our daily calories should come from these foods for a healthy, well-balanced diet.

RICE

Oryza *sativa* – the world's most important staple food yet in general we know so little about it. It nourishes over half of the total population each day, although in world trade it accounts for only about 3% of the whole crop grown. Most rice is eaten within 20 miles of where it is grown: what reaches our shores and stores is a minuscule fraction. Of the tens of thousands of rice varieties grown (estimates range from 7,000 to 80,000) you can categorise the grains into three main groups, depending on the starch levels and types:

Long-grain rice for savoury dishes: curries, chillis, pilaffs
Short-grain rices for puddings, desserts, sushi, chopstick eating
Medium-grain rices for risottos, paellas, stuffings

In addition to these categories, rices can be classified by textures: dry and fluffy; sticky and glutinous; and starchy and creamy. It is important to remember these groups when deciding which rice to use in cooking. Those unused to cooking rice who are disappointed with the result may simply have used the wrong type of grain. Price is a good guide to quality.

Easy-cook rice
There is one other consideration that affects the texture, a process that can be applied to any rice. The unrefined grain (known as cargo rice or paddy, the true name for the whole grain) is subjected to a few seconds of very high temperature steam. This hardens the outside of the unhusked grain (and gives

it a characteristic yellowish colour). Grain treated in this way is described as being 'non-stick', but the process also removes some of the natural flavour of the grain and makes the texture chewy. It is popular in certain communities but not among Asian or gourmet rice eaters. It is ideal for rice recipes that require long cooking without the risk of breaking down, as in West Indian cooking. Brand names include Uncle Ben's, but any rice described as parboiled or easy-cook will have been subjected to this treatment. These rices also take longer to cook.

AMERICAN LONG-GRAIN RICES

These are excellent quality rices, sometimes described as having a popcorn flavour. Normal long-grain rices (i.e. not parboiled) do have a good natural flavour of their own, particularly rices grown around the Mississippi and Arkansas. Their grains are longer than those of Thai rices and need up to 12 minutes cooking time.

BASMATI RICE

Deemed to be the 'prince of rices', basmati rice can be classed as the connoisseur's grain. The reason is simple – it is slim, elegant, cooks beautifully and marries well with a host of dishes from the simple to the sophisticated, savoury and spicy to sweet and creamy. 'Basmati' translates to 'fragrance' in Hindi, and that should be the first quality you notice about a good-quality grain. The fragrance is legendary, and justly so.

There is a saying that 'a house that smells of rice cooking is a home of warm welcome'. When you put a pot of top-quality basmati on to cook the first indication of its special nature is the wonderful aroma that wafts through your kitchen and indeed your house.

Basmati is highly prized in Indian and Middle Eastern households because it complements the highly sophisticated aromatic dishes typical of these cuisines. The natural fragrance of basmati grows within the grain and other factors affecting its quality are climate, soil and farming methods (as with grapes for fine wine). The best comes from the Haryana state in the Punjab where it is literally watered by pure snow-fed rivers of the Himalayas. It's a delicate grain and the best can crop only once a year. Attempts to grow it elsewhere in the world do not produce the same quality – you may have a nice rice, but not a good basmati. For the best quality, look for a good brand name such as Tilda – supermarket brands are packed to a price not a quality. The price difference is negligible when you consider that a 500g package serves 8–10 people.

Cooking basmati rice

Basmati grains expand to three times their length in the course of cooking and develop a characteristic corkscrew texture. Many cooking methods exist, depending on the cuisine of the country: in Iran, for instance, where basmati is highly esteemed, the grains are first parboiled then drained and steamed in a tightly covered pan until the base forms a golden crust called a *tadeeg*. Indian cooks often rinse and soak basmati grains to remove any residual starch and lighten the grain. It's not vital but it does make for a more tender grain. Forget tipping rice into a sieve and running under a cold tap. The best way is to tip grains into a big bowl and cover with lots of cold water. Swish with your hand, allow 30 seconds or so for the grains to settle, then tip out the water when the grains sink to the bottom. Repeat 2–3 times more. The final time, let the grains soak in the last change of water. Drain and cook as you choose.

THE EASY BOILING METHOD

Bring about 2–3 litres of water to the boil in a large pan. Add 2tsp of salt, then tip in about 250g of basmati rice (soaked or unsoaked). Return to the boil, stirring once or twice, then cook on a medium boil for 10–12 minutes. To tell if the grains are cooked, lift out a few with a fork and press one or two between your finger and thumb. If they break quickly and feel tender they are done. Drain the rice immediately in a colander and stand this over the pan in which the rice was cooked for 5 minutes (rice needs standing time to firm up and absorb moisture). Stir with a fork, add a good knob of butter if liked and some chopped fresh parsley, dill or coriander or a nice mixture of all three herbs.

COOKING IN A MICROWAVE

Measure the rice in a jug or cup. Transfer to a microwaveable container and stir in one and half times the amount of cold water to rice plus some salt (basmati, being delicate does not need as much water or cooking time as other long-grain rices). Cover and cook on high for 4 minutes. Uncover, stir once recover and cook on defrost for 8 minutes. Uncover, stir with a fork and serve as above.

COOKING IN A COVERED PAN

Measure one and a half times water to rice and place in a saucepan. Bring to the boil, cover and lower the heat. Simmer for 10 minutes, then remove from the heat without lifting the lid. Leave, still covered, for 5 minutes then stir and serve. Note: rice cooked like this has tiny steam holes on the surface.

SAFFRON RICE

Allow a pinch of saffron strands to steep in 4tbsp of boiling water in a cup while the rice cooks by the easy-boiling method. Drain the rice, leave it to stand for 5 minutes, then trickle over the saffron water and strands. Gently fork through so the golden grains mingle lightly with the dazzling white for a speckled effect.

BROWN OR WHOLEGRAIN RICES

These are any rices that have their outer bran layer still intact. This generally applies to American rices but basmati can also be brown. Brown rices have a nice nutty flavour but do take a long time to cook. Brown pudding rices seem to take even longer to cook and they never really become creamy, merely soggy and chewy. Brown rice is naturally a good source of fibre, brown basmati the best of all. Easy-cook brown rices are chewy with little flavour. I am not a huge fan.

CARMARGUE RED RICE

A fairly recent introduction to the rice world. The story goes that a French rice farmer noticed some of his cultivated rice had reverted to a red colour (red being a natural wild rice colour). So he hybridised them to produce an unusual nutty flavour and texture – *et voilà*! A new red rice was born, one that is relatively easily available as a speciality rice. It cooks to a starchy consistency with a flavour reminiscent of buckwheat. It's good with game meats and rich stews.

ENRICHED RICES

Vitamins and minerals are added to white grains by law in the United States – you may see the description used on packets in Europe. It was a requirement brought in after the First World War to nourish poorer families, but given today's very rich diets their relevance is arguable.

GLUTINOUS RICE

Short-grain, sticky rices used for sushi, oriental puddings and for wrapping in lotus wraps, bamboo leaves or for pounding into a paste to make New Year mochi cakes. It is soaked overnight, then steamed rather than boiled.

JAPANESE RICES

Japanese rices are small, medium-grained and have a pearly lustre. Those we buy in the west are often grown in California from Japanese varieties – Nishiki is one brand name. When cooked the rice is shiny, slightly sticky and has a nutty aroma. Check the packet instructions as these rices usually need a light rinsing before cooking in not much water.

PUDDING RICES

Pudding rices are short-grain rices, at one time imported from Carolina, USA, but now likely to come from the Po Valley in northern Italy. Pudding rices are high in starch but not much else. Other varieties such as Thai, basmati and risotto rices also make nice puddings.

RISOTTO RICES

Every Italian eats pasta or rice or both each day and the rice industry in Italy is based on producing excellent quality rices of medium- to short-grain length and starchy to creamy texture. Italian rice is grown around the Po Valley. Risotto rices are similar in nature to Spanish rices but varieties abound and it is all a very serious business – some rices are produced and milled by centuries-old traditional methods, others use the most modern technology.

Risotto rices are graded into superfino and semi-fino qualities – a 'DOC' of rices, if you like. There are three risotto rices that chefs like to use: *arborio* is a superfino quality and is the most widely available; *carnaroli* is also superfino but is not as abundant. Both of these rices are plump and retain a good bite to the grain when cooked even though risotto dishes are smooth and creamy as a result of the naturally higher starch levels in this variety. Carnaroli rice may have a narrow edge in that the grains have a slightly firmer bite, but it's marginal: it does, however, hold up better in a restaurant kitchen and can be parcooked ahead then finished for the last five minutes' cooking time with extra stock and a good dollop of mascarpone cheese or butter. However, the gourmet's choice is more often the third choice, the *Vialone Nano* grain, which although classified as semi-fino is smaller in grain size and, being slightly wholegrain, has a nuttier bite to it.

Risottos rices also make good desserts or fritters. This is where a dish of risotto is left to go cold, then divided and shaped into little cakes to be egged, crumbed and fried until crisp. The Italians call these *suppli.* I once enjoyed *suppli al telefono* balls stuffed with nuggets of mozzarella cheese – which go stringy like telephone wires when you bite into them.

REAL RISOTTO

This takes up to 20 minutes to make in the time-honoured way. Do use a proper risotto grain, otherwise you will not get the correct creamy texture. Stirring in the stock in stages encourages this creaminess. If you oven-bake a risotto it will become stodgy You can add flavourings to this risotto such as seafood, shredded chicken, sautéed mushrooms of any type, blanched baby vegetables, or asparagus tips with grated lemon rind.

Have about 2 litres (3½pt) of a good stock on gentle simmer For a quick and easy risotto you could use a good stock powder stock such as Marigold, but homemade stock, please, for special meals!

In a large saucepan, gently fry a large finely chopped onion in 4tbsp of olive oil with two crushed fat garlic cloves. When softened, after about 10 minutes, stir in 250g (9oz) of risotto rice and cook for about 5 minutes until lightly toasted. Pour in a glass of dry white wine (or red wine for a red risotto). Stir this until it reduces right down.

Pour in and stir a third of the hot stock, bring to the boil then lower the heat and continue stirring until it is all absorbed. (If you haven't the inclination for constant stirring, then frequently will do, but you need to get the starch out of the grain and into the dish.)

Add another good slurp or ladleful of stock and again stir until reduced right down. Carry on adding stock in ladlefuls until it is all gone. By now the rice should be plump and just tender with a good *al dente* bite to the grain. If you need any extra liquid add boiling water. The whole process should take about 18–20 minutes.

Finish the dish by stirring in a generous knob of butter or dollop of mascarpone cheese and some freshly grated Parmesan cheese. Season to taste and serve instantly. A risotto waits for no man.

SPANISH RICES

It was the Moors and the Venetians who developed the now thriving Spanish rice industry. The idea then was brought to northern Italy via the South of France, establishing the Carmargue rice industry along the way. Now there are many excellent Spanish rices that are medium-grain in length and starchy in texture. Look for *Calasparra* or *Bomba* varieties for true paella rice or try cooking baked quails on a bed of saffron Spanish rice in the oven and notice what a difference a real rice can make! Once the stock has been added, Spanish rices are shaken in the pan during cooking rather than stirred and then left to slowly absorb the liquid without additional stirring.

TEXAS RICES

The American rice industry is highly mechanised, whereas Asian rices are still harvested by hand. The USA exports a lot of rice and has an open mind to modern marketing. Texas grows aromatic Asian rices, though they do lack the delicate fragrance of the originals.

THAI RICES

These are long-grain rices that are lightly sticky or glutinous – not an accurate description really, as rice is gluten free, but its texture can have the stickiness of gluten. (Just because a rice is called sticky, it doesn't mean it's soggy: there will still be a good bite to the grain.)

There are many grades of Thai rice: those exported are generally of good quality. They are described as fragrant because, like basmati, they have a natural fragrance that grows in the grain. One of the nicest is *Thai jasmine*, a tender, slender grain that needs only a short cooking time, and if cooked by a measured amount of water, just 1¼ times water to rice in under 10 minutes.

WILD RICE

This is not a true rice as we know it because it's a different species from the *Oryza* family but the grains look oh so similar. It's a North American lakeside grass known originally as 'Indian Rice' because it was a favourite grain of Native Americans introduced to European settlers in the early days of colonisation. Like turkeys, cranberries and other New World delicacies, it soon became incorporated into American standard fare, especially around Thanksgiving Day, and now, it is said, around 75% of all wild rice is eaten on just that one day in America.

True wild rice is still grown wild, and often organically around lakes in Canada and north-west America, where the native Americans still have the right by treaty to harvest the grain as their ancestors did. The wild rice plant is tall, about 4 metres high, and the panicles (grain-bearing branches) dip gently towards the water. The grains are knocked into canoes by hand and what falls into the lake is next year's harvest. Genuine wild rice is long and sleek with dark, shiny brown grains. It is best sold packed in boxes, inner wrapped so the brittle grains don't break. Don't buy it loose – it costs too much to waste. Best in boxes with an inner pouch vaccuum-sealed.

Most European chefs don't understand that many of the grains should burst open to release their natural aroma. Wild rice smells heavenly during cooking, like sunshine on a green meadow or a newly mown lawn. Do cook genuine wild rice fully – it can take up to 50 minutes boiling, but you can reduce this time by soaking the grains in cold water overnight, then boiling them gently for just 20 minutes.

Cultivated wild rice is grown in California. The grains are smaller and lighter in colour and often they are passed through metal rollers to scratch the surface of the grain so it cooks quicker, a process called scarification. It is sometimes sold mixed with easy-cook basmati or long-grain rice. The nicer blend is with basmati, in which East meets West.

OTHER GRAINS

Apart from rice, all grains belong to the same cereal family of grasses except for the two known as pseudo-cereals, namely buckwheat (see pages 217–8) and the Inca grain quinoa (see page 223), both of which are members of the Goosefoot family, as is, strangely, beetroot.

ARROWROOT

A thickening starch little used now except by top pastry chefs because it dissolves very easily and makes a crystal clear gel, ideal for spooning on to summer fruit flans. You can buy arrowroot fairly readily in small drums from the baking sections of supermarkets. Basically you dissolve it in a sweetened liquid, such as apple juice, then heat and stir it until it is clear. Use it quickly before it sets. In days of yore it was used as an invalid food because it is easily digested.

BARLEY

One of the oldest grains cultivated by man (historians say nearly 10,000 years ago) and still in use in many marginal parts of the world. We associate barley with traditional cooking although it is sometimes used in restaurants and mentioned in cookery books to make interesting variations of pilaff and risottos. Otherwise we use it in soups, as a stuffing, as a flour in baking and in the semi-medicinal barley water, recommended by Hippocrates, the father of medicine, as a miraculous cure-all. Like rye, barley has a low gluten content so it's tricky for risen bread, and the grains do take some cooking – upwards of a couple of hours of simmering. It gives a slight jellied texture to soups, such as Scotch broth.

Barley grains are sold whole as *pot barley*, with the germ and bran intact, or polished as *pearl barley*, with most bran and germ removed. *Barley flakes* add interest to breakfast cereal mixes. But possibly the greatest use for barley is as *sprouted malt grains*, used in Scottish whisky distilling, in beer brewing, in baking and for malt extract. Yeast produced as a by-product of malting was used in the making of wheat bread until our baking techniques were revolutionised in the 19th century by the introduction of pressed yeast.

BUCKWHEAT

You will mainly find buckwheat in health food stores as it is much in vogue with macrobiotic cooks and buckwheat recipes have become popular with wholefood advocates. There are two forms of buckwheat: the first is the *wholegrain roasted buckwheat*, which has a distinctive flavour, and the second is *buckwheat flour* known as *blé* or *sarrasin*. Roasted buckwheat is one of the kasha dishes of Russian cooking – the demise of the Cold War opened our eyes to a previously little-known cuisine. The Japanese make a buckwheat noodle called *soba*; the French Bretons and Normans use buckwheat flour in their wafer-thin galettes; and the Russians use buckwheat flour to make yeast-risen blinis, the true accompaniment to caviar. In America buckwheat pancakes, trickled with maple syrup and topped with crispy sweetcure bacon, are a must for breakfast. I find when I use buckwheat flour (greyish, with tiny black speckles, best mixed with wheat flour), it has quite a 'short' crumbly texture.

BULGUR WHEAT

To produce bulgur wheat, also known as cracked wheat or pourgouri, wheat grains are parboiled, spread out to dry (traditionally in the sun), then passed between stone rollers until they crack into a fine meal. Because it is partially cooked bulgur is very easy to prepare requiring, little to no extra cooking. It is popular in the Middle East where it is the grain used for tabbouleh, or soaked and mixed with minced raw lamb for kibbeh. Packets of bulgur will tell you to soak the grain in a measured amount of boiling water until absorbed and cool.

TABBOULEH
To make a tabbouleh, simply add lots of freshly chopped parsley, mint and salad onions plus garlic, lemon juice and olive oil to cooked bulgur as it cools. Finally, stir in some chopped fresh tomato, season well and serve chilled.

CORN/MAIZE

The only original grain of the New World, although we still refer to grains collectively as 'corn' for some reason. In its natural state, as fresh corn cobs, corn is gluten free, but check packs for cornmeal flour to be sure. We are all familiar with yellow corn but may not be aware that there are many other colours – blue, purple, red to mention some. Snazzy delis or chic food halls sometimes sell different Mexican corns as either flours or tortilla chips.

There are three maize products: for thickening, cornflour; for popping, popcorn; and as a vegetable, sweetcorn and, increasingly as regional Italian and American food become popular, as cornmeal or polenta.

Cornmeal, introduced into Africa as part of the two-way slave trade, is now a traditional grain there, where it is pounded with a pestle and mortar and called mealie-mealie or oogali. In the southern states of America, white and yellow cornmeal is cooked like a porridge, long and slow in water, and eaten as hominy (corn with the hull and germ removed). Grits is broken hominy grains served with eggs and bacon, or shaped into hush puppies and deep-fried as fritters to be served with catfish or chicken. Ground maize cannot be made into traditional bread as it is too crumbly: instead American cornbread is an oven-baked batter of cornmeal and eggs poured into corncob-shaped baking tins – very moreish – and a substitute for higher protein gluten. Flavoured with a little chilli and topped with melted butter – baby, are they good!

Masa harina, sold as blue or yellow, is finely ground corn used to make tortillas and as a thickener for sauces. It is also mixed into a dough, wrapped in corn husks – with or without additional sweet or savoury ingredients – and called tamales.

Cornflour is a light, gluten-free starch that makes light, glossy sauces with less risk of lumps, ideal for light tempura batters and Chinese stir-fry sauces. This is also the flour to use in sauces or stews you intend to freeze, as corn starch (retrogrades) does not break down. For baking, a 1:3 mixture of cornflour and wheat flour makes lighter, crisper biscuits.

Fresh corn sold 'on the cob', has a limited shelf life and ideally should be picked, sold (still in the pale green parchment-like husks to keep the cobs fresh and juicy) and eaten the same day. I do wish our supermarkets would stop stripping off the husks and thereby hastening their staling. To cut fresh corn from the cob, strip off the leaves and silks then, holding the cob upright on a board, cut down each side with a sharp knife. The kernels will fall off instantly. When very fresh these are delicious eaten raw, like juicy peanuts.

Cook fresh sweetcorn, on or off the cob, for just a few minutes. Overcooking makes the kernels toughen.

Now to the designer grain – *polenta*, Italian cornmeal. To be fair, it's 'designer' only in cosmopolitan cities: it still retains its peasant purity in northern Italy. Polenta is served wet and steaming, like a savoury semolina, flavoured with butter and Parmesan cheese to accompany rich stews, roasts, vegetables etc. There are many grades of polenta, and even a new season's polenta favoured by the discerning. You can now buy instant polenta meal for serving wet (ready in 5 minutes), and set polenta in rolls or rectangles ready to be sliced and grilled: the texture of both is acceptable, but the flavour is a bit musty and disappointing.

MAKING POLENTA

Whatever the grade, all polenta is cooked in the same time-honoured way. Bring a large pot of salted water to the boil, then let the polenta meal fall from one hand in a steady stream while all the time stirring enthusiastically and in one direction with a long-handled spoon in your other hand. Keep stirring until the mixture thickens and starts to 'plop', sending out spurts of the hot mixture – stand well back! Eventually the mixture will be thick enough for serving as porridge. It can be flavoured with blue or creamy cheese, pesto, sun-dried tomatoes or anything else delicious and Italian.

Leftover polenta is spooned flat on to a tray to solidify, when it can be cut into wedges then grilled and served drizzled with olive oil or butter. A dual-purpose food.

COUSCOUS

This grain, unlike bulgur, is not parboiled, but you can buy pre-cooked grains that need just soaking and a light steaming. This may sound confusing! The difference is that couscous in its natural state is a semolina of wheat, in other words the grains have been ground to a certain coarse stage. It undergoes a further process of being dampened, then dried and coated lightly in flour. Traditionally it is then soaked in cold water, spread out to swell on trays, rubbed frequently by hand to keep the grains separate (during which time more cold water is sprinkled over), then finally when the soaked grains have plumped up it is steamed for further plumping. This gives you a very light grain with a delicious natural flavour. Pre-cooked couscous has been soaked and partially steamed so it is easier to use, but has less of the finesse of freshly cooked couscous. The steaming is generally in a couscousière steamer over a pot of gently bubbling aromatic stew. Harissa is often stirred in to flavour it.

GLUTEN-FREE FLOUR

If you have an allergy to gluten, wheat-based products are denied you, which is grossly unfair. In one fell swoop, you cannot enjoy 'normal' bread, pizzas, cookies and cakes or sauces thickened with wheat flour. I have occasionally been asked to demonstrate at health food exhibitions using a gluten-free flour – a mixture of soya flour, oats, cornmeal and rye. It makes a passable bread and pizza base, a nice cake mixture and good short biscuits. It is certainly not cheap, and you have to use it in conjunction with a gluten-free baking powder, but it does enable those sensitive to gluten, particularly children, to enjoy many foods their peers eat.

GRAIN WHEATS

Wheats are broadly divided into bread wheats and durum wheats, the latter having a higher level of the elastic gluten protein, which is useful in dried pasta making. However, by a variety of processes, wheat can also be eaten in granular forms.

MILLET

Millet, also known as sorghum, is still one of the world's most important staple crops in countries where rainfall is uncertain. In the West we may associate millet with budgie food and cheap cattle feed, but it is used like rice in the regional cuisines of China, Japan and India as well as in many African countries such as Nigeria, where its name translates to 'hungry rice', and Ethiopia, where it is known as teff and made into bread. You can buy *millet grains* or *flakes* in health food shops.

One of the chief characteristics of millet is that it is very absorbent and soaks up a great deal of liquid. Although the flavour may be bland to our sophisticated palettes, millet does make a nice light pilaff mixed with vegetables, stock and maybe a hint of meat. In Southern India they make little pancakes with a millet gram called *dhosas* (which you might see occasionally in restaurants). Millet makes a passable sweet milk pudding, should curiosity overtake you. Sorghum is used to make a syrup and in beer making, but little of it comes on to the open world market other than as cattle feed.

OATS

Wheat is a precious grain and grows only in temperate climates where summers are dry (or dryish) and the water supply reasonably consistent. So in northern areas or uplands with short, wet summers other crops are traditional because their supply was assured – at least the people wouldn't go hungry. Oats were an established crop in parts of Highland Scotland, rain-swept Ireland and parts of northern Europe when many religious and fertility rites evolved to celebrate the harvest – and from whence we get the expression 'sowing wild oats' presumably.

Traditional uses for oats still remain and they're popular in breakfast foods and baking. It is a highly nutritious grain, full of carbohydrate, B-group vitamins and minerals such as iron and potassium. Oatmeal also enjoyed something of a revival during the health-conscious 1980s when the medical profession informed us that oats were one of the best sources of insoluble fibre: they dissolve easily in our guts and pass directly into the bloodstream to lower cholesterol and keep our veins running clear. Now we have a proliferation of oat-based or oatbran enriched breakfast cereals.

Oats are milled into various forms. The traditional use of oats is as *oatmeal* (groats), available in a number of grades which you can still buy in health food stores. The coarsest is pinhead, followed by rough, medium and fine. These are used in baking for oatcakes and bannocks and to thicken stews, soups, sauces and puddings. Fine oatmeal makes good pancakes or a coating for frying. Medium grains make the best porridge, traditionally cooked overnight in a 'porringer' on the side of an old range cooker, but it can be cooked normally on the stove for around 30 minutes, or for 5 minutes in the microwave (possibly the main reason for porridge's recent return to popularity). Tins of Irish Oatmeal sold as 'steel cut' are considered to be finer quality because the grains are cut without heating or crushing.

Oatflakes, sometimes called rolled oats or porridge/porrage oats, have been partially steamed, kiln dried and rolled. These are the oats sold in packs with pictures of a perfect Highland man tossing cabers. They are mixed into muesli, bound with other grains and seeds, nuts and sugar for crunchy oat cereals, and they are an ingredient of chewy snack bars and the like.

Oatbran is the outer husk of oats ground until fine and sold either added to rolled porridge oats or on its own as a baking ingredient. Oatbran is one of the best sources of the cholesterol-lowering insoluble fibre.

QUINOA

The ancient supergrain of the Incas, quinoa (pronounced *keen wa*) is now popular with wholefood followers. It's believed to be extremely nutritious and easy to digest, making it ideal for those with allergies. Like buckwheat, it is known as a pseudo-grain (again, a member of the Goosefoot family). It is cooked in a ratio of 1½ times water to grain, then used mixed with other ingredients to make a soft pilaff-style dish. There is increasing interest in this grain (personally, I find it a little flavourless). Should you hunger for more quinoa knowledge, then read a book called *Quinoa, the Super Grain* by Rebecca Wood.

RYE

Rye is another of the marginal crops grown in poorer climates by farmers who lived a hard, precarious life. It is important in Scandinavian, Russian and north European cooking, it's main use now as a flour. Rye flour, however, has little gluten and so cannot rise like wheat to form a light texture or hold moisture: but it does make excellent crispbreads. Bread made with 100% rye flour is very heavy and dense, with a characteristic slightly sour flavour – pumpernickel is a classic rye bread. But if mixed with wheat it is possible to make a risen loaf with a rye flavour. Eastern European immigrants took rye-baking techniques with them to the United States and popularised classic sandwiches such as pastrami on rye and Reubens.

Rye can be sold as flakes for mixing into mueslis or into multigrain breads. There is a storage problem with rye, not significant nowadays because of better conditions. However, rye is subject to a fungus called ergot, which in centuries past was associated with witchcraft and a condition known as St Anthony's Fire that produces hallucinogenic symptoms and miscarriage. Nowadays the fungus has medical uses in drugs for inducing labour. Rye is also used in the making of American whiskey, a Dutch gin and Russian kvass.

SAGO

Sago is also known as pearl sage. It is simply a starch extracted from the sago palm, which grows freely in the freshwater swamps of South-East Asia. In Europe it is used to make a creamy milk pudding.

SEMOLINA

Semolina is a stage of wheat production using hard durum wheats. It is coarsely ground wheat (generally yellow in colour) used in the manufacture of pasta (see pages 234–5). You can also use it to make fairly quick sweet, mild puddings. The Italians use semolina to make a thick cold paste to cut into shapes for savoury gnocchi flavoured with butter and cheese, then baked and served with tasty tomato sauce. You can also mix in some chopped fresh spinach – a favourite family dish of ours.

SPELT

Spelt is an ancient form of wheat, still produced in the Balkans and slowly
becoming popular among wholefood devotees. The Roman legions were
supposed to have marched to their glorious victories on spelt. It is a higher in
protein and has more vitamins and minerals than ordinary wheat. It makes a very
nicely flavoured bread but for a time it slipped out of favour with millers because
it was hard to mill and easier strains of wheat were developed. Now, however,
speciality flour mills are not so daunted by the challenge. You can buy spelt flour
in health food shops. Doves Farm make spelt flour, as do Sharpham Park.

TAPIOCA

Tapioca, also known as cassava, is an important root crop in the tropics. There
are bitter and sweet cassavas: the former is poisonous if eaten raw but the juice
can be extracted to make cassareep, which is used in West Indian sauces as a
syrup. Tapioca is a flour made from cassava – the 'frog's spawn' milk pudding
some of us may remember from school dinners. (I loved it!)

WHEAT FLOURS

See pages 232–4.

BREAD

Bread is both a sustainer of life and a great delicacy. The three crucial
influences on bread are the flour, the raising agent, and the method of baking.
Within these simple parameters the scope for variation is endless. Sadly,
most of the bread we buy is monotonous and boring, eaten as a cheap filler
and more often than not hardly noticed. The situation is slowly changing as
previous speciality bakers close their high street outlets and start supplying
supermarkets direct. Ethnic bakers supply Arab, Greek, Italian, Spanish and
Indian breads to a rapidly growing number of stores. Each country has its
staple loaf. Now one country's staple loaf has become another's speciality so
we are as familiar with baguettes, ciabattas, pumpernickel and pittas as we are
with our own bloomer.

BREAD FLOURS

The type of flour determines the texture and flavour. For bread to have a light texture it needs a high percentage of the protein gluten, found in so-called hard wheats. This basically forms a framework around rising bubbles of gas given off from the leavening agent. Light and crispy French bread has a higher gluten level than softer sandwich bread.

Wheat white flour is produced from the endosperm. The germ and bran are removed. Until fairly recently, white flour (70–78% extraction) was chemically bleached white. Consumer pressure now ensures it is available as a softer creamy unbleached white. *Wholemeal* and *wholewheat flours* (100% extraction) contain practically all the grain. The bread is slightly heavier but the flavour is fuller, almost nutty. *Graham flour* is further milled wholegrain flour, developed by Dr Graham a 19th-century American health food enthusiast. *Brown flour* or *wheatmeal flour* is a slightly lower extraction rate of 80–90%, so the texture is midway between white and wholemeal – Hovis is the most popular brand. *Granary flour* is a trademarked wheat flour with added cracked grains. The generic name is Multigrain.

Rye flour is the world's second most popular bread grain. The grain however contains an inhibiting substance that impedes the development of gluten. Bread made with all rye flour will have a heavy close texture and bakers frequently mix it with some white flour. Rye flour made from only the endosperm will be paler in colour while rye flour mixed with wheat gives lighter loaves with a pleasantly tangy rye taste. *Barley flour* is low on the important gluten protein too and is a pale grey in colour. So, barley loaves are generally made with part wheat flour. Similar story with *oatmeal, cornmeal* and *buckwheat flours*. (Always read the label.)

The way the flour is ground can affect flavour and texture too. The old method of crushing between stone rollers (known as quernstones), which is described as 'stoneground', is still deemed to be the most wholesome because stones do not generate as much heat as in modern milling, thus the wholegrain is left more intact.

RAISING AGENTS

Raising agents add not only lightness but also flavour. Before the advent of commercial bakers' yeasts all bread was made with a chunk of the previous batch of bread dough, known as *sourdough starters*. This imparted a mellow sourness with a refreshing flavour and was the normal flavour in bread over a hundred years ago. An increasing number of speciality bakers are returning to this practice and sourdough breads are a feature of revivalist cuisines found in the best chic food halls, American and French included. Sourdough leavening (the term for raising) takes time so flavour develops at a leisurely pace.

Chemical raising agents are used in parts of the world where gluten-high hard wheat was originally in short supply so using yeast was not feasible, and breads were made with flours from corn or softer wheats. Now the breads are so ingrained in the food culture they retain their popularity despite competition from mass-produced yeast risen wheat loaves. Many corn-belt American states still enjoy cornbread (spoon bread) and Ireland has its soft brown soda bread, both made with *bicarbonate of soda and/or baking powder*. The texture is more cakey and the flavour has slight salty metallic taste.

Bread can also be made 'unleavened' – that is with no raising agent, like many of the Arab and Indian flat breads. Or the Scandinavian crispbreads, which in times past were simply breads with a central hole, hung up to dry in the wind. Flat breads are basically a flour and water dough rolled thinly and simply slapped on to a very hot dry pan or inside the walls of a searingly hot tandoor oven. The air trapped in the dough by kneading acts as a raising agent and gives it lightness while the sudden intense heat causes the dough to puff. Unleavened bread is popular in country areas where ovens are a luxury. They can also be made over an open fire.

A BRIEF RESUMÉ OF THE WORLD'S BREADS

BRITISH AND IRISH
Cottage, bloomers, split tins, Coburg, Vienna, soda, wheaten, bannocks, baps, bara brith, malt loaf.

FRENCH
Baguette, pain complet (wheatmeal), petit pain, brioche, croissant, pain de campagne.

GERMAN, AUSTRIAN AND SCANDINAVIAN
Brot (the generic German name), Brod (Scandinavian), Landbrot, Vollkornbrot, Pumpernickel, Knackebrot, Kleinegeback (little breads, e.g. pretzels), Stollen,Vienna roll, Gugelhupf, Danish pastries, plus many rye speciality breads.

ITALIAN
Pane (generic name), ciabatta, focaccia, pane integrale (wholemeal), panettone (sweetened), panino, pizza.

AMERICA
Corn breads (pone, spoon bread, Johnny cakes, Hush Puppies), sourdough, rye breads, bagels, Parker House rolls, English muffins, tortillas.

MIDDLE EAST
Flatbreads including pittas and lavash, manakeesh, semit, sesame breads.

INDIA
Roti (generic name), chapatis (gram flour), parathas, puris, naan.

BEST BREAD AND BUTTER PUDDING

Almost any bread will do, but textures and flavours will differ according to the bread. Brioche or panettone make devilishly wicked ones. Or try sliced malt loaf or chocolate bread.
Serves 4–6

4–6 slices white sandwich bread, medium sliced
about 50g (1¾oz) unsalted butter, softened
3–4 tablespoons raisins or sultanas
2 tablespoons chopped mixed peel
2 medium eggs
1 egg yolk
2 tablespoons caster sugar
½tsp vanilla essence
300ml (10fl oz) milk
200ml (7fl oz) double cream

Spread the bread with butter then remove the crusts and cut the bread into triangles. Lightly grease the sides of a medium-size oven-proof oval dish. Make sure it has sides at least 7cm (2¾in) high.

Arrange the bread in the dish, pointed ends up, scattering the dried fruit in between. You may not need all the bread, depending on the size of your dish. A 1 litre (1¾pt) capacity should be fine.

Whisk the eggs, yolk, sugar vanilla essence, milk and cream together then slowly pour over the bread. Press the bread into the mixture to make sure it is all soaked then set the dish aside for at least half an hour so the liquid is absorbed into the bread.

Preheat the oven to 150°C/gas mark 2. Place the dish in a roasting pan containing hot water that comes about halfway up the sides of the dish (a bain-marie).

Bake the pudding for 1–1¼ hours until the top is puffy and golden and the liquid set to a light custard. Remove carefully from the bain-marie and let the pudding cool a little. Serve with trickles of more cream.

Instead of dried fruits, you could spread the slices with marmalade and use pinches of cinnamon instead of the vanilla.

ADDITIONAL FACTORS

Other variables in bread-making that determine shape and flavour include additions such as fat and sugar, dried fruit, nuts and seeds. These will enrich a dough but also slow down its rising. Brioche or Danish pastry doughs, for example are rich wheat flour doughs with a delicious melt-in-the-mouth texture and buttery flavour. They are still technically breads. Much Italian bread is made with added oil, cheese or eggs giving a slacker dough that forms a flatter shape like ciabatta (Italian for slipper).

Shaping and baking give softness or crispness. Long thin loaves have proportionally more crust, large round or deep shapes more dough for softness. Slashing the dough as it rises exposes more crust, brushing with salt water helps crispness, sprinkling with flour or grains gives a softer crust while egg and sugar glazes make for a shiny crust. If bread is baked covered with an earthenware pot it is paler and softer. Breads baked in tins have softer sides and higher shoulders. Wood burning ovens impart a delicious flavour and crisp crust to breads, especially pizza doughs. Old bakers' ovens from France are highly prized and sought after. They are often bought by (and reassembled in) chic inner city bakeries.

WHEAT FLOURS, PASTA AND NOODLES

Over the centuries farmers have continually developed new strains of wheat and millers new techniques in grinding grains and making flours that reflect changing tastes and fashions. The process has been gradual but the wheat flours we use now are different from those of our ancestors. Our flours are finer in texture (for smoother sauces and lighter cakes), higher in protein (for pastas and crusty breads) and easier to mill.

Wheat grains contain not only starch but also a protein known as gluten. When mixed with water it becomes quite elastic and stretches as it is kneaded. It forms a coating around bubbles of gas formed during bread-making and helps pasta doughs hold their shape and texture as they are rolled thinner and thinner.

FLOUR VARIETIES

Hard wheats are richer in proteins and gluten than soft wheats, which have a greater proportion of starch. Botanists describe both of these as 'bread wheats' though they are used in all forms of baking.

As flours are milled, the outer bran layer and the wheatgerm are removed. What is left is the endosperm. Within this endosperm are starches and proteins. *Bread flours* (sometimes sold as 'strong' flours) have a higher proportion of gluten. This is the flour you would use to make your own bread at home, kneading either by hand or in a domestic machine. *Soft flours* are best used for cakes, most pastries, biscuits and as an all-purpose thickener for sauces, gravies etc. By law, bread must contain certain nutrients lost during milling: these are iron, thiamine, nicotinic acid and calcium in the form of chalk.

When flour is milled it is a natural cream colour. Before the days of modern milling, flours were coarser and darker ground and milled between large heavy mill stones called quernstones. Paler coloured flour was associated with fine living and so people began to demand *'white' flour*. Flour does also whiten naturally as it ages and older flour makes better bread but, of course, this takes time. Millers found a way of bleaching flour chemically to make it white and of adding chemical 'improvers'. It is these two processes that many food 'purists' do not approve of, preferring to seek out unbleached, *stoneground flour*. Bread stales quickly without additives: the recently introduced longer-life breads contain improvers to delay staling for up to a week.

Flours are also categorised according to the extraction rate, that is the amount of bran and wheatgerm still remaining after milling. **Wholemeal**, or *wholewheat*, flours are made from 100% of the grain. Flours of between 80 and 90% extraction are called *wheatmeal* or *brown flours*. White flours have extraction rates of 70–75%, though some of the very fine cake flours can be as low as 40%: this means they are capable of absorbing more liquid and sugar during baking, making cake textures soft and moist.

Self-raising flours have chemical agents added during milling which, when mixed with liquid, give off gases and make the mixture rise during cooking – fine for cakes but not so good for pastries that need a crisper texture. Self-raising flours should always be used well within their use-by dates as the chemical agents can lose their effectiveness in time. Unless you are a frequent cake-maker, it makes sense to buy self-raising flour in small bags.

Sponge flours: with the current trends in home-baking, attention is paid to lighter sponges. Millers have been quick to jump on the band wagon. In fact, any high-quality self-raising flours, such as Doves or even supermarket own-brand self-raising organic flours, give excellent results.

FLOUR GRADES AND ALLERGIES

Like all grain foods, wheat comes in many variations that affect the end use. Most of these involve the wheat protein gluten, which stretches in bread making to enclose microscopic bubbles of air from yeast fermentation or air beaten into cakes during mixing. Some wheats high in gluten are classed as 'Hard or Strong' flours, especially for bread making, including automatic bread machines to make open-textured loaves. Similar wheats called durum semolina make perfect pastas that cook until just tender (al dente) without softening. For those who like to make their own pasta, choose doppia zero (or '00') superfine ground flours perfect for egg pastas and pizza bases.

Home cake bakers who require softer (self-raising) wheat flours and pride themselves on light and even sponges should buy Supreme or Sponge flours that have the benefit of 'super sifting', or you can use ordinary self-raising flours and give them a double extra sifting before folding into the creamed fat, sugar and egg mixture.

For most of us these hard or strong bread wheat flours cause no allergic problems. But a minority reactions can be so bad as to be life threatening. So sufferers (often called Coeliacs) seek out gluten free alternatives not only in wheat but in many other grain foods – oats, barley, corn etc. Their life styles involve constant checking of labels for the magic words 'gluten free', in case food processing plants might have been exposed to tiny traces of gluten. Eating out can be misery even if restaurant kitchens swear their sauces are flour free. Most gluten allergy sufferers know how to manage their condition but some are so extreme they have to ensure their own kitchens have dual toasters, bread bins etc. So gluten allergy sufferers beware, check all labels on packages, canned and bottled foods states 'gluten free'.

PASTA

Having established the flour types we can now have a better understanding of pasta making. Pasta means 'paste' in Italian and that is all a basic pasta is – flour and water. Italians pooh-pooh stories that Marco Polo brought pasta techniques back with him from China in the 15th century, pointing to many examples of pasta-style recipes from the days of early Rome onwards. Certainly many Mediterranean countries have long traditions of pasta making going back centuries – it was, after all, the big waves of Italian immigrants to the United States that helped to popularise pasta so much during the early 20th century. No matter where it was born, pasta is now firmly one of the world's most recognised foods, made in countless countries, though Italy is still numero uno when it comes to high-quality pasta.

Pasta is made with the hardest of all wheats, a separate species known as 'durum', which is milled into a coarse meal called semolina (also known as *semola di grano duro*). When semolina is mixed with water it forms the paste from which pastas are rolled and extruded. If you want to make homemade pasta without eggs, then use '00' (doppio zero) quality for its higher gluten content. Hard durum semolina wheat likes a hot, dry climate and low rainfall, such as occurs around the Abruzzo and Apulia regions of Italy. Canada and the USA also grow durum wheat of this quality and much is exported to Italy to be blended with local durum wheat (and then presumably exported back to the up-market delis of metropolitan America as the ultimate chic pasta).

It is the mixture of these wheats with their levels of gluten-high proteins that determines the quality of a pasta. The way a dough is rolled and extruded will also have an effect, as will the length and style of drying (the nearer the natural air-drying state and the longer the time the better). Both of these can affect the absorption of water during cooking and ultimately the texture of a pasta. Pasta dough extruded from plastic moulds will have a shiny, smooth surface, but dough pushed through old-fashioned perforated bronze dies will have a pale cream, slightly floury texture that absorbs sauce more easily. Compare bags of pasta on a well-stocked deli shelf and you'll understand. The best Italian brands – San Martino, Delverde and De Cecco – coincidentally all come from the same river valley in the Abruzzo region of Italy.

Fresh and dried pasta

Fresh pasta is not a better quality than dried but it does have a different texture and is more suitable for filled raviolis, tortellinis etc. In Italy, fresh pasta is just that – made freshly either at home (*fatta in casa*) or in a special store to be sold for early consumption. Fresh pasta is made with a superfine wheat flour, called doppio-zero or '00', not to be confused with our soft wheat all-purpose flours which have a different ratio of starch to gluten (although you can make a passable homemade pasta with them, just not quite as good as '00').

The concept of vacuum-packed 'fresh' pasta is a relatively recent marketing exercise mainly confined to British and other European supermarkets. The dough is made with a durum flour, eggs, water etc. but not to such a high quality as some of the very best dried pastas.

Italian friends inform me that they will either eat 'real' fresh pasta (as Mama used to make) or good-quality dried pasta.

Flavoured pastas

Add egg to a dough and you have a richer, more yellow pasta: *all'uovo*. By law this must be 5 eggs per kilo of flour (leaving not a lot more for water). *Pasta verde* or *con spinaci* has added spinach purée; *con pomodoro* has tomato purée. *Intergale* is a wholewheat dough probably similar to the coarse country pastas made until the 19th century. Other flavourings include squid ink, dried mushroom (porcini), beetroot, pumpkin and even saffron. However, much of the flavour is leached out during boiling so the use of these flavourings is mostly a novelty factor.

Buying pasta

Outside Italy, supermarket own brands now dominate sales of pasta. While a number are made in time-honoured fashion with the right sort of wheat, correct methods etc., there is little way of knowing which ones are good quality except by price or by trial and error. (Though I once bought embarrassingly expensive speciality pasta from a smart food hall only to find it broke up in the pan, so a high price is not necessarily an indication of quality.) Enlightened stores will offer the discerning customer a choice of brands: otherwise, frequent your local Italian food store and ask for advice. Italians love to talk about food!

Brand names to check out are San Martino, De Cecco, Delverde (all gourmets' choices), Barilla and Buitoni.

Cooking fresh and dried pasta

Pasta needs lots of water so it can roll freely. A good rule of thumb is to allow 1 litre (1¾pt) of water per 100g (3½oz) of pasta. Bring the water to a good boil, adding salt to taste – say a scant teaspoonful to every litre (2 pints). Add the pasta all at once and stir it occasionally as it returns to the boil. Do not break long pasta to fit: simply hold it upright in the water and as it softens you will be able to push it further into the water. Stir the pasta occasionally during cooking.

Cooking times will probably be anything from 5 to 15 minutes, depending on the shape of the pasta, so check the packs first and always time from the moment the water returns to the boil after the pasta has been added the pan. Thin strands will need a shorter cooking time than thicker twists. Homemade fresh pasta will need much less cooking time, but I have noticed that bought 'fresh' pasta needs about the same cooking time as dried pasta.

Pasta is cooked when it is soft on the outside but still has a good bite in the centre – what the Italians call *al dente*. This is where quality shines through: quality dried pasta will still have this al dente bite even if slightly overcooked; poorer quality pasta will fall apart and even stick to the pan.

Once cooked, drain the pasta in a large colander, giving it a couple of quick shakes but without overdraining. Pasta should be served slightly wet so either tip it back into the cooking saucepan or into a pan with sauce. If serving simply with, say, pesto or garlic and olive oil, you might like to add a little of the pasta water back into the pan (assuming, that is, that you had the foresight to save any). Spaghetti is traditionally lifted out of the pan of water with two long-handled forks or a spaghetti fork and held aloft for a few seconds before adding to a pan of sauce or serving bowl rather than being tipped into a colander, but I reckon this takes practice to perfect.

Pasta shapes

This is the subject of many pages in cookery books, with long descriptions of what are often just simple translations of names – bows, shells, ears, tubes, strands and so on. Choose your pastas according to your own sense of style, but remembering a few guidelines. Long, thin pasta (e.g. *spaghetti, linguine, vermicelli*) suits thin sauces or light dressings such as pesto, white wine and seafood such as clams (*vongole*), or thin tomato and herbs. Pasta with hollows, ridges (*rigati*) or in tubes (e.g. *shells, rigatoni, penne, macaroni*) is good for trapping puddles of sauce. Wide, flat pasta (e.g. *wide tagliatelle, pappadelle, lasagne*) suits rich creamy or meaty sauces. Tiny baby-sized pasta (e.g. *orzo, alphabetti, fiori di sambuco*) are nicest in soups (*brodo*). Ironically, the best known pasta dish outside Italy, spaghetti Bolognese, is a prime example of a bad match of pasta shape to sauce.

A BRIEF GUIDE TO THE KEY PASTA SHAPES
Over 300 have been recorded and still more keep coming:

Short and Stocky Pastas
Gnocchi (shell or dumpling), conchiglioni (shells), penne (quills), anelli (rings), rotelle (wheels), maccheroni (macaron), lumache (snails), farfalle (bows), fusilli (twists), orecchini (little ears), stelline (stars), tubetti (tubes).

Long Rounded Pastas
Spaghetti (strings/strands), bucati (holed), ziti (bachelor), capelli d'angelo (angel's hair), vermicelli (worms).

Long Flat Pastas
Pappardelle, tagliatelle, fettuccine (flat ribbons), chitarra (guitar strings), lasagne (sheets), linguine (tongues), garganelli (flat squares rolled into quills).

When a name ends in *-ini* or *-etti* you can generally reckon it to be a smaller or thinner version of the parent pasta.

Filled pastas

These are sold fresh, vacuum-packed or dried. Basically, they are flat sheets of pasta filled with a meat or vegetable paste, often with added Ricotta cheese or a mushroom purée to hold the mixture together. The stamped-out shapes can be left as they are for *ravioli* or twisted into further shapes such as *cappelleti* (little hats) or *tortellini* (twists).There are many Italian cookbooks that tell you how to make your own fresh pasta, and fill and shape it. Once you've mastered the technique, ravioli is a good dish to try yourself because you can create your own delicious fillings. Stuffed pastas don't have to be small sizes, either: the trend in restaurants is to make large sizes, allowing one per person, filled with mixtures of chicken, lobster, prawns, wild mushrooms, pumpkin and so forth.

RAGU BOLOGNESE

Perhaps the most famous pasta sauce. Made in the original way it is a far cry from the dreary mince and canned tomato sauce that tries to pass under the same name. Two ingredients make all the difference – chicken livers and cream. And it's not to be served with spaghetti because it is too rich and thick a sauce for thin pasta strands. Instead toss it with rigatoni, penne or shells or layer it with lasagne sheets.

Heat 2tbsp of olive oil in a large saucepan with a good knob of butter. Add 300g (10½oz) of lean minced beef, 125g (4½oz) of chopped chicken livers and 125g (4½oz) of chopped pancetta or lean streaky bacon and stir well until browned and crumbly. Add a chopped onion, 2 crushed fat garlic cloves, a small chopped carrot and small chopped celery stick. Cook these for about 5 minutes until softened, then stir in a small glass of dry white wine and cook until it has all evaporated away.

Now add 500ml (18fl oz) of crushed tomatoes or passata, 4tbsp of tomato purée, a large bay leaf, a little freshly grated nutmeg and salt and freshly ground pepper to taste. Bring to the boil, cover and simmer gently for 20 minutes until reduced down. Check the seasoning and mix in about 3tbsp of double cream just before serving. Like many meat sauces, this is best made the day before to allow flavours to mellow and develop. In which case, stir in the cream after reheating and just before serving.

OTHER PASTA-STYLE PRODUCTS

Non-wheat pasta

As the problem of allergies becomes more commonplace, so speciality manufacturers are looking at non-wheat alternatives. Two of the most noteworthy are corn and rice pasta. At the moment I have seen these only as short shapes, probably because as they lack gluten they cannot hold up as long strands. They can be cooked and served in the same way as traditional pasta, but do not have quite the same al dente texture. But, what the heck – if you like the idea of eating pasta but you're sensitive to gluten or you want to avoid eating wheat products as you follow a de-tox diet, then try and enjoy them.

Panne carasau

As the hunt for more regional Italian specialities intensifies, supplies of this light and crisp durum wheat bread from Sardinia are appearing alongside pasta packs. Eat it as you would any crispbread (it's good with creamy Italian cheeses) or soak it in water and use like softened pasta. Use it to make a quick lasagne, or like stuffed pancakes with fillings. You can break it into soups, brush it with olive oil and sprinkle with grated cheese and heat it lightly in the oven.

Spatzle

If you holiday in Germany, Austria or the German part of Switzerland you may come across irregularly shaped noodles served in a variety of ways but often in a broth. They are generally made fresh from a pasta-style dough that is extruded straight into boiling water. You can imitate the process by pushing the dough through a colander with the back of a ladle. Messy, but quite rewarding if you persevere.

NOODLES

As I've said before, debate continues about who 'invented' pasta and noodles – the Orientals or the Mediterraneans. I expect the idea evolved simultaneously as mankind learned to mill wheat and grains and mix it with water to a dough. If he or she slapped the dough on to a hot stone it baked into bread: if rolled out, cut into strings, then tossed into a pot of boiling liquid it became pasta/noodles.

Noodles, however, are definitely oriental, using varying grains or pulses as a dough base. Wheat noodles are the most popular (and widely available in the west) but other grains include buckwheat (soba), rice, gram flour (chickpeas) and even mung beans. It is thought that the idea for noodles first developed in China then spread to Japan and down towards South-East Asia, undergoing various refinements as it travelled. Noodles are not only the popular street food of these countries; they're also embellished with countless stories, myths and legends. The noodle is very much part of the Buddhist attitude to life – the principle of yin and yang. Noodles are yin, calming and light: sauces to match are yang, full-bodied and sometimes fiery.

Chinese noodles

Chinese noodles (found also in South-East Asia) are mainly made of wheat, rice or mung beans. *Egg noodles* are wheat flour mixed with egg. They come in thin and medium thicknesses and are sold in pleated sheets or twirled into nests. They can be dressed in a light broth with accompanying shredded vegetables, tofu, thinly sliced meat or seafood to be further flavoured with soy sauce. They cook in 5-7 minutes, depending on the quality. They can also be served cooked and stir-fried.

Bean thread noodles (also known as *cellophane* or *Chinese vermicelli*) are made of mung bean starch and look like thin fishing rod lines. They usually come wrapped in little bundles and have a delicate flavour best suited to rich sauces. They just need to be soaked in hot or warm water before use.

Rice noodles are made from rice flour and can be found fresh or dried. They range in size from wide, flat noodles to long, thin, delicate strands. They are normally served in stir-fried dishes and acquire a nice crispy coating as a result. Rice noodles come with a light oily coating which needs to soaked off in hot water before use but require little to no cooking thereafter. Dried rice noodles have a firmer bite than fresh. Thin rice noodles can be deep-fried and used as a crispy garnish and any leftovers can be used for filling spring rolls.

Japanese noodles

Japanese noodles owe their origin to Chinese inspiration but, as in most things, the Japanese proved to be masters of the art of further refinement.

Their noodles fall into four main categories: *fat, white udon wheat noodles*; the more refined *thin, somen wheat noodles*; *thin, light brown soba noodles* made with buckwheat or blended with buckwheat; and the more popular thread-like *ramen noodles* bound with egg and sold in many guises in takeaway shops throughout Japan. The ramen noodles are the noodles of bawdy Japanese folklore. However, as noodle culture continues to evolve and hybridise so the classic distinctions blur and definitions become irrelevant. It's all very exciting – and very Japanese, as is the politely acceptable way of slurping them from the bowl directly into your mouth with the minimum use of chopsticks or spoon.

Cook Japanese noodles lightly in boiling water according to the packet instructions, then serve in a light broth with vegetables, slices of fish, prawns, tofu, chicken, even raw egg yolk. Classically this should be dashi, a clear fish and miso broth.

HERBS AND SPICES

Take herbs and spices away from cooking and food becomes monochromatic. Many archaeological excavations reveal remains of the aromatic plants that were the forerunners of herbs and spices now used the world over. For thousands of years Man has gathered seeds, leaves and stems from aromatic wild plants not so much for goodness and nutrition but because he/she liked the taste. Since written records began, the medicinal properties of herbs have been also noted: sometimes a herb or spice will aid digestion, cure flatulence, or brighten our skin, eyes and hair, for instance. Many herbs and spices are associated with legends and folklore. It is worth noting this background when we consider the origins and uses for herbs and spices.

The same aromatics, such as basil, cinnamon, thyme and coriander, are used in worldwide cuisines in quite different ways, but in the main we include these natural substances because we like their taste. Herbs and spices are also associated with legends and folklore. Herbs are leaves or stems, while spices are berries, stalks, barks and roots. Both can be used fresh or dried, though some dry and store better than others.

HERBS

Classic herbs in Western cooking are of Mediterranean origin and in the wild can be found clinging to cliff tops or along arid roadsides. Herbs can be woody like shrubs, or leafy like garden plants. Sunshine brings out the best in herbs: not only does it help them grow vigorously but it warms the leaves and releases delicious aromas to tempt us and attract bees who suckle on the nectar for their aromatic honey.

Herbs can broadly be divided into *umbellifers* (with seed heads like umbrellas) and leafy labiates.

When a classic recipe calls for a *bouquet garni*, it requires a small bunch of fresh bay leaves, parsley sprigs (including stalks), thyme, a thin stick of celery and leek, tied tightly together.

BASIL

This leafy herb originated in South-East Asia and is as popular there as in Italy, the country we generally associate with basil. It is one of the aniseed-flavoured herbs with a very distinctive aroma. Pots of basil were suppose to bring young maidens sweet dreams of their lovers.

In many Greek islands and Italian villages you will see succulent basil bushes growing rampantly in old tomato cans, ready to be picked almost every day to be tossed into salads or scattered over tomatoes. Basil is the original herb used in pesto, and, although some chefs experiment with other herbs, the original to my mind is still the best. Thai cooks add whole leaves to their curries, soups, salads and chilli-spiked stir-fries. Their varieties include *light* and *dark holy basil* and the reddish stemmed *sweet basil*. Basil wilts easily so keep it refreshed with water and bagged in the fridge. I prefer to buy basil in a pot because packet leaves seem to turn mouldy quickly or have tell-tale signs of damage – basil bruises very easily. If you buy pot basil, don't throw it out once the leaves have been plucked: keep it on a light sunny window sill but out of direct sunlight and water it. Keep the plant going and replenish the leaf stock.

BAY LEAVES

Another of the bouquet garni herbs, used in cooking as a flavouring as a whole leaf, rarely snipped up – it's too tough. The flavour of bay is warming and sweet. Dried bay leaves are more aromatic than fresh, bigger ones better for flavour than small. If you have a garden, it's worth planting a small bay shrub – it will grow quickly and well and will only need pruning lightly once a year to give you a good supply of leaves for cooking. My Granny used to make rice puddings adding two or three big leaves from her garden and I've always had happy memories of the flavour. Add a bay leaf to the milk you scald before making béchamel sauce or the poaching liquid for fish or chicken. Small sprigs are good for the stockpot or tucked into the cavity of a roasting chicken. I slip bay leaves into the belly of a whole salmon before baking and skewer small leaves with meat balls or cubes on satay sticks for kebabs.

CHERVIL

A delicately aniseed-flavoured herb that looks a little like dainty parsley. One of the classic French *fines herbes*, it is almost impossible to buy on a retail level except from up-market greengrocers' stores but it will grow fairly easily in a sheltered spot in the garden. Chefs seems to be able to lay their hands on it readily enough through catering suppliers so maybe the more they use it the more likely we are to be able to get it in supermarkets. I keep looking. It is sometimes added to sauces during cooking but more often stirred into a dish at the point of serving or scattered lightly over a salad. Little individual sprigs laid on the top of a crowning stack of sliced medallions of fish or lamb are a wonderful garnish.

CHIVES

One of the onion family and found all over the temperate world, sometimes wild but mostly cultivated in gardens. It's widely available in major supermarkets. I prefer to buy chives when they are thicker stemmed in packs rather than pot chives, which are more tender but do not have such a pronounced flavour. However, I have found that pot chives do root well in the garden or window box and, despite what growers say, appear each year, fresh and full flavoured.

Just snip the long stems with scissors straight into soups, over salads, into soured cream or cottage cheese for spooning into baking potatoes. In the mid-summer chives start to sprout little purple onion heads. Gardeners pinch these out to encourage thicker growth, but cooks like to pick them to use in salads. Not only do they look pretty but they also have a good strong oniony flavour.

CORIANDER LEAVES

Coriander (also known as cilantro) and flat leaf parsley look very similar and are often mistaken for each other. Fresh coriander is a plant of three culinary uses: the leaves make a good garnish; the leaves, stems and roots can all be used for flavouring; and the seeds are dried to be crushed and used in spice pastes or in general cooking.

Whole coriander can be sold with roots, mostly in ethnic stores. Don't cut these off, simply stand them in a jug of water like flowers. Again, if you find fresh coriander looking bedraggled, don't despair – a cold bath and time in the fridge work wonders. Chop fresh coriander roots finely and add to stews or stir-fries at the same time as vegetables, then finish with a leaf garnish. Don't restrict coriander to Asian and Oriental cooking: it certainly is indispensable in Indian, Chinese, Thai and Indonesian recipes but it also enhances many Western dishes. They're wonderful added to pâtés and grilled fish. The possibilities are almost endless. (See also Coriander berries, page 257)

COTTAGE GARDEN HERBS

I list here herbs that you may not as yet find in stores or supermarkets, but – who knows? – they just might become popular.

Borage is known as the 'bee-keeper's friend' but it attracts aphids as well as honey bees, so watch out. Its dainty star-shaped blue flowers are sometimes added to Pimm's. Younger leaves can be shredded and mixed into cucumber salads or cucumber sandwiches.

Sweet Cicely, known as the 'sugar saver', tastes like a cross between aniseed and angelica. It has very pretty feathery leaves, which country cooks would add to rhubarb or gooseberries to help reduce the sugar needed in the days when it was still a luxury item. Sadly it wilts quickly so it's unlikely to be a commercial commodity.

Lovage looks like very dark celery. It's very aromatic with a strong aniseed/ caraway flavour, which means you need only a couple of leaves at a time. It does make fresh tomato soup taste sensational and it's good snipped over eggs, cheese, chicken and rich fish.

Angelica is often spotted growing wild. It's a majestic umbelliferous plant with fleshy hollow stems. Commercially you can buy it candied for adding to creamy desserts (essential in tutti-frutti ice cream) or for decorations. Rinse the sugar off candied angelica under tepid water. It's one of the herbs used in the liqueur Green Chartreuse.

Hyssop is one of my personal favourites. It has a hint of lavender about it and is lovely used in summer fruit cups. Or add a sprig when cooking pan-fried liver.

Geranium leaves are nice laid on top of summer trifles as a garnish. Used as an infusion they make nice ice creams and sorbets.

CURRY LEAVES

Occasionally you might see Indian curry leaves on sale, tied in small bunches. If you love curries, then buy them and use them – in curries! Even if you just chop some to add to a creamy cheese sauce or smooth carrot soup, they will add a lovely fresh spice flavour and are well worth trying. Again, if you have any left over, just allow them to dry naturally and continue to use them. Or buy dried bunches from ethnic or halal shops.

DILL

In Middle Eastern stores it is possible to buy big bunches of this bright green aromatic, aniseed-scented herb. Its feathery leaves and succulent stalks are both used in cooking. It's a very versatile herb for which I find all sorts of uses, especially blended with parsley or mint. Pick the fronds of dill weed from the stalks and snip them over new potatoes, chicken salads or egg mayonnaise. Dill is a classic herb with cream cheese and essential to make gravalax, the Swedish home-salted salmon served with a honey-mustard dressing. Chop the stronger-flavoured stalks and add them to stews. Dill seeds are from the umbellifer head and are simply dried. They are more pungent than the leaves – good in winter soups and stews.

DRIED AND FROZEN HERBS

There are only a few dried herbs I bother using: oregano/marjoram, tarragon, dill weed, sage, rosemary, mint and thyme. Their flavour is pretty near the fresh original and they don't lose much pungency in processing. The others seem to me either too overpowering (like basil) or they smell of dried grass (like parsley and chives). If there is no fresh supply of a herb then I would rather go without or substitute a similar dried one that does store well, dried oregano or thyme instead of fresh basil, for instance.

TIP: STORING DRIED HERBS

Store dried herbs in a dry cupboard and certainly out of any light.

Displays of jars of dried herbs look pretty but the contents soon lose both

their colour and flavour. Check use-by dates: I will frequently throw out

a dried herb even within its use-by date if I feel the flavour has gone.

It's worth spending a little extra to get good flavour.

FENNEL

Fennel is a stocky plant with leaves and seeds similar to dill. This is a plant you can see growing wild in many sunny wasteland sites, both in Britain (great in gardens) and over much of Europe. It's another herb I pick on self-catering holidays. The herb is nice chopped into a Waldorf celery, apple and walnut salad. The bulbous root, known as Florence fennel, is used as a vegetable (see page 106).

FENUGREEK

One of the milder aromatic curry herbs, which Indian cooks call *methi*. Buy it fresh or dried from ethnic foods stores or halal butchers. The seeds are an essential ingredient in any curry blend or garam masala, and also are excellent soaked and sprouted (see page 93).

MARJORAM AND OREGANO

Marjoram has pretty white or pale purple flowers that appear around June and attract busy bees. Oregano, frequently called wild marjoram, has slightly smaller leaves and is more pungent when crushed Both of these herbs are associated with Italian cooking but are also good all-rounders with many meat, fish, egg, vegetable and cheese dishes. They are both good tomato herbs in that you can snip the leaves over sliced tomatoes, trickle over a little olive oil and serve for a simple and memorable salad.

Oregano is a herb used much in Mexican cooking with dried cumin, coriander and chilli. Golden varieties of the herb are as useful as the green and can make attractive garnishes. Dried oregano is frequently sprinkled over pizzas before baking, but too often in commercial pizza bars they use herbs way past their best and all you get is a musty stale smell.

MINTS

Mints are labiate herbs with lush all-green or streaked green and white or yellow leaves. The scores of varieties all have very pretty leaves that can make a country-style garden look so fresh and wholesome. Mint seems to grow brazenly anywhere and everywhere it is let loose. Gardeners often contain it in a sunken pot to stop the roots from spreading and, while it likes sun, it also grows well in shaded spots.

Mints on sale in stores for culinary uses are generally *spearmints* or *peppermints:* good speciality herb growers will have a delightful array of mints should you wish to get carried away. Look out for *pineapple mint* and the *mossy leaf apple* or *Bowles mint.* If they are wilted give them the cold water bath and fridge treatment.

The fragrance of mint is well known and mint extracts are made into aromatic oils used in cooking as well room fragrances, teas and drinks. Peppermint oil is a pain reliever. Mint is one of the few leafy herbs that dries well, though its smell becomes more aniseed as a result. Dried mint gives salty cheese such a Greek Feta a good balance of flavour. Fresh it is often associated with a sauce for lamb or cooking with new potatoes, but try it in generous amounts mixed with parsley and dill to stir into cooked rice, with soaked bulgur in tabbouleh and over a tomato, cucumber and grated carrot salad.

CUCUMBER RAITA

Mint and cumin make this classic Indian fresh relish magic.

Coarsely grate a cucumber, including the skins and seeds. Allow to drain in a colander for 20 minutes.

Meanwhile, chop a good handful of fresh mint leaves (picked from two large sprigs) and a few stems of fresh chives. Beat into a 200g (7oz) tub of thick Greek-style (whole milk) yogurt with ½tsp ground cumin.

Stir in the cucumber and season to taste. Chill before serving. If the cucumber leaks a little, simply mix it well into the dressing. Classic with spiced grilled meats or to cool down burning palates.

PARSLEY

The most used herb in European cuisine and found in many food stores and gardens, though it's a tricky herb to grow from seed – folklore has it that out of every seven seeds sown, six go to the devil. Better to buy one or two plants ready potted. Parsley is high in vitamin C and the stalks contain more flavour than the leaves, so don't discard them, simply chop finely. There are two main types – the curly leaf, thought to have most flavour but regarded as a passé garnish, and the flat leaf or continental parsley used extensively in Mediterranean and Middle Eastern countries.

If you buy leafy parsley that has started to wilt, simply dunk it in cold water, shake it dry, bag it in a polythene food bag and store it in the bottom of the fridge – it will soon perk up. Use it for making stock or for adding extra flavour to a stew: it's one of the classic herbs for a bouquet garni. It is also supposed to be an antidote for garlic breath: just chew a few stalks and breathe freely again. Ethnic or halal stores are the best places for good, bushy bunches of fresh flat leaf parsley, far cheaper than the little packs sold in supermarkets. Use chopped parsley in big handfuls – it does have a lot of flavour.

ROSEMARY

The name means 'rose of the sea', and judging by the number of times I have spotted rosemary while on Mediterranean holidays it certainly seems to grow well on wild rocky cliffs and in poor soils. With woody stems and spiky leaves, the aroma from the essential oils lingers even after it has been dried for some months. Maybe that is why it is also called the herb of remembrance – the lingering smell is hard to forget. Herbs bought ready-dried, if they are a good brand (try Bart's, Fox's, Schwartz), will have come from hot countries and have a stronger smell than our own homegrown, although home-grown packs a powerful punch too.

Rosemary features in the Herbes de Provence mixtures and is in Italian mixed herbs too. Like mint, it is best known as a herb for roasted lamb, but it is also delicious with baked fish, spiked into roast pork, tucked into roasted chicken cavities and snipped over vegetables roasting in olive oil. Perfect with roast potatoes. Talking of oils, why not slip a large sprig into a bottle of olive oil to scent it, although just to be on the safe side heat the oil and sprig together to boiling then transfer to a clean, sterilised bottle. I have also used rosemary snipped over homemade biscuits and in creamy ice creams and added it to poached fruits. If you grow rosemary (and there is a West Country saying that rosemary grows well where the mistress is master of her house) look out for flowering time and pinch off the pretty pale blue flowers to scatter over tomato salads or freeze in ice cubes for drinks.

SAGE

Another Mediterranean herb with a pungent aromatic oil, associated with pork, goose and the English cheese Sage Derby. Sage bushes have attractive green or purple leaves which chefs like to use, deep-fried as a garnish or rolled into veal escalopes with cheese as saltimbucca. And, best of all, bees love it. I find dried sage crushed and sold in jars too pungent and prefer to dry either my own few branches from the garden or fresh sprigs bought from a store. Tie up the sprigs with kitchen string and hang them up: within a week the leaves will be crisp enough to crush in small quantities over pork chops or potatoes or into omelettes or even to make homemade sage and onion stuffing by mixing it with fresh breadcrumbs, eggs and grated lemon rind. If you like offal, do sprinkle a cautious pinch of dried sage over pan-fried liver or kidneys.

SAVORY

Winter and summer savorys are popular with chefs but like chervil are not often seen in stores – yet! Summer savory is sometimes known as wild thyme or sarriette. In Germany it is known as the bean herb, which should give you a clue as to its best use – yes, tossed into hot butter-dressed beans. Treat savory like thyme.

TARRAGON

Aniseed-scented and very pungent, tarragon is served with fish, chicken, eggs and cheese. If you buy it in pack s then use the leaves from just one sprig – that will provide plenty of flavour. When I can't use a whole pack before it wilts, I simply allow the leaves to dry naturally to use later. Keeping them covered in the fridge is not very successful: they could turn black and slimy. The variety French tarragon has a stronger flavour than the spindly Russian variety.

THYME

There are many varieties of this popular herb. Common thyme can grow anywhere and is the one readily on sale, semi-dried, in open-air markets. It's widely used in European and West Indian cooking – it's one of the essential herbs for rice 'n' peas. Thyme blends well with chilli spices and garlic, and mixes with lemon. Along with parsley and bay it is essential in a bouquet garni and nice as a fresh ravioli filling. Lemon thyme is more delicate, with spindly soft stems and tender leaves that look dainty arranged in long, elegant sprigs to garnish grilled chicken, escalopes, grilled vegetables and chargrilled fish.

WILD GARLIC

If you go down to the woods in early spring, you are probably sure of a nice surprise. Along pathways and roadsides, you'll find rows of dark green clumps of lily-shaped leaves and white onion-head flowers. This is wild garlic, a great favourite with country chefs and cooks. The leaves (washed and thinly sliced) perk up salads and vegetable dishes, and the flowers make a starry garnish. They can be grown in home gardens, alongside fences or walls in dappled shade, and obligingly come up every year.

SPICES

The history of mankind has been shaped over thousands of years by the quest to find more efficient ways to obtain much sought-after spices. The ancient spice trails with their fabulous cities can still be travelled. Some of the great cities are long gone but many – built of mud upon mud – still stand strong and are important sites of world heritage.

The rise and refinement of Western Civilisation began with the quest for quicker routes to the spice islands. Columbus set off from Spain in 1492 to find a back route to the spice islands of the East Indies and stumbled over the New World instead. Trading companies were established and wars fought to ensure European cooks always had a consistent supply of spices to make their food and drink palatable, and merchants' profit margins increased accordingly.

Buying and storing spices
The flavour of spices is due to natural volatile oils. These lessen with time and on exposure to light, heat or damp. Unless you know the source of supply I would suggest sticking to well-known proprietary brands or buy from busy and buzzy ethnic stores. I wouldn't buy spices, or herbs for that matter, from a trader who weighs the contents out of a large jar displayed in strong daylight. You don't know how old the contents are. Ethnic stores are good sources of supply if the spices are well sealed and within their use-by date. But sometimes the packs they sell are bumper bundles and more than you can use within a few months. So, a well-sealed smaller jar from a supermarket might be a better bet.

The golden rule is to buy little and often and store in airtight containers in a cool dry cupboard away from light – not on a wall-mounted spice rack. Properly stored spices should be vibrantly coloured and have fresh, well-developed aromas.

Cooking with spices
Today, many of us remain cautious about using spices and require guidance.

Because of their volatile nature, spices are generally best heated briefly before use to release the aromas. This can be done by gentle frying in a little oil, dry-frying or roasting, just for a minute or two. Most recipes will instruct you to fry wet, chopped or puréed spices in a little oil, then stir in a dry spice mix before adding the remaining ingredients for the dish.

Don't add dried ground spices to a casserole or simmering sauce without a little pre-frying or they will taste pasty and do little for the dish. Alternatively, if you buy a quality spice or curry paste, the spices will have been ground and pre-fried, so you just add whatever quantity you require straight into the cooking pot.

Whole spices, such as a piece of cinnamon stick, a blade of mace or a slice of dried ginger, can be popped straight into a simmering pot to give a gentle flavour. Many Asians dishes contain whole spices and diners simply leave them on the side of their plate.

AJOWAN

An Indian spice available as small, light brown, oval seeds. They have a strong thyme-like flavour, so you can use dried thyme as a substitute.

ALLSPICE

Allspice, also known as Jamaican pepper and pimento, is a New World spice which curiously does smell like a mixture of many popular spices – cloves, nutmeg, cinnamon and even black pepper. The small mid-brown berries are added to syrups and crushed in rich fruit puddings, mincemeats and punches. In old seafaring days, allspice was used to help preserve meat and fish, and during the late 19th century walking sticks made from allspice wood were all the rage. Allspice is still popular in German and Scandinavian cooking.

ANNATTO

Not a spice you come across in powder form to use in home cooking but it's found in many foodstuffs, chiefly as a natural orange colouring – so-called red cheeses are coloured with annatto. It is, however, popular in South American cooking, where it is called achiote.

ASAFOETIDA

You may not have come across it before, but in fact asafoetida is a popular spice in Indian cooking. Well, calling it a spice is misleading: it's more of a flavour enhancer, adding a sharpness or piquancy to dishes. It is the creamy sap of a fennel-type plant which hardens to a brown resin. Buy it ready ground, which is easier to use than the resin, and use it in little pinches. One word of warning, until cooked it smells of the school chemistry lab. The Romans used it frequently as a medicine – one only hopes they heated it first.

CARAWAY SEED

A small seed that looks like cumin but to my mind does not possess its charm in terms of flavour. In short, not a favourite spice of mine, being rather too strong on the aniseed front. But it's popular in European cooking where it's used with cabbage, in cheese and in breads and sweet baking. It's another breath freshener spice. Sweetened caraway seeds are sometimes included in Indian digestive spice mixtures that are sucked after rich meals.

CARDAMOM

Native to India and Ceylon, the sweetly aromatic cardamom is often described as the 'rice spice' because of its affinity with rice dishes. There is also a 'turpentine' hint to its fragrance and, indeed, it does have medicinal uses too. It's sold in green husked pods, which contain strongly flavoured black seeds. For a subtle flavour, use about three whole pods in a whole spice pilau or, for a fuller taste, grind about ½tsp of seeds from 1–2 pods into the rice. It's wonderful cooked with milk puddings, especially *kheer*, an Indian rice dessert, and makes a delicious ice cream. White cardamoms are bleached green pods. The spice known as black cardamom is not related and has a cruder flavour than green, though it's acceptable for stews.

CASSIA BARK

A relative of cinnamon, but less fragrant. It is sometimes sold as cinnamon bark but, though it looks more like bark than cinnamon quills, it's not the same. It's used by the Chinese in pickles and spicy dishes and is more associated with savoury use than sweet.

CINNAMON

A native of southern India and Sri Lanka. In the wild, cinnamon trees can grow to quite a size. But commercially cinnamon is cut as shoots from the plant after two years and the bark peeled off and curled into quills. Continuous harvesting ensures the plants never grow more than the height of a man for easier picking. The dried bark is also ground into a powder for baking: the leaves and broken bark yield oil for medicinal use.

Cinnamon is used throughout the world by nearly every major cuisine. It is popular in Indian and South-East Asian food, in China, the Middle East and North Africa, all over Europe from Italy to snowy Scandinavia and over the Atlantic to America, Mexico and South America. In fact there is probably no country that does not use cinnamon in at least a few dishes.

In the West, cinnamon is a classic in punches and mulled wine (whole quills can be reused if the first use was just a brief steeping in a light syrup), but it is also good added to everyday beef, pork or lamb stews to add a hint of aromatic spiciness without fiery heat. Indians like to add little pieces of broken bark to plain rice as it boils along with a few cardamoms and two or three whole cloves. Ground cinnamon is essential in too many baking classics to list. Mix ground cinnamon with sifted icing sugar to shake over homemade biscuits or cakes, sprinkle it over cappuccino coffee, make it into ice cream and mix it with chocolate in baking.

CINNAMON ICE CREAM

Heat 250ml (9fl oz) milk and 250ml (9fl oz) double cream with 100g (3½oz) caster sugar, 1tsp ground cinnamon and ½tsp vanilla essence until the liquid starts to froth and creep up the sides of a saucepan. Remove from the heat stirring briskly until the sugar dissolves.

Meanwhile, beat 6 egg yolks in a large mixing bowl. Pour the scalded spicy milk in slurps on to the yolks, whisking hard then pour back into the saucepan.

On the lowest heat setting, stir the mixture with a wooden spoon until it starts to coat the back of the spoon, this might take about 5 minutes. Do not let it even simmer or it will surely curdle.

Remove from the heat and pour through a sieve into a shallow freezer proof container. Cool and chill stirring occasionally.

Freeze the custard either using an ice cream machine or in a shallow tray in the freezer, beating the mixture a few times. When creamy and slushy, cover and allow to freeze completely. Use within 1 week and allow to sit at room temperature for 10 minutes before scooping.

CLOVES

Zanzibar is back on the tourist map, if you are looking for an exotic holiday, and one of the best ways to approach it is by boat because as you steam towards the shores you should detect the rich, almost musky fragrance of cloves, the island's most famous export. Where would many of the world's great dishes be without this precious spice?

Use cloves, generally whole, sparingly because they can be overpowering – two or three cloves are all that are needed to impart their flavour. For a subtle hint in a white sauce, stick a small onion with three or four whole cloves and steep it in a pan with milk that has just boiled to infuse. Traditionally cloves are stuck into a roasted ham coated with honey mustard for a decorative effect as well as for their flavour. They were one of the spices in the orange pomanders carried by ladies of fashion in Tudor and Stuart times and they are still used in warm spicy punches. Ground cloves is a very strong mixture to be used very sparingly, often mixed into rich fruit cakes and puddings, generally in pinches. Oil of cloves is the powerful essential oil used to soothe toothache, and some breath fresheners contain clove essence.

CORIANDER SEED

Also known as *dhania* and *dizzycorn* – because the aroma from the freshly crushed seeds can make you feel a little dizzy – this is another aromatic rather than fiery heat spice. It's widely used in Indian, South-East Asian, Chinese, Middle Eastern and Greek cooking and is a popular spice with modern-day chefs. Coriander seed is good with oranges, particularly crushed in a marmalade. Like cumin, it's a very useful spice. Add whole dried berries to stock and use them in salad dressings. They're wonderful added to pâtés and grilled fish. The possibilities are almost endless. (See also Coriander leaves, pages 244–5.)

TIP: USING DRIED CORIANDER BERRIES

While I was working alongside Michelin-starred chefs, I picked up a tip

for using dried coriander berries. They crush about 1tsp freshly each time

they need it rather than using ready-ground coriander. The difference it

makes to flavour is remarkable. I soon retrieved my old pestle and mortar

from the back of a cupboard and now keep it by the peppermill with a jar

of coriander berries at the ready.

CUMIN

Aromatic and pungent but not fiery, cumin (also known as jerra) is one of the spices with a distinctive curry flavour but with many other uses other than in Indian cooking. It is used throughout Asia and the Middle East and is popular, too, in Mexican and Spanish cookery (the Moorish influence again). I find it has an affinity with paprika, chilli and oregano. It's also used in many middle European dishes, for example a good pinch of cumin seeds in a batch of beetroot borscht gives a convincing authentic flavour. My favourite, though, is to sprinkle ground cumin on scrambled eggs or mix into mayonnaise. Cumin is one of the German and Dutch cheese spices which you will spot as little flecks. It is sold as small seeds or ground and is always best freshly roasted in a hot dry pan.

EPAZOTE

Epazote, also known as wormseed, is a Mexican spice used in the cooking of beans. It's also good as a tea. It is said to alleviate intestinal gases. Bay leaves are a vaguely similar substitute.

FENNEL SEEDS

Fennel seeds are similar to caraway but are somehow less pungent and slightly sweeter in flavour. Cool Western gardens often have fennel plants, and their seed heads sprout in the summer. It's the same plant, so pick those seed heads. Fennel seeds are popular in many Mediterranean dishes such as the classic French *bouillabaisse* soup and scattered throughout an Italian salami called *finocchiona*. Indian chefs use fennel in some of their spice mixtures, and it can be sweetened for chewing as a digestive. Fennel is delicious sprinkled into a homemade tomato soup as it bubbles. A small pot of fennel seeds will last a good time, so don't overbuy.

FENUGREEK SEED

Like cumin, this is one of the classic curry-blend spices, aromatic, quite mild and sweet in flavour. A favourite with Indian cooks and now beginning to appear in its own right in fusion food recipes where European chefs cook dishes with Eastern influences. The seeds are used lightly ground, but are best given a slight roasting first. Fresh fenugreek leaves are called methi and are sold in halal butchers to be chopped and added to meat and vegetable dishes (see page 247). Fenugreek seeds make dainty, tasty sprouts (see page 93).

GALANGAL

This is a milder relative of ginger, only recently sold fresh in the West as we become keen on Thai and South-East Asian food. There are two varieties, *greater* and *lesser galangal*. Greater galangal is the fleshy white root with thin pink rings most frequently on sale. It has a slightly lemony hint with a pungent rather than fiery flavour. Store it like ginger and use it like ginger too, that is grated or chopped or in thin shreds in sauces, stir-fries and stews. It's traditionally used in conjunction with fresh lemon grass or the flowery kaffir lime leaves. It's one of the old medicinal spices, still popular in herbal medicine today.

GINGER

This ia a rhizome sold fresh as roots, dried in flakes, ground, and steeped in sweet syrup and crystallised. Ginger is also credited with health-giving properties and is said to be good for the digestion.

Fresh root ginger needs fertile soil and good rainfall. It grows well in South-East Asia, where it is still a hand-tended crop. In Australia, however, ginger is grown and harvested by modern methods. Used fresh, it is a main spice in almost all Asian and oriental cooking – the Chinese like to grate fresh ginger using a wooden grater which looks like a doll's wash board. But, until air transport made fresh supplies possible, in Europe ginger was only used dried, so there are many old European recipes that use ground ginger in baking and desserts. The original gingerbread from the 16th century was simply a mixture of ground ginger blended with ground black pepper and stale breadcrumbs bound together with honey then pressed into flat cakes.

Buy plump fresh ginger roots, as large and juicy as you can. Avoid any that are shrivelled or feel dry. The skin should be thin and silky, as if you could almost peel it with a fingernail. It keeps very well if loosely wrapped in a food bag at the base of a fridge. Break off a large knob at a time and peel it thinly with a potato peeler, then grate or slice thinly into discs and chop or cut the discs into shreds. I like to make up a batch of ready chopped ginger which I store in a jar topped up with dry sherry then add in teaspoonfuls to quick and easy stir-fries. Ginger is pre-fried with garlic and green chilli for Indian dishes, often referred to as a wet spice paste, before dried spices are added later on. Ginger juice adds a delicate fragrance to sauces: simply finely grate a little unpeeled ginger and squeeze the juice from the pulp – just a little adds good flavour. And ginger is, of course, the base for that old-time favourite, ginger beer.

TIP: MORNING SICKNESS

Some women eat ginger to counter the miserable nausea of early

pregnancy. I was told a story of a woman who developed a craving

for ginger in every available form: ginger preserve on Melba toast for

breakfast; ginger tea instead of coffee or ordinary tea; ginger ale, ginger

beer and ginger cordial for cold drinks; stir-fried rice heavily laced with

ginger for supper; and stem ginger straight from the jar throughout the

day. On really bad mornings, when nothing could pass her lips, she'd

break off a piece of root ginger and sniff the raw surface. It seemed to

help, and with no side-effects or implications for the baby.

HORSERADISH AND WASABI

Is this a herb or a spice? Horseradish is a branch of the wallflower family and is thought to be one of the bitter herbs eaten by the Jews during the first Passover.

You can't buy dried horseradish except as the Japanese wasabi powder. Sometimes you may find fresh horseradish roots in stores. It has a dirty brown, netted skin and a smell so powerful it can irritate your nostrils and make your eyes smart. The most readily available form is grated horseradish mixed as a relish, a sauce or as creamed horseradish (the mildest). The sharp and mustardy-hot flavour is good, we all know, with beef but it's also tasty with smoked rich fish such as mackerel, trout and salmon. It's nice mixed into beetroot salad or if just a hint is stirred into creamy mashed potatoes.

Wasabi is a relative of horseradish, with a similar pungency but slightly sharper flavour. You buy it as a green powder to mix with water to a thick paste. Serve very small mounds of it with Japanese sushi or sashimi. It's often eaten in conjunction with pink pickled ginger, a surprisingly good combination.

JUNIPER

Small, charcoal grey/purple semi-soft dried berries with a slightly pine-scented odour. They're not widely available, so if you spot a jar grab it because juniper stores well. There are several legends about juniper warding off evil spirits and it is extensively used in herbal medicine and aromatherapy. They're classic with game, especially hare and wild rabbit. Juniper is the flavouring for gin, Dutch gin and Schnapps.

LEMON GRASS

Flowery and fresh, these juicy stems with bulbous bases impart an exotic citrus flavour whenever they are used. Classic in South-East Asian cuisine, they are now catching on fast in the West. It's a fragrance known since the time of the ancient Romans and Greeks, who used it in bathing. Lemon grass is grown in many parts of India, South-East Asia, South America and South Africa.

Personally, I do not recommend the dried or puréed forms of lemon grass: can't see the point when it is nearly always available fresh and it keeps well, bagged and in the fridge, for a couple of weeks.

Use one stem at a time for general flavouring. Strip off any hard outer layers, trim the base and chop or slice finely. (If the stem is woody split it down the middle to the bulb.) Add whole to whatever dish you are cooking, then remove it after. Lemon grass makes a heavenly scented light salad dressing steeped in vinaigrette.

LIME LEAVES

The fantastically fragrant lime flavour of these leaves, also known as Kaffir lime leaves, are another essential of South-East Asian cooking. The leaves look a little like dark, glossy green bay leaves. The tender leaves can be finely shredded and used in Thai green curries but they're also good in any chicken, seafood or pork dish, and nice in puddings too. Whole leaves add colour but should not be eaten. They dry well, so a pot in your dark and dry storecupboard is recommended. Or buy a bunch of fresh leaves and let them dry naturally uncovered in the fridge.

LIQUORICE

Originally from the Middle East, liquorice spread all over Europe and was grown by monks in many monastic gardens. The strong aniseed flavouring is extracted from the rhizome roots and is used to make confectionery (both sweet and salty), in drinks (Sambuca liqueur and stout), and even in cough medicines. Liquorice sticks are the dried stems of the plants.

MANGO POWDER

This is also known as *amchoor*, a powder from sharp, under-ripe mangoes. It is used in a similar way to tamarind as a sweet-sour flavouring for curries, vegetables, chutneys and marinades. One teaspoon is equal to the juice of one lemon.

MUSTARDS

Like peppercorns, mustards come in varying strengths and colours – white, brown and black. Not only do the seeds vary but so do the mixtures they are blended into, depending on additional ingredients.

Black mustard seeds (from a plant related to wallflowers) are the most pungent and are often used in Indian cooking for simple vegetable side dishes or dhals. Because they are very bouncy, tip them gently into the hot pan for pre-frying, then be prepared for them to start popping madly – you might like to cover with a mesh frying pan cover. Apparently they are also rather tricky to grow and can be harvested only by hand. *Brown mustard seeds* are less pungent but can used in the same way as black seeds. *White (or yellow)* mustard seeds are the whole seeds used not just in mustard mixtures but also in pickling spice blends.

The 'mustard' seed in salad cress punnets is often not true mustard but a rape seed, unless the pack is labelled 'traditional hot mustard and cress'.

Mustard blends

Mustard pastes are blends of ground powder, or flour, with salt, vinegars, sugars and sometimes horseradish. *Dijon mustard* is a blend of brown powder with a sour grape juice or wine. *Bordeaux* (also known as French) mustard is black and brown powder mixed with vinegar and tarragon. *Meaux mustard* (the speckled French mustard) is the mixture of lightly crushed seeds also called wholegrain mustard: good brands are Maille, Pommery, Grey Poupon, and the English company Gordon's. *Honey or sweet mustard* is spicy mustard seeds, crushed and blended with fragrant honey, a variation on the sweet–spicy flavour barometer. *German and Finnish mustards* suit mildly salty cured sausages or aromatic cheeses. The Italian sweet mustard-preserved fruits – *mostarda di Cremona* – complements ham or boiled beef, although to my mind it is an acquired taste but I do know a leading Michelin-starred chef who will happily eat almost a whole jar in secret! *American mustards* are mild and creamy with a gentle tanginess: French's, in squeegee bottles, is the best-known name and the one we see squirted over hot dogs. *English yellow mustard*, as in Colman's, is a blend of ground seeds, a little flour and a touch of yellow turmeric.

Using mustard

Black mustard seeds are good fried then tossed into coarsely grated carrots mixed with fresh lemon juice for a simple salad or curry relish. Blend wholegrain mustard with soft brown sugar as a glaze for roasted ham and whisk French mustard into a vinaigrette dressing with clear honey.

Mustard powder can be used as a thickener, but do so sparingly because it will blow your head off in large amounts. It also enhances flavour in a dish – try adding a little mustard to cheese sauce, or sprinkle dried mustard powder over beef before roasting.

NIGELLA

The little black seeds of nigella, also known as *kalonji*, are sometimes mistaken for black cumin or black onion seeds. They're used in Indian cooking. Heat them first to release their slightly fiery but quite mild and aromatic flavour before tossing with grated vegetables or mixing into vegetable dishes.

NUTMEG AND MACE

At one time a European gentleman would carry about his person a little silver nutmeg-shaped container. One side would contain a whole nutmeg and the other a little miniature grater. The idea being one would grind a little fresh nutmeg into hot toddies and mulled wine. A native of the famous Molucca Islands, nutmeg is now commercially grown in Indonesia and Grenada, West Indies.

Nutmegs are fleshy, yellow-skinned fruits containing a hard central nut enclosed in a fibrous casing. The fruit is discarded, the casing carefully peeled off to be dried and sold as blade mace and the nut is, of course, what we call the nutmeg. Both spices last a very long time.

Nutmeg is an all-purpose flavouring: it's chiefly used in sweet dishes but is also wonderful freshly grated over pasta, spinach and over crisp cabbage or buttery carrots. It's good, too, grated directly on to whipped cream or cappuccino coffee. Mace is generally used for savoury recipes, such as mashed potato, fish sauces and ketchups, but take care not to add too much or it will taste bitter. If you are keen to learn about how spices affected the course of history, read Giles Milton's book *Nathaniel's Nutmeg*.

PEPPERCORNS

The world's most popular spice, essential to practically every cuisine. Peppercorns grow on vines, sometimes even up existing trees, in several parts of the tropical world. It is thought the plant originated along the south-west coast of India and the province of Kerala is still one of the best production areas. Until the introduction of chillies into India in the 16th century, peppercorns were the main source of spicy heat and they still feature prominently in Indian dishes.

Varieties of peppercorns
All colours of peppercorns come from the same plant and differ in strength according to the degree of ripeness.

Green peppercorns are the unripe berries and taste more aromatic than fiery. You can sometimes buy them fresh still attached to a vine stalk: otherwise you will see them dried and lightly shrivelled or pickled in brine or vinegar, although this has an effect on the flavour of the berries. They are popular in Thai cookery and are also used in European foods, often in pâté mixtures or pressed on to the surface of steaks. Add a quick spicy aroma to a simple chicken casserole by adding ½–1tsp of lightly crushed green peppercorns to the pot, then serve with a swirl of double cream and a sprinkling of chopped fresh coriander.

Black peppercorns are green berries that have been spread out to dry in the sun for about a week until the skins turn black and shrivelled. They can be coarsely ground and used as a coating. Creole-style blackened cooking requires cracked pepper, so either set your pepper mill to a loose setting, or crush whole peppercorns in a pestle and mortar.

White peppercorns are ripened whole peppercorns that are soaked and left to soften in running water. This loosens the outer skins, which can be rubbed off, and the inner peppercorns are then sun-dried. This makes the peppercorns hot and spicy rather than aromatic. White peppercorns are traditionally used with white fish or in creamy sauces when you don't want dark flecks to show.

Black and white peppercorns are sold not just whole but also ground. Ground pepper, black and white, has quite a fiery flavour with less aroma. It's better to buy whole corns and grind them yourself but, as they're quite difficult to find, when you see them buy a pack. They keep a long time.

Pink peppercorns are not of the same botanical family: they are the berry of a plant from the North American poison ivy family. At one time, pink peppercorns were all the rage in trend-setting restaurants until reports of ill-effects caused the fashion to nose-dive. But, moderation in all things: a little of what you fancy will do little harm. Limit the use to around ½tsp at a time. They're available dried or pickled.

Sichuan pepper (also known as Farcheiw spice) is not a true peppercorn but the dried berries and stalks of a prickly ash tree. It's perhaps one of my favourite spices, popular in Chinese and Japanese cooking, but I find its delicious woody aroma useful in many Western dishes too. Use it in the same way as whole peppercorns – for example, it's wonderful ground over scrambled eggs or smoked salmon.

TIP: PEPPER BLENDS

You can buy a mixture of black, white, green and pink corns to use in pepper mills. Professional chefs, however often prefer to make up their own personalised mixtures and you might like to do this too. Use a base of half black peppercorns then add in varying proportions according to your own tastes white peppercorns, some all-spice berries, a few whole cardamoms, some crushed cinnamon bark, a few cracked star anise, some whole cloves – in fact anything that will grind. Make up a large batch and store in a jar.

Seasoning with pepper

When tasting a dish to check on seasoning take care not too add too much. Pepper develops its flavour gradually so, after you have added a sprinkling of ground pepper, wait for 5 minutes or so for the flavour to develop before adding more.

One of the common causes of over-seasoning is adding too much pepper. Peppercorns can be used in all savoury dishes, but are good too in sugar syrups – at one time it was fashionable to grind pepper over strawberries, but try it over pineapple or fresh figs.

SAFFRON

This has the distinction of being the world's most expensive spice because it is estimated that it takes some 70,000 saffron crocus flowers to make a pound of spice. The best quality saffron is the Mancha coupe grade from south-eastern Spain. The saffron produced in Iran and India is ideal for Iranian and Indian dishes but is not, I find, suitable for European recipes. I've even come across Yemeni 'saffron' which had a curiously unfamiliar aroma (I mention this out of loyalty to my birthplace). Saffron used to be a very important crop in England

and during the 16th century was considered to be the finest in the world. Now all we are left with are place names – Saffron Walden, Saffron Hill and so on.

Quality saffron will have mostly red stamens and a very distinctive deep, sweet, flowery, aromatic fragrance. Buy it in the tiniest amounts because all you need are a few stamens at a time, say 6–8. Sometimes saffron is sold in a small coloured cellophane wrapper within a tall jar, other times you can buy about 0.5–1g at a time in small plastic pots. It's a lovely gift to give keen cooks.

USING SAFFRON

To use saffron you have to heat it slightly to release the aroma. So either heat a small dry frying pan, crush in a few stamens, heat for a few seconds then add to the dish, or dissolve a pinch of stamens in about 2tbsp of boiling water, then loosely stir the yellow/gold liquid (including the stamens) into cooked rice for the rippled effect you get on good Indian pilaus. Saffron is the classic spice to use for real paellas, risotto milanese and, of course, Cornish saffron cake. Try it too stirred into creamy mashed potatoes, sauces or a fish soup.

SPICE BLENDS

There is an increasing number of these now, from traditional British ground mixed spice to Indian garam masalas. *Garam masala* is simply a general Indian term for spice mix, and most Indian cooks use their own blends and strengths depending on the dish. Spice blends are mostly mild and aromatic, to be added at the end of cooking to spike up the spice aroma. *Chinese five spice* is a blend of anise pepper, cassia, fennel, star anise and cloves all ground to a fine powder. It's used in rich sauces and relishes such as the barbecue hoisin sauce. There are traditional spice mixes from other countries, such as *Mozambican peri peri, Moroccan ras el hanout* and *Japanese seven spice powder* (aka *shichimi togarashi*), a blend of sesame seeds, ginger, Sichuan pepper, seaweed and orange peel, used in *yakitori.*

STAR ANISE

One of the magnolia family, native to south-east China. The highly aromatic star anise is a little, woody, five-pointed star containing small shiny brown seeds. Often just one star is enough to add a sweet, woody pungency to a dish. It's good in sweet and savoury dishes – in Chinese braised red-cooked dishes, also in homely casseroles – and popular with French chefs in game dishes and to flavour rich red wine sauces. I break up a few and add them to a peppercorn mixture for grinding in a peppermill. Sprayed silver or gold, they also make good Christmas decorations, especially for the front door Christmas wreath! The essential oil is burnt as an incense in Japan.

SUMAC

An Iranian wild red berry which is dried and ground to a powder. It's often sprinkled over dishes just before serving to add a sweet sharpness. I especially enjoy it over buttery basmati into which I have mixed a little fresh chopped dill weed and a few broad beans. Barbaries are similar berries. Sumac, the tree (aka Staghorn) is a popular plant in many British gardens. I found I have one. The dried small berries can be used in cooking.

TAMARIND

Another flavour enhancer of the Indian kitchen sold either 'fresh' as pods (the tamarind is a legume), dried or in a paste which you dilute with water. The distinctive tamarind flavour adds a sharpness to curries and sauces. It's good, too, in chutneys and relishes. Lemon juice is an acceptable substitute. But a pot of paste costs very little and lasts and lasts.

TURMERIC

Turmeric (also known as **haldi**) is generally sold ground as a bright yellow ochre powder, but occasionally you can find fresh turmeric sold as light brown skin roots with bright yellow flesh and a fresh, mildly spicy flavour. Although a very gentle spice in terms of heat, turmeric has a lingering aroma and an overwhelming ability to stain anything that it comes into contact with, including your hands. Another of the curry spices, turmeric is popular in many cuisines as a gentle colouring and flavouring agent. It is sometimes unfairly thought of as the poor man's saffron, because a tiny pinch does an awful lot of colouring in rice pilaus, soups, sauces, piccalillis etc. Take care not to get too carried away using it because the colour deepens to a dull brown if you use too much. Start with ¼tsp and then let your mixture stand for a few minutes before you decide if more is needed.

VANILLA

Occasionally you might come across an unusual souvenir – an ornamental crocodile shaped from a vanilla pod. It's one of the speciality crafts of the island of Madagascar, the world's largest producer of this vital spice. A member of the orchid family, vanilla pods have to undergo a lengthy drying process before they achieve the familiar dark and delicious, glossy black sheen and sweet, slightly smoky fragrance. You can buy vanilla as pods (the gourmet's choice) or as a highly concentrated and expensive extract. If you buy it in liquid form and it appears cheap, check the label – it may be an artificial flavouring.

Vanilla is one of the main sweet flavourings for ice cream, custards, cakes, biscuits, yogurts, and much more. To use the pods whole (one per recipe is ample), slit them lengthways and open out. Inside you will see a sticky mass, which you should scrape out with the tip of a sharp knife. These are vanilla seeds: they give a characteristic speckled black appearance to real vanilla ice cream and sauces. The scraped pods can be steeped in hot milk or cream. French chefs use vanilla in light cream savoury sauces to serve with fish: it's good, honest.

SAUCES AND PASTES

It is possible to vary the simplest of stews, marinades and dressings just by the addition of a sauce. Many countries have their own specialities stretching back centuries. Now with the globalisation of foodstuffs we can have an eclectic selection on our shelves. Most of them keep for years, but why store them unused? Experiment, mix and match!

ORIENTAL SAUCES AND PASTES

BEAN SAUCES

These are sold under various names. These are Chinese-style sauces such as yellow bean or black bean garlic. They are generally thick pastes flavoured with fermented soya beans, garlic, spices, sugar etc. Genuine oriental bean sauces are really condiments to be used 1–2tbsp at a time, not thinner versions of pour-over sauces. I mention this because I've come across first-time users who have used a whole jar of paste in a recipe with overwhelmingly powerful results.

BONITO AND DASHI

Bonito – shaved and dried tuna flakes – is one of the essentials in Japanese cooking. It's used to flavour dashi, the traditional Japanese broth made from dried kelp. Instant dashi is sold in sachets or jars, or you could make your own fresh with the help of a Japanese recipe book.

HOISIN SAUCE

Hoisin sauce is a soya bean paste mixed with sugar, salt, garlic, chilli peppers and other Chinese spices such as a hint of star anise. The name apparently means 'flavour of the sea'. Most Chinese food lovers associate it with crispy Peking duck, spread quickly on steamed pancakes to be topped with shredded duck and onions, but its potential goes far beyond this. Like oyster sauce, it can be used with meat, seafood, vegetables and noodles. Play around with hoisin (sparingly, at first) and use it in salad dressings, dipping sauces, as a barbecue sauce, etc. Good hoisin is a dark, reddish-brown, syrupy and very glossy. It is very concentrated so a little goes a long way.

LAKSA

Laksa means 'soup' in the Malaysian or Singaporean kitchen but it's now used as a term for a spicy paste added to noodles, vegetables and other tasty variations on a Malay theme. The main ingredients include dried shrimp, fish pastes, chilli, garlic, lime and palm sugar. It was made popular in the West by Australian chefs. You use the paste by diluting about 2tbsp with a little boiling water. *Laksa lemak* is a coconut milk sauce that can be found fresh in some supermarket chill cabinets and sold as a noodle sauce.

MISO

Miso, or soya bean paste, is made from soaked, boiled beans mixed with fermented grains, usually barley or rice. Each region of Japan tends to have its own version of this essential ingredient, the grains and proportions of other ingredients used determining the varieties. Miso is generally served as a broth combined with dashi and is very nutritious, rich in minerals and proteins. I particularly like the sachets of instant miso soup, adding finely sliced mushrooms or a few sprigs of watercress to a cup of hot broth. Look out for the rich and dark Mugi, Genmia and Hatcho miso brands and the lighter and sweeter Shiro. Miso is also available in paste form: slake them down with a little water before using. White and yellow pastes are sweeter and milder for summer food: red and brown add richer flavour to winter stews and soups.

NAM PLA

This Thai fish sauce might be an acquired taste for Westerners but they soon learn to enjoy it. Nam pla is made from fermenting small fish and is a speciality of Thailand increasingly used over many parts of South-East Asia. Fish sauce is to Thai cooking what soy sauce is to Chinese and Japanese food, or what garum was to the ancient Romans. It has a distinctively pungent aroma that mellows on cooking. It's sold under many brand names in a variety of amber hues. The lighter the colour, the better the quality though it does darken once opened so use it up quickly. The Vietnamese version is known as nuoc mam and is a little stronger in flavour.

THAI-STYLE SALAD DRESSING
Good for tossing into crisp green leaves or as a dipping sauce.

120ml (4fl oz) sunflower oil
3tbsp rice wine vinegar
1tbsp dark soy sauce
1tbsp Thai fish sauce (nam pla)
1tbsp sweet chilli sauce
1tbsp crunchy peanut butter
1 garlic clove, crushed
1tsp freshly grated galangal or root ginger
½ tsp sea salt
1tsp caster sugar
freshly ground black pepper

Place all the ingredients in a small saucepan, adding pepper to taste, and heat slowly until dissolved, stirring. Remove, allow to cool, then store in a screw-topped jar. This dressing will keep for two weeks in the fridge.

OYSTER SAUCE

Oyster sauce is an example of one of those (apparently) happy culinary accidents that became a classic dish or ingredient – after all, good cooks are constantly experimenting. In 1888, a Mr Lee Kum Sheung let oysters simmer for too long in the pot. Instead of throwing them out, he found the rich, concentrated juice that formed was ideal for flavouring. He had created the first oyster sauce, which is now produced all over the Far East by many other companies though the original is still marketed by Lee Kum Kee.

So, unlike the ancient soy sauce, oyster sauce is a mere babe with a history of not much more than a hundred years. It differs from soy sauce in that it has a more pronounced sweet-salty balance and has a slightly thicker texture. However, oyster and soy sauces are often used in combination.

There are qualities of oyster sauce. The label of a genuine sauce will say 'oyster flavoured', meaning it contains extracts of real oysters. Vegetarian oyster sauce is made with shiitake mushrooms.

PLUM SAUCE

Plum sauce is a pale, sweet/savoury, thin, sticky sauce flavoured with plums and a hint of garlic and ginger – not to be confused with plum chutney or even hoisin sauce. It's another sauce for spreading on Chinese pancakes with duck or for adding to stir-fries as in the chicken with plum sauce dish found on menus.

SHRIMP PASTES

The salted fish theme is echoed around the Orient not only as liquid sauces but also as salted and dried prawns. Whole dried shrimps (*kung haeng*) are actually very useful to have in store – soaked in brine then dried they keep almost indefinitely and need only be soaked in a little boiling water to reconstitute. But make sure you buy brightly coloured ones, if possible, as they are fresher. Use them tossed into Thai-style fried rice with diced pineapple, Thai fish sauce, lemon grass and a little coconut milk.

Malayan and Singaporean cooks use a paste called *belacan* that is highly pungent and needs to be flattened and lightly fried before use. Open the kitchen windows wide when cooking with this.

Kapi is the Thai equivalent of belacan. You buy it fresh (so keep it chilled and use it soonest) or dried. Thai producers go to great lengths to stress how high in vitamin B and proteins these products are – I just think they taste good.

SOY SAUCES

Soy sauce (not 'soya' for some inexplicable reason) is the product of the humble but versatile soya bean, which benefits man in very many ways, nutritionally and commercially. It not only nourishes, it can also add flavour.

The brewing of soy sauce is thought to go back over 2,500 years. The rise of Buddhism led the new vegetarian disciples to seek non-meat flavourings. It was found that by fermenting mashed soya beans and mixing them with salt, a well-seasoned condiment resulted.

There are three ways soy sauce can be produced. The best-known method is 'naturally brewed', made by fermenting soya beans and wheat in water and salt. There are three main stages: first, adding the koji – the starter; second, the brewing and fermentation which takes up to six months and involves enzyme activity; and finally the refining, where the resultant reddish-brown 'mash' is pressed to release the liquid which is then pasteurised, matured further and bottled. Sauces made by this method have a greater depth of flavour and more natural balance of sweetness to saltiness. Of the naturally brewed brands, the best known is Kikkoman – but beware of imitations: I have been in Chinese restaurants where the distinctive Kikkoman bottles are placed on the tables, but the sauce inside is definitely not naturally brewed. You might also find the Chinese brand Lee Kum Kee. *Shoyu* is the general name for Japanese soy sauce made in the natural way and matured for up to two years in cedarwood casks, giving it a unique depth of flavour. A good brand name is Sanchi. *Tamari* is a Japanese soy sauce made without wheat. It's popular with health food followers and served with sushi.

Non-brewed soy sauce is made by a more rapid (and cheaper) process that involves blending hydrolysed plant proteins with water, salt, corn syrup and caramel colouring, producing a sauce within three days. Or you can buy soy sauce that is made by a combination of the two styles.

Other Far Eastern countries have their own styles of soy sauce. *Ketjap* is a rich, sweetened Indonesian soy sauce.

Soy sauces are made in two strengths, light and dark. The first is used in vegetable, egg, fish and rice dishes: the second is richer and with a slightly sweet flavour that is ideal for beef, duck and richer sauces. It's also good as a dipping sauce.

Don't limit the use of soy sauce to Chinese or Japanese food. It's a good all-purpose seasoning and especially useful for adding quick flavours to stews or soups instead of stock cubes. Reduced salt soy sauces are increasingly available.

Soy sauce marinades

Various companies produce ready-made marinades that are basically added-value soy sauce. Kikkoman Teriyaki and Sukiyaki are two, the Lee Kum Kee Chicken Marinade another. Check the label for added sweetener, vinegar or spices. They're good all-purpose marinades ideal for all grilled and pan-fried dishes, not just oriental style

---

COOKING WITH ORIENTAL SAUCES

Chinese, Japanese and South-East Asian cooks use many ready-made bottled sauces as condiments, unlike Europeans who, until recently, did not rate bottled sauces too highly or confused them with ready-made pour-over sauces.

Many of the authentic oriental sauces are highly concentrated: you need to add just two or three spoonfuls or even smaller amounts at a time. Oriental cooks prepare a selection of fresh meat or fish and vegetables, then toss them into delicious dishes adding sauces in the same way as artists mix colours on a palette. I mention this because I have noticed that many Europeans are put off buying genuine sauces because of the marginally higher price. In fact they are much better value, lasting twice or three times as long as ready-made pour-over sauces.

SWEET CHILLI SAUCE

This is found in many parts of South-East Asia and is used as a dipping sauce. The best-known Thai sauce comes from a town called Siracha. Sweet chilli sauce is sold as red or yellow and in varying strengths. It's very good as a quick crudité sauce if you're entertaining or if you've bought some heat-and-serve spring rolls.

TOM YUM

Another soup paste, this time from Thailand. Tom Yum is based on the same type of ingredients as laksa and needs diluting in the same way – about 2tbsp of paste with a little boiling water. Toss into noodles or stir straight into a bubbling pot of water, then add chopped or finely sliced mushrooms, tomatoes, prawns or cooked chicken, some sliced lemon grass and fresh coriander for a traditional Thai soup.

XO SAUCE

This is a very expensive specialised Chinese paste made from shredded dried scallops, dried prawns, chillies and other Chinese flavourings. I love it, especially a small spoonful stirred into a bowl of steaming Jasmine rice for a light lunch. It's also good as a dim sum dipping sauce and on noodles, sushi and so forth. Lee Kum Kee is a good brand.

NON-ORIENTAL SAUCES AND PASTES

The orientals aren't the only creators of rich seasoning sauces. Over in Britain, cooks add splashes of flavourings to dishes such as mushroom ketchup and anchovy essence. And where would we be without wonderful Worcestershire sauce?

ANGOSTURA BITTERS

Angostura bitters was created in 1824 as a fever cure by a Dr Siegert, a young German surgeon with General Bolivar's liberation army in Venezuela. Using tropical herbs and flavourings, including gentian, quinine, spices, rum and citrus peel, he called his sauce after the town where he made it, Angostura (now Ciudad Bolivar), though the company later upped sticks and moved to the safer haven of Trinidad. The perfect partner for pink gin, for those who drink it, Angostura is also delicious shaken over fruit and ice creams and used in mincemeat, Christmas pud etc. The makers also recommend adding it to savoury sauces and stews, which I've yet to try.

HOT PEPPER SAUCES

These are a feature of West Indian, Mexican and Louisiana cooking. They are basically variations on the theme of chopped red hot chillies steeped in vinegar and salt. The most famous is Tabasco, made by the McIhenney family on Avery Island in Louisiana. Tabasco is the name of the actual variety of chilli used (see page 103), which is mashed and left to ferment in barrels for three years then blended with vinegar and matured again. The same company also makes a milder green *Jalapeno sauce*. Cajun chefs like to use a pepper sauce called *Louisiana Gold*. Encona makes a similar sauce in Jamaica, using the decorative Scotch bonnet chillies – possibly the world's hottest chilli.

All these sauces should be added a little drop at a time unless you are an experienced chilli eater or a masochist. *Harissa*, from Morocco, is not a sauce as such, more a paste mixed with garlic and spices such as caraway, cumin, coriander and salt. You dilute it with a little water and stir into couscous or add it to stews and tagines to liven them up a little – or a lot.

MUSHROOM KETCHUP

If you salt mushrooms and drain them, in time they exude a liquid which when boiled down becomes a 'ketchup'. It's particularly good added at the end of a nice steak and kidney casserole or shaken over pan-fried liver or kidneys. Look for the Watkins brand name on a distinctive Victorian-style label.

PATUM PEPERIUM

Another of the highly flavoured condiments to come from 19th-century Britain – well, to be exact, from an Englishman living in Paris. In 1828, John Osborn made a rich paste of salted anchovies, butter, herbs and spices to spread on toast. It apparently took the Parisians by storm and became such a favourite of the English gentry that it acquired the nickname Gentlemen's Relish.

WORCESTERSHIRE SAUCE

Britain has its own 'happy accident' sauce story. In the early 1800s a governor of Bengal returned to his native shores with his cook's recipe for a relish. It included salted fish, garlic, chillies and soy sauce. He asked the local chemists in Worcester – Lea, Perrins & Smith – to make it up for him. They made too much and put the remainder in their cellar and promptly forgot about it until three years later when it was rediscovered and sipped. The maturation had turned it into a mellow and rich sauce that soon had them rushing back to their records for the recipe. Nowadays the recipe includes tamarind, cloves, shallots and the original anchovies, garlic and chillies. But no soy sauce – that was dropped during the Second World War. Now other manufacturers make the sauce but the original is still the best.

The company think most of the sauce is used as dashes for Bloody Marys, but you will find it in Chinese supermarkets, in Arab shops and presumably there are Indian cooks who must find it vaguely reminiscent of a sauce 'back home'. Worcestershire sauce (not Worcester, please) enhances many sauces, stews and soups from the mild and cheesy to the rich, aromatic and beefy. A few years ago, I remember, Lea & Perrins suggested marinating chicken breasts in a whole bottle of Worcestershire sauce before grilling. It actually tasted good, although a little on the spicy side. Worcestershire sauce continues to mature once opened so unless you use a lot of it, buy in small bottles.

OILS, VINEGARS AND SALTS

Opposites attract but if mixed together can blend into a harmonious emulsion. Certainly this is the case with all oils and acidic liquids. Both of these substances have been part of Mankind's food chain since he learned to mix foods together. Oils come from animal and vegetable sources, vinegars from vegetable and fruit sources. Both vary greatly in terms of availability and eating and cooking quality.

OILS

The difference in classification between fat and oil is that at room temperature, normally around 20°C, oil is liquid while fat is solid. They are both a combination of fatty acids and alcohol, normally glycerine. The fatty acids have an odour that gives the oil its distinguishing characteristic. Oils are also categorised according to their saturation level of fatty acids, which determines how healthy they. are. Saturated fats can raise cholesterol levels in our bloodstreams: at the other end of the scale are polyunsaturated fats, which can help lower cholesterol levels. In between are the mono-unsaturated fats, which are beneficial as they regulate our blood cholesterol levels.

Cholesterol is further divided into two groups of lipoproteins, which nutritionists divide into two camps. The goodies are high-density lipoproteins (HDL), which perform the function of clearing arteries: the baddies are low-density lipoproteins (LDL), which can clog up our arteries. An oil high in mono-unsaturated fats can be beneficial in reducing the build-up of harmful cholesterol in our bloodstream. So, when you check the nutritional label on an oil bottle, look for the percentages of the various fat levels. This, I find, is also a good indication of the eating quality of an oil. Oils with a higher level of polyunsaturated fatty acids tend to be lighter.

When it comes to calorie levels, however, all oils have around the same value, i.e. 800 calories per 100ml (or, put another way, about 80 calories for each dessertspoonful). So they are all as fattening as each other. The difference in terms of health is the role they play in reducing cholesterol levels in your bloodstream.

VEGETABLE OILS

Vegetable oils are pressed from the nuts, seeds and fruits of oil-rich plants. If you press or crush them just as they are you will get a fairly small amount of readily available oil, a process known as cold pressing. If you then lightly heat the residue of crushed pulp and press that again you will receive a further amount of oil, not as pure (or virgin) as the first pressing but still of good quality. Further heating, washing and crushing of the residue will result in yet more oil but of an inferior quality. It's more worthwhile subjecting oils with delicious aromas and flavours to an initial cold pressing as they can command a premium price. This helps explain the differences in qualities and prices. Let's look at specific oils.

OLIVE OIL

The best-known oil, possibly also the oldest cultivated by mankind. It is thought that the eastern Mediterranean was the birthplace of olives six thousand years ago, and they've been significant in history ever since.

Olives grow on medium-height trees in quite arid conditions. The main growth areas in the Mediterranean are Spain (Europe's largest producer supplier), Italy, Greece, Turkey, the South of France (Provence), and North Africa. Oils also are made locally in the eastern Mediterranean and further afield in California and Australia. Olive trees can grow to a great age, certainly over a hundred years, and still produce fruit of excellent quality. If you ever have the opportunity to visit an olive oil mill during the harvest around November, the first aroma to reach your nose, curiously, is that of freshly picked tomatoes. Ripe olives do indeed smell of this fruit, which is quite appropriate given their affinity with tomatoes.

Olives grown for commercial purposes are harvested in a semi-mechanical way, involving various methods of shaking the branches and collecting the olives in nets. Prime quality olives, however, are hand picked which, of course, adds to the end cost. Olives for the table are pickled in brine – black or purple fruits being riper than green ones.

The flavour and quality of an olive oil depends on the variety, the growing climate and soil and the farming methods. Much olive oil is blended, but the top qualities will come from individual estates and be crushed and bottled locally. You can pay a high price for such olive oil but if you choose wisely the benefits are enormous. Olive oils do differ from one region to another in terms of characteristics, flavour and viscosity.

Classification of olive oils

Olive oil is a subject of great passion and debate. Classifications can reach the same intensity of study as fine wines and cheeses. Novices can gain an initial broad outline from the bottle label.

Extra virgin cold pressed olive oil should come from the first initial pressings of olives and in theory you should be able to detect a definite aroma and character to the oil.

Tasters also note the colour of the oil. Often very first pressings will be a slightly cloudy olive green, but a lighter-coloured oil is not an indication of inferior quality: Provence oils, for instance, are lighter in colour than Tuscan but both can be classified as being of excellent quality, just different in style.

It is worth being aware of the difference between the phrases 'bottled in' and 'produce of' on a label. There is much trading between olive oil countries. The region of Andalusia in southern Spain, for example, exports much of its oil to neighbouring EU partner Italy, where it can be refined and bottled. The label may say 'extra virgin' and 'bottled in Italy' (or even Tuscany), but the oil inside may be Spanish. That is not to say it is a poor-quality oil, indeed it is probably an excellent one, but you could be forgiven for thinking it is oil from Italian or even Tuscan olives.

TASTING OLIVE OIL

Professional tasters will slurp a little oil at the front of their mouths to detect flavours, then swallow the slurp and note any residual after-effects. Novice tasters have been known to slurp too quickly and be hit with a fiery, peppery sensation at the back of the throat. One can also test an oil aroma by the safer method of rubbing a small amount between warm hands and smelling deeply. Tasters use descriptions such as appley, buttery, grassy, peppery, metallic and almondy.

Experts also use a grading system according to the level of acidity, which you can check on the label. The best acidity level is below 1% – these are the top extra virgin oils. Those in the next category, pure olive oils, fall between 1 and 1.5%, Finally, basic blended olive oils, at between 1.5 and 3%, are ideal for everyday cooking.

As our supermarket shelves expand to accommodate greater numbers of bottles of olive oils from all over Europe (and beyond), you may enjoy sampling them until you discover one that suits your palette and pocket. Spanish oils for example, once thought of as 'rank' and powerful, are now marketed according to fine qualities or single growing regions. We are seeing more Greek oils, single-estate oils from Tuscany, Auplia, Arbruzzo and so on – all with their own little characters. Indeed, I buy my oil from an ex-pat Briton living in Spain (www.mothersgarden.org), who sends me 10 litres a year of the most divinely fragrant extra virgin oil.

Grades of olive oil

The first pressing of the freshly picked olives is done cold, and is known as cold pressed oil. This is a complex classification but, broadly speaking, the main label name will give you a good idea of what is inside the bottle, and on the label.

Extra virgin olive oil The classification depends on the initial process of the pressing of the olives (one harvest batch can go through two or three times) and the level of acidity of the olives, generally around 0.8%. Worldwide, this quality accounts for only about 10% of production, although Mediterranean countries have 30–80% of their national crop at this category.

Virgin olive oil can also be first pressed but might have a higher acidity level, up to 1.5%. Still very good.

Pure olive oil is usually a blend of refined oils (see below) and virgin production oil. Fine for cooking and dressings. Oils labelled simply as olive oil might have a tiny percentage of extra virgin oil topped up with refined production olive oils from anywhere.

HOMEMADE MAYONNAISE

Please note that this recipe uses raw eggs, and observe the precautions on Storing and using eggs on pages 65–6.

Put 2 organic free-range egg yolks into a deep medium-sized bowl with 2 good pinches of sea salt and a few grindings of black pepper (you can also add one or two crushed garlic cloves). Stand the bowl on a damp cloth to hold it steady.

Measure 150ml (5fl oz) of light olive oil and 150ml (5fl oz) of sunflower, safflower or groundnut oil into a jug. Trickle 2tsp on to the egg yolks and beat well with a wire whisk until smooth. Add another 1tsp of oil and whisk again.

Continue like this, slowly at first, adding the oil very, very gradually so it has time to blend into an emulsion (the gritty seasonings help the binding process). I find it easier to dribble the oil off the teaspoon and just dip it into the oil pot rather than pour it out in such tiny amounts.

The mixture should become thicker, pale yellow in colour and glossy. If it stays thin and separates out when you stop whisking then you have added the oil too quickly, in which case you should start again by beating another yolk in a separate bowl with seasoning and slowly trickling the curdled thin mixture on to that, whisking well.

Once the thick emulsion is established, you can gradually add the oil in larger amounts, 1tbsp at a time, but it is essential to get a thick emulsion first. Finally, when most of the oil is added, whisk in 1–2tbsp white wine or rice wine vinegar or the juice of ½ lemon plus 2tbsp of water if the emulsion is very thick. This will thin down the sauce, and you then add the rest of the oil. Cover and set aside in the fridge to rest.

Using olive oil

Extra virgin olive oil has a fine aroma when heated and it is generally regarded as a waste to cook with it as such. However, this does not mean you can't trickle it over hot food as a flavouring or use it in the same way as butter. There is nothing more delicious than a good plate of perfect *al dente* pasta dressed with fine extra virgin olive oil plus a little garlic and maybe some chopped fresh parsley. Or try it over new potatoes, sliced ripe tomatoes or roasted peppers. Mediterranean folk like to dip fresh bread into good olive oil in the same way that we butter bread. The list of uses is endless.

If you intend cooking with olive oil, then use a pure olive oil, not extra virgin. It's wonderful for frying a lovely fresh organic egg or for sautéeing sliced potatoes. For mayonnaise it's best to use a pure olive oil or half pure olive oil mixed with half sunflower or some other more neutral oil (extra virgin oil is too pungent and gives a green-hued sauce). Some manufacturers have done just that and sell an oil blend called SunOlive, a good all-purpose, high-quality cooking oil.

Mayonnaise is the best summer sauce in the world. Making your own is wonderfully therapeutic and rewarding and is a classic example of blending oil into an emulsion with eggs and vinegar. To shorten the process you can use a food processor or electric blender. Homemade mayonnaise is quite, quite different from shop-bought mayo, which tastes of inferior, bland oil.

BLENDER MAYO

The same basic principles apply as with mayonnaise made in a bowl, except you use 1 whole egg and 1 yolk. Blend these in the jug with the blades running with a little seasoning and a tiny trickle of oil. Get a good emulsion established first then, with the machine still running, trickle in the rest of the oil very slowly – dribbling from a spoon is a good hint. Some new food processors have an oil-dripping hole fitted to the funnel which is ideal for mayonnaise making. The resultant sauce is a little paler in colour than handmade mayo.

OTHER OILS AND COOKING OILS

(See also separate entries under Nuts and Seeds, pages 197–207.)

These include sunflower, corn/maize, groundnut/peanut, safflower, coconut and vegetable oil blends. A good cooking oil will have a fairly neutral flavour and be able to heat to a high temperature without breaking down. This causes an accumulation of fatty acids and leads to a rancid flavour, increasing with each time the oil is heated and cooled. Shallow-frying requires only a small amount of oil that is used just once and usually incorporated into the dish.

Deep-frying is best done with oil that can withstand being used a number of times as each time it is heated it deteriorates further. To minimise this, the oil should be cooled, then strained through a muslin-lined sieve (or a clean J Cloth) to ensure no debris of crumbs or food remains. The best oils for deep-frying are groundnut, vegetable blends and corn oil because they can be heated to a higher temperature without breaking down. Sunflower oil is OK for occasional deep-frying but becomes sticky with prolonged use. Animal fats (i.e. solid fat such as lard, beef dripping, goose fat and ghee) are good for deep-frying so long as they are clarified (or strained) of any residues that might burn. Olive oil is not really suitable unless it is a light blend of oils and used just once or twice, though it does impart a good flavour and is a favourite oil of haute cuisine chefs.

Cooking oil varieties

Sunflower oil is high in polyunsaturates and is thus regarded as a 'healthy' oil. It has a good neutral flavour which makes it ideal for all-round kitchen use – frying, salad dressings, greasing cake tins etc. If you can find it, try extra virgin cold pressed sunflower oil: it has a pleasant taste of sunflower seeds without the bitter or sharp flavour associated with other seed oils.

Safflower oil, extracted from safflowers, is a light, healthy oil and high in vitamin E. It's sometimes found in health food shops but I've not yet seen it in supermarkets. It's popular in France and is one of the oils used in vegetarian ghee. Safflower oil is yellow in colour.

Vegetable oil (aka *rapeseed oil, colza* and *mustard oil*) is a really good all-purpose oil. I have two oils by my cooker – olive oil and this one. It's also good used in dressings. Now sold as cold pressed rapeseed oil to use like extra virgin oils.

Grape seed/pip oil is a nice, light oil chiefly used for salad dressings. Again, it's more popular in France than in the UK. It's good in a half-and-half blend with olive oil for vinaigrettes and nice, too, for frying fish or other light meats.

Pumpkin seed oil is very much one for the niche market. The best is a speciality of the Styria region of Austria, made from a particular variety of huskless and roasted aromatic pumpkin seeds to produce a rich, dark green oil. Use it in the same way as other aromatic oils for trickling and flavouring, though not for frying.

Soya oil is one of the world's most important sources of vegetable oil. It is high in polyunsaturates and mono-unsaturates but has a rather definite flavour. Still – a good all-purpose, healthier cooking oil. Use it sparingly in dressings.

Groundnut oil (also known as arachide or peanut oil) is popular with oriental cooks because you can heat it to a high temperature, up to 218° C. It's high in mono-unsaturates but not so high in polyunsaturates.

Palm oil is popular in West Indian and African homes. It has quite a pleasant flavour but is high in saturated fat, so use it sensibly.

Cottonseed oil is not sold as on its own in shops but is often part of a blend of oils or used as a background oil for canned foods. It's popular in Egyptian cooking.

Hydrogenated oils are oils of polyunsaturates and mono-unsaturates that have been heat-treated to change their molecular structure so they become semi-solid. These are the white cooking fats used in pastry making. Recently, there have been health concerns about using too many hydrogenated oils (or transfats) in our diets.

Blended vegetable oils are variable blends of oils (corn, safflower, soya, rapeseed, cottonseed and even coconut or palm oil) recommended for general frying purposes.

VINEGARS

If you allow a fermented liquid prolonged exposure to the air it will start to turn sour because of the action of bacteria, and produce acetic acid – a good example of beneficial bacteria. No doubt you will have found this out for yourself if you have ever forgotten to recork an unfinished bottle of wine. (Vinegar is different from the centuries-old ingredient verjuice featured in old recipes, which is soured grape or apple juice preserved with salt.)

Vinegars are made from alcoholic beverages of less than 18% alcohol – wine, beer, cider, rice wine, sugar and malt. They are measured in percentages of acetic acid, generally 4–6% but it can be higher if the vinegar is further reduced by boiling or evaporation. Chefs will reduce vinegar by deglazing a dish during cooking to concentrate the flavour. Vinegar is used to preserve foods and to enhance flavours. Cheap coloured vinegar can be just a soured sugar and water mixture with added colouring.

JAM JAR VINAIGRETTE

So easy, it's embarrassing, yet I still see recipes for oil and vinegar dressings made in a jug with a whisk. Working on the basic principle of using three parts oil to one of vinegar, you simply add a mixture of salad-quality oils (e.g. sunflower or grapeseed with a pure olive or extra virgin olive oil) to a clean, screw-topped jam jar. Spoon in about ½tsp of sea salt, ½tsp of caster sugar or a trickle of clear honey (if liked), a touch of French mustard and a few grindings of black pepper. Now add wine or rice wine vinegar in the proportion of 3:1 (so for 3tbsp of oil, add I tbsp of vinegar). Screw on the lid and shake well. Use what you need and store the rest in the jar, then simply shake again when required. In this way you can make up a big batch of dressing to use at any time. I fail to understand why people buy dressings that are full of water alginates, inferior oil and vinegar when their own homemade can be so easy to make and delicious.

VARIETIES OF VINEGAR

Malt vinegar is based on beer but without added hops or coloured with malt or caramel. Malt vinegar is used in combination with spices in pickles of onions, eggs and red cabbage. It's frequently distilled to make it stronger than 6%, which is essential in preserving vegetable pickles, otherwise they can start to turn bad. Malt vinegar is the only vinegar to sprinkle on thick-cut chips, especially those fried the old-fashioned way in beef dripping!

Wine vinegar is made from red or white wine but not necessarily the cheapest. The gourmet vinegar of Orleans is made with fine wine added at intervals to vinegar maturing slowly in vats. Wine vinegars can be further flavoured with tarragon, garlic, chilli and rosemary.

Fruit vinegars are often white wine vinegars that have been steeped with soft berry fruits such as fresh raspberries, currants and strawberries. If you intend making your own at home, allow a good four days' steeping, strain through muslin and boil the vinegar for a good 10 minutes to kill any potentially harmful organisms. Store in sterilised glass bottles.

Champagne vinegar is, of course, regarded as one of the finest wine vinegars and is popular with chefs. Often a chef's recipe will call for 1 or 2 teaspoonfuls of reduced Champagne vinegar – fine for a busy kitchen but I find it more useful to boil down a whole bottle to reduce it by half, then cool and re-bottle. Then you can simply trickle out the tiny amount needed to make all the difference.

Cider vinegar is made from apple juice that has been exposed to the air. It can range in colour from pale brown to cloudy green. It has quite a high acetic content, up to 6%, with a good apple flavour. Cider vinegar is good in full-bodied beef or pork casseroles. If you use it in dressings, it might benefit from a little diluting. My mother used to enjoy it as a long drink diluted with chilled sparkling water and sweetened with a little honey. Fine organic vinegars, as made by old companies such as Aspall, have been matured for a good four months. Cider vinegar (from apples) is very popular in America.

Sherry vinegar from Spain has a wonderfully mellow, slightly oaky flavour. It's gaining in popularity and is already a favourite with chefs for adding a mystery piquant touch to a sauce. Just a few drops are all you need. Such speciality vinegars make great gifts for any keen cooks.

Rice wine vinegar is my personal favourite. Gently acidic, slightly sweet and very versatile, this vinegar is popular throughout all Asia and is sold in many forms from dark and spicy to colourless and delicate. Use it in vinaigrettes as you would a wine vinegar – it makes a much lighter dressing. The Japanese flavour rice wine vinegar for further uses and varieties will include added mirin (a sweet wine), dashi (dried fish stock), ginger and sesame seeds. A good all-purpose, rice-wine seasoned vinegar with added salt and sugar is essential throughout Japan for salads and for tossing into hot rice for sushi. This is occasionally sold in our more cosmopolitan food halls or, if you have one of the state-of-the-art oriental hypermarkets near by, you might track down a bottle there.

Brown rice wine vinegar is a golden amber brown and has a nicely mellow flavour.

Chinese rice wine vinegar can have added spices (such as star anise and cinnamon) plus sugar and colouring. It's good in rich Chinese braised dishes cooked in the Sichuan red style or 'drunken' chicken. Brands to look out for are Mitsukan, Sanchi, Lee Kum Kee.

Black rice wine vinegar (also known as *chinkiang*) is a mixture of fermented rice, wheat and millet that makes a rich, dark, sweeter, smoky flavoured mixture. Red Chinese vinegar is slightly lighter but used in the same way — for dipping, in dumpling broths and hot and sour recipes.

Finally, the ultimate in vinegars – *balsamic* (from the Italian word for 'balm', meaning mellow). This can be made only in and around the northern Italian city of Modena where for centuries families have concentrated a grape juice over a low heat to then be fermented slowly in a succession of wooden barrels each of differing character. This process can take anything from ten years to a hundred. I do marvel at the patience and ingenuity of cooks over the centuries to perfect such a process – it's like planting majestic trees as saplings for future generations to enjoy. As balsamic vinegar ages and is transferred from one type of wooden barrel to another (chestnut, oak etc.) so it mellows and develops unique characteristics. The more you pay for a good bottle of balsamic vinegar the greater the ultimate flavour, like a rare wine. Sprinkle balsamic vinegar not just over salads but also over a plate of sliced ripe strawberries, in season. Use it to deglaze thinly sliced pan-fried liver, and trickle it over vegetables or chicken.

SALTS

Can you imagine a diet without salt? It is now so freely available and relatively cheap that we take it for granted yet until modern times salt was sold in block form and had to be ground for cooking and table use.

Salt is a by-product of the sea and is obtained either directly from coastal works where it is evaporated, cleaned and dried, or from inland mines where it comes from ancient rocks that once, millions of years ago, were sea beds. Salt is used as a preservative (as in brine for bacon, salt cod and Moroccan salted lemons) and as a flavouring, especially in commercial food production.

There are many salts that have flavour. The one we commonly refer to as 'salt' is sodium chloride, but others are calcium carbonate, magnesium sulphate and potassium. Sodium chloride is the salt that can cause diet-related problems by raising blood pressure. Low-salt products include other chemical salts that don't cause such concern. However, their flavour is not as intense. Having acquired the taste, it takes time to wean your taste buds off edible salt, which is why nutritionists try to persuade mothers not to add salt to children's food. We don't necessarily need to add extra salt to our food: the recommended amounts are just 6g a day for men and 5g a day for women – as much as is contained in around 1tsp of soy sauce.

Salt is vital, though, for our body metabolism. If you lose too much through sweating on a hot day, you will begin to feel faint and may pass out. The remedy is simple – a fizzy drink containing salts will quickly restore the balance.

TYPES OF SALT

Rock salt (as mined in Cheshire or the ancient salt mines of Germany and Austria) can be sold as tiny chips or crystals to be hand ground in salt mills – popular with chefs and gourmets alike. Or it can be diluted below ground by high-pressure water and the resulting brine evaporated and milled.

Table salt is produced by evaporation under vacuum pressure, which gives it virtually 100% purity, but it has to be mixed with a little magnesium carbonate to stop it from caking. This, along with cooking salt, is the cheapest though it leaves an aftertaste which many people find unpleasant. *Iodised salt* has added iodine, which is useful for people with thyroid problems.

Sea salt is made the world over on commercial scales and in more localised areas, retaining characteristics that add extra flavour. If sea salt is allowed to evaporate naturally it may be known as *gros sel marin* or bay salt. It may also contain additional minerals that can colour it. Highly prized by chefs is the French *Le Guérandais*, a pale grey, lightly moist, granular salt. Sea salt can be evaporated into salt flakes to be crushed in the fingers over food as a condiment. The most famous, and the favourite of many international star chefs, and also mine, is from *Maldon* in Essex. A similar sea salt is made in Anglesey. If you enjoy seaside holidays in salt-producing areas, you may like to buy a batch of local sea salt as a souvenir and taste the difference. A recent personal indulgence was a drum of *Pacific crystal salt* sold specifically for margaritas – the idea is to dip the wet rim of a glass into the salt. However, the salt was so expensive I couldn't afford the margarita mixes to go with it – but the flavour was good in my cooking.

ESSENTIALS AND EXTRAS

OLIVES

Botanically olives are regarded as fruit. Apart from the oil, the fruits make fine eating, but not fresh.Olives need to be treated so they soften and develop an appetising flavour. Olives are sold as green, purple or black (either the natural colour or processed black). They come smooth-skinned or wrinkled, with stones or pitted, stuffed or plain. Olives sold in jars or cans will generally be in brine, but can be covered in oil or vinegar. If you buy them loose, store in the fridge for only a few days.

Olives are an important element in the cuisine of all Mediterranean countries and each has its own varieties. The array can be quite bewildering when displayed in a food hall (or even better outside in a Mediterranean market while on holiday). If you are unsure about what olives to buy, ask for a taster from whatever batch catches your eye – it is expected. Olive trees can grow to a great age, even a thousand years, and it takes a few years for them to begin producing fruit. All olives are the same colour in that they start as green and ripen through to purple and black. September is the month when farmers start to harvest green olives, November and December when they pick purple or black ones. Wrinkled olives are olives left on the tree over winter before picking.

If you eat an olive straight from the tree, chances are you will almost immediately spit it out: it will be mouth-puckeringly bitter. Olives need to be soaked either in a brine (the simplest method for sweeter varieties) but more often in a lye or weak caustic soda solution. (Lye is an alkaline solution of carbonates of potassium and sodium and has been used for centuries in the manufacture of soap and olives. It is harmless but needs to be thoroughly rinsed away after it has performed its function.) The olives soften in the solution and change flavour. They are then rinsed in several changes of water.

Green olives can be turned black by alternate soaking in lye and exposure to air for oxidisation. They have a characteristic smooth, glossy skin and can be bought pitted (whole or sliced) or unpitted. They are used for general cooking, the type you would find on a commercial pizza.

Spain is a great producer of good-quality olives of varying sizes and colours. The fattest, from Andalucia, are called *queens*. The small *manzanilla olives* are pale green, and sold whole with or without stones, or stuffed with almonds, pimento or – my favourite – anchovy. (The pitted manzanilla is the correct olive for a Martini cocktail, should you wish to impress). The South of France offers a glorious selection of olives, especially from the region of Provence, which range from the tiny, *semi-wild purple olives* to *fat juicy green fruits* and *glistening black olives from Nyons*. They are dressed in either oil or brine and invariably tossed with dried herbs, garlic and strips of lemon. If you are ever in Nice or Nimes, visit their open-air markets and just gaze at the olives piled high. Olives from Greece include the fine, plump *purple Kalamatas* and the *smaller wrinkled black olives from Crete*. Olives from North Africa will often be flavoured with lemon and spices. A nice Moroccan way of serving oranges is as a salad dressed with olive oil and scattered with black olives. The two fruits have an affinity with each other. As do tomatoes. In fact, if you walk into an olive shed, the smell that hits you is 'tomato on the vine'.

CAPERS

I thought the seed pods from my summer nasturtiums looked familiar and then I read that capers were the unopened flower bud of a similar Mediterranean creeper. Capers are mainly imported from Spain and Italy but some of the nicest come from Provence. The name of the classic olive, caper and anchovy paste, *tapenade*, is derived from the Provence word for capers, *tapeno*. Capers can be fat and large or small and dainty; sold in vinegar, in brine or loosely packed in coarse salt. Some salted capers can be used as they are but others are quite powerful and need a little rinsing first.

The main function of preserved capers is as a piquant flavouring: they marry nicely with meat in stews and sauces (tasty with fried liver and onions); they are good tossed into salads, sprinkled on pizzas and nestled into tuna sandwiches; and they're nice with roasted sweet peppers. I love capers with rich meaty fish such as halibut or salmon. The classic way of serving skate is with a brown butter and caper sauce. Lightly chopped and mixed into a béchamel-based onion sauce they make a nice old English sauce for roast lamb. In short, it pays to keep a jar always to hand. They have a long shelf life.

NICOISE CAVIAR (TAPENADE)

Finely chop about 300g (10½oz) of pitted black olives, 3tbsp of capers (rinsed if salted) and 3 anchovy fillets. (You can do this in a food processor but make sure you do not overprocess them to a paste. Use the pulse button.) Transfer to a bowl and add 2 crushed garlic cloves, 1tbsp of chopped fresh basil and lots of freshly ground black pepper. Gradually work in about 150–200ml (5–7fl oz) of extra virgin olive oil and that's it. Spoon into a screw-topped jar and pour a thin layer of oil on top to keep it fresh. Use it within a week to ten days. It's scrummy spread on crisp toast with chopped tomatoes. Or spread it thinly on grilled fish or chicken just before serving.

MONOSODIUM GLUTAMATE

MSG is a flavourless white powder with a bad press, but it's actually of some benefit in cooking if used wisely and in moderation. Chinese and Japanese cooks have used flavour enhancers such as *ve-tsin*, made from wheat, for centuries. It was a Japanese scientist at the dawn of the 20th century who, while researching kelp, isolated the glutamate ion and found it had the ability to enhance other flavours.

It has no harmful side-effects in the way that salt, alcohol, fats and sugar do and can be beneficial for those following a no-salt diet as it makes food more palatable. The problem, nicknamed 'Chinese restaurant syndrome', can arise when it is eaten or absorbed on an empty stomach. Then head and chest pains and a burning feeling can develop. These sensations pass after an hour or so but can be quite unpleasant while they last. Westerners mostly eat Chinese food in large quantities in restaurants; they may have saved up their appetite to do justice to the meal and then tucked into a large portion of tasty Chinese soup or dim sum or whatever on an empty stomach. Well, that's the case for the defence anyway.

MSG is used in many proprietary Chinese products so check the labels if you want to avoid it. There are also Western uses for MSG, such as in stock cubes and sauces sold as 'liquid seasoning'.

PICKLES

Pickled vegetables

The days of spending time pickling vegetables from garden gluts seem to be golden memories for many of us now. Even if I do find odd hours to indulge in a spot of country-style preserving, I rarely get the opportunity to use the fruits of my labour during the year before they start to turn soft. Alternatively, I can and do donate spare jars to my local village fete. There are many proprietary brands you can buy, though they lack the charming homemade touch.

Pickled onions are baby silverskins in clear malt vinegar or the larger shallot size in a darker brew, often seen perched on a chip-shop counter. If you see Italian pickled onions (borrettana), buy to try – they just might be the delicious pickled wild hyacinth. *Shredded red cabbage* is another salad pickle that some diehards enjoy with cheese or cold meats. The cabbage is crisp but the pickle often too sharp for my taste. *Sweet pickled cucumbers* come in a variety of sizes, whole or sliced, and often flavoured with dill. *Gherkins* too, in sizes ranging from the baby French cornichon to the pungent larger sizes. *Sauerkraut*, I know, has its devotees. 'Sour cabbage' is the translation of its name and sour cabbage is an exact description. In fact, it is fermented, brined cabbage and, unless you are used to it, stand back when you open the jar. Instead of spooning it straight from the jar, it is then cooked further – for what seems like hours – with fatty bacon, onions, cooking apple, vinegar and whole spices. After that it is served (miraculously still intact) with stiff mashed potato and a slab of boiled meat or sausage. Well, that is what a German flatmate would treat us to once a month in our heady student days.

Other pickles are *walnuts* (good with real farmhouse Cheddar), eggs, and certain fruits, like *peaches* and *pears*, in a sweet and sour dressing. All worth a try, if only on a need-to-know basis.

Oriental pickles

The Chinese, Koreans, Japanese and South-East Asians are great pickle eaters. *Pickled ginger*, found throughout Asia, is cured in brine then packed in a sweet-sour pickle, often coloured a pale pink. It's traditional with sushi but is also good used as a light pickle for cold meats and smoked fish. *Sichuan preserved vegetables* is a generic name for a variety of Chinese-style pickles including kohlrabi, mustard greens, cabbage and turnip. They all have a spicy-salty taste flavoured with chilli or Sichuan peppercorns. The Chinese enjoy them for breakfast. Some need rinsing before use and a number are best cut into thin shreds or slices to serve. *Kimchee*, from Korea, is often pickled napa cabbage but it can be other vegetables. The pickling liquor is garlicky, salty and spicy. A bit on the whiffy side, but worth taking a deep breath and trying if you enjoy the rich diversity of oriental food. Pickles are an important part of the Japanese diet – you will see a lively selection if you shop in Japanese stores, including many vegetables we are familiar with. They use similar vinegar pickles but include other flavourings such as soy sauce, MSG, mirin, mustard and sesame seeds. *Umeboshi* are dull red, salty, pickled plums popular with rice for breakfast, and believed to be good for the digestion.

ALCOHOL

Not a resume of fine wines, but a few hints on using alcohol in cooking to add flavour. In most cases, they should be brought to the boil for at least a few seconds to burn off the alcohol. Wines should be boiled until well reduced to concentrate the flavour.

Wine
It is often assumed that wines for cooking can be of an indifferent quality, but a bad wine with poor flavour will not be transformed into a great wine when cooked down. The better the flavour you pour into the pot, the nicer the end result. That is not to say you have to cook a boeuf bourguignon with a Chambertin, but use a better full-bodied red than plonk rouge.

If you have wine left over from a dinner party and wish to save it for cooking rather than downing it for breakfast, then pour it into a small screw-topped jar to keep out as much air as possible, or freeze it. Wine for cooking is often boiled to reduce it anyway, so I boil leftovers to a concentrate and freeze it in ice cube trays, ready to pop a quick rich flavour into gravies or simple pan-fry sauces. Certainly this is a good way of not wasting flat Champagne.

Fortified wines
Fortified wines are generous with their flavours and, unlike wine, once opened will keep for some time. The most useful is *dry vermouth*, particularly Noilly Prat – a favourite in haute cuisine kitchens. Just a splash makes quite a difference to fish, poultry and meat dishes. Otherwise a *dry sherry – fino*, *amontillado* or *manzanilla* has uses ranging from adding to the meat pan to trickling over fruits and trifle sponges or using in marinades and even Chinese sauces as an alternative to rice wine. *Ruby port* adds a rich, mellow flavour to pork, lamb and liver dishes as well as being good sprinkled over fruits.

Marsala from Sicily is a must for zabaglione but is also good served with cheese or the almondy cantucci biscuits that you dip into the perfumed sweet wine. It is classic with pan-fried liver and good added as a small spoonful to devilled kidneys. *Madeira* from the Canaries can be used in the same way.

Spirits

Spirits are an excellent way of adding rich flavour with just a spoonful or two. If you've already got a bottle in the drinks cupboard then it's actually quite a cheap way to add a little quality flavour.

I don't use cooking brandy: it is better to buy a small bottle, even a quarter size, of a good *French brandy*. Chefs will often add just a teaspoon or two of brandy or *Armagnac* to the juices of a pan. It deglazes in seconds and imparts a heavenly fragrance to the meat, then you can swirl in a little stock or water.

Rums are wonderful for sweet dishes and macerating dried fruits. *White rum* is finer, but the slightly fudgy *dark rums* are good for baking with bananas. *Kirsch* is the classic cherry spirit to use with many fruits including strawberries, pineapples and peaches. It tastes nothing like cherries but does have a distinctive flavour. The clear Kirsch is finer than the darker liquor of the same name. *Maraschino*, from the Italian Adriatic coast, is made with the crushed fruit and kernels plus a little honey; I have to confess to being rather partial to cherries in this spirit. *Cherry brandy* is simply cherries steeped in spirit. *Pernod* is another favourite spirit in a chef's kitchen, again used in cautious splashes not over-indulgent slashes, whatever TV cooks may advise – alcoholic overkill is the ruination of many a dish.

Whisky is fine with game or fruits and is a must for Scottish flummery, but I find *gin* has few uses apart from sprinkled over freshly sliced oranges or steeped with wild sloes. *Vodka* is a novelty spirit as far as cooking is concerned: I've had it in a pasta sauce, steeped with baby tomatoes as a cocktail delicacy and mixed with melted chocolate and frozen for an after-dinner liqueur.

Eaux de vie

This is a generic name for fruit spirits that use the sugars of the fruits for fermentation. Many are quite strong and alcoholic. *Poire William* (pear), Kirsch (cherry) and *Calvados* (apple) are all technically eaux de vie. Fruit brandies are spirits steeped with fruits after distilling: *Crème de cassis* is one example, *Southern Comfort* another. *Eau de vie de marc* is a more 'basic' spirit made from the leftovers (or marc) of wine making. Clever wine makers don't waste the crushed skins, pulp and pips: the leftover mush is turned into alcohol and distilled but has to undergo some purification to render it drinkable. The Italians call their eau de vie *grappa*, the Portuguese *bagaceira*, the Germans *Tresterbrantwein*. Some marcs are actually quite good.

Oriental alcohol

The Chinese have an aromatic red-brown wine called *mi chui* that is made from fermented glutinous rice and millet. It is then aged for anything between 10 and 100 years. The finest quality comes from Shao Hsing. These wines are generally added at the end of slow-cooked and braised dishes, such as drunken chicken.

Japan's national drink, *saké*, a rice wine, is often used in cooking. Like wines, there are many styles, regional varieties and qualities. It has a clean, lightly sweet flowery taste and can be served warmed or cold. It adds a depth of flavour when added towards the end of cooking time. *Mirin* is an essential ingredient in Japanese cooking; it is rather like a light sweet sherry but is in fact made from glutinous rice. It is used only in cooking. *Hon-mirin* (sweet sake) is naturally brewed: *Aji-mirin* is made with alcohol, corn syrup and salt. Use both in the same way.

FLOWER WATERS

These are gradually making a comeback as we dabble in Arab- and Turkish-inspired cooking. But in fact flower waters were an essential ingredient in many fine British kitchens until the end of the 19th century when Victorian chauvinism discouraged anything but plain cooking. The best-known flower water is *rose water*. But don't use the light liquid you dab on your skin as a tonic – rose water for recipes should be triple distilled and exotically fragrant. The most obvious use is to add it to fruits, but try a few drops in chocolate mousse (like the perfumed flavour of Turkish delight), with rhubarb, milk puddings and even chicken dishes. *Orange flower water* is delightful in orange mixes or stirred into whipped cream and piped into brandy snaps. I also like to add it to sugar syrup and even homemade lemon sorbet. Both can be bought in Middle Eastern or Greek delis, and some larger supermarkets stock them.

WATER

And don't forget the cheapest liquid of all! Plain tap water is indispensable in cooking to lighten sauces, soups and liquids that have thickened or concentrated too much. The most fragrant stock I ever tasted was made from a selection of vegetables that had just been brought to the boil in a large pan of water and left to steep overnight then strained. French chefs call this a *nage* – meaning to swim – because that is all the vegetables have done. Just add a splash of water to the meaty deposits left in a pan after you have roasted a joint or pan-fried some steaks, stir briskly, season then strain, and taste a pure uncomplicated light sauce, or *jus*.

COOKS' AIDS

These are the small kitchen helpers that lift our breads and cakes, set our jellies and mousses, and generally refine many of our cooking techniques.

Raising agents
A collective term for baking powders and yeasts. In all cases it is carbon dioxide gas that rises as bubbles and lightens the texture of cakes or breads. How the gas forms is dependent on what agents are used. Chemical reactions are one method, live yeasts another.

Baking powders
When you mix an acid and alkaline together in the presence of moisture and heat, carbon dioxide results. Until the mid-19th century the only way to give cakes a light texture was to beat them long and hard to get air into the fat and sugar manually (see 'maximum specific volume' on page 308). There had been a few experiments with carbonate of potash or bicarbonate but these left a residual soapy flavour. Then it was discovered that if you mixed tartaric acid (cream of tartar) with bicarbonate of soda in the ratio of 2:1 bubbles of carbon gas appeared. But you had to work fast because when water is added to bicarbonate it starts to fizz. Bicarbonate works quite effectively on its own in wet, strongly flavoured mixtures such as gingerbread or in pancakes made with an acidic milk such as yogurt or, more commonly, buttermilk. Nowadays a more stable acid/alkaline mixture is bicarb mixed with a slower-reacting acid like diophosphate. However, these baking powder mixtures have a limited shelf life as the chemical reaction becomes ineffective so check the date on

the drum. It is also useful to have a drum of bicarbonate in the cupboard for medicinal purposes – to settle acidic tummies and also in a weak solution so soothe skin rashes, insect bites etc.

Yeasts

Yeasts are all around us floating in the air, living on leaves and fruit skins and even on our own skins. They are natural single celled microscopic fungi. There are countless numbers of yeasts and we owe them a lot. We need different yeasts for brewing, for making wines and in baking. When you add water to flour, enzymes called amylases are activated and turn some of the starch into glucose. If the flour and water mixture also contains some yeast it feeds on the glucose and give off carbon dioxide and alcohol. If there is no oxygen in the dough, the yeasts carry on producing alcohol, so air is introduced 'mechanically' by the action of kneading. (This also has the added benefit of stretching the gluten that traps the bubbles of CO_2.) This is why bread dough smells a little like beer. During baking the alcohol evaporates out.

Yeasts are quite tough organisms and can survive chilling, pressing, drying and freezing. They simply bounce back again when conditions return to their normal. To grow and multiply (and give off the vital CO_2 gas) they need moderate warmth, moisture, food and a slightly acidic medium. For home baking use you can buy yeasts as a fresh compressed rubbery paste, as dried granules or in sachets as fast-action/easy-blend yeasts. With the first two yeasts the dough needs to rise twice for the proper open structure to form when the bread is baked. The second rising is known as 'proving'. Fast-action yeasts have been developed to eliminate the first rising, thus cutting down on time before baking. But they do have to be used in a slightly different way.

Fresh yeast (the experienced cook's choice) is bought by weight (allow 20g per kilo of flour). You will find it in chill cabinets in health food shops but you could also sweet talk your local baker if he still makes his own bread instead of having it delivered part-baked. It should smell sweet and slightly yeasty and have a nice clean crumbly, rubbery texture. Buy slightly more than you need – if well wrapped it keeps up to a month in the fridge or can be frozen if divided into small portions and wrapped well in cling-film. When you come to use it again, allow about a quarter as much again of the necessary quantity (i.e. 25g per kilo) to allow for a few dead cells and dissolve from frozen as it liquefies on thawing. Fresh yeast needs first to be blended with a little liquid to get it going, then mixed into the flour.

Dried granular yeast has to be mixed with a little tepid liquid plus a pinch of sugar as food to kick-start the yeast growth into action. This is ready when the mixture starts to foam. If it does not foam, then the yeast is dead. Sorry. Throw the rest of the batch away.

Fast-action/easy-blend yeasts are specially formulated to be tipped straight from the sachet into the flour (allow one sachet per 750g of flour). They should not be mixed with liquid first. If you have spices to add or fat to rub in, do this first and then mix in the yeasts followed by the liquid.

Yeast needs a liquid temperature of 25°C and a slightly acidic medium of 3.0–6.0 pH to multiply, which is why vitamin C (ascorbic acid) is added to fast-action yeasts. Salt is added for flavour but also to stop yeasts from growing too fast. For fresh and dried granular yeast don't be tempted to add a higher proportion of yeast to flour, it will only give the dough a strong yeast aroma. Long, slow rising, even overnight in the fridge, makes for a better texture. Fast-action yeasts, though, can be used in slightly higher ratios without affecting the flavour. In other words, you don't have to worry about getting the proportions exactly right – that's why they are called easy-blend. Follow the label instructions and you shouldn't have any problems.

YEAST EXTRACTS

It's well known that the UK has its favourite *Marmite* spread but every Aussie prefers *Vegemite*. Extract is a misnomer because these spreads are really concentrates created by a process known as autolysis, the destruction of body cells by their own enzymes. Basically the proteins are turned into amino acids, which are neutralised with a little caustic soda to form salt. Other flavourings are added to make the yeasty paste taste nice and the whole lot is reduced right down. A tiny dab is all you need at one time. Foreigners cannot understand why we Brits enjoy the stuff, but then they have probably never dunked yeast extract toast soldiers into soft-boiled eggs. *Bovril* is a beef extract with a strong, almost soy sauce flavour. It has a slightly pasty texture, I find both make wonderful quick hot drinks or emergency stocks for stews.

STOCK CUBES AND POWDERS

Manufacturers produce a huge array of concentrated dried food powders, some from natural sources, some artificial. Stock powders are simply a mixture of whatever recipe each manufacturer specialises in and will include salt, sometimes MSG (see page 294), and in the case of stock cubes, a binder. Some smell quite artificial, others are more natural.

The ones I have to hand are *Knorr, Just Bouillon* and the vegetarian *Marigold* powder (also available in a vegan version). If you holiday in France or Italy, then pick up *wild mushroom* flavour stock cubes or veal stock powder. In general, I tend to use a vegetarian stock, as it is more versatile and less pungent than meat-based varieties.

SETTING AGENTS AND THICKENERS

Gelatine

Gelatine is a protein obtained from an animal source, generally hides and bones. When you make stock at home with fresh bones (especially veal or beef bones), you will notice it sets on chilling. In 'olden' days cooks would use hartshorn (antler) shavings to set mixtures: the modern commercially extracted gelatine is much easier. You can buy gelatine as crystal powder or in clear, transparent sheets.

Crystal gelatine is mainly sold in sachets but is sometimes also available in tins. Allow 1 sachet for each 500–600ml of liquid depending on the strength of set needed. Gelatine dissolves in water at just under boiling temperature. For small amounts (1 sachet's worth) you can dissolve the crystals by sprinkling them straight into the hot liquid and stirring briskly; the mixture is ready when you can feel no grittiness on stirring. For larger amounts, you need to stir the crystals in a cup with a little cold liquid and let it 'sponge', that is go solid with a texture of wet sand. You then dissolve the set mixture by standing the cup in a pan of boiling water until the crystals dissolve.

Leaf or sheet gelatine is a more professional product, popular with chefs, though it is becoming easier to use. Depending on the size of sheet, you need to allow about 1 sheet for each 100ml of liquid, generally 5 or 6 per 500–600ml. The sheets need to be soaked in a bowl of cold water until they soften. Tip all the cold water out and then stir the soft sheets straight into hot liquid. It dissolves almost instantly. Irritatingly, there is no standard weight or size of gelatine sheets. Some are thicker than others, and some manufacturers even change pack sizes, making it a problem if you stick to the same brand.

TIP: AVOIDING LUMPY GELATINE

To stop the dissolved gelatine (of either type) going lumpy (chefs call this

roping), blend some of the cooled liquid or mixture it is to set with the

gelatine then stir that back into the main mix. Don't be tempted to stir it

in straight after it has dissolved.

Liquid pectin

Pectin is derived from carbohydrates yet it has the ability to set fruit liquids, like flour thickens a sauce. It occurs naturally in fruit pips, skins and membranes. This is why when we make marmalade we save the pips, tie them in a muslin bag, and add them to the boiling pot. Under-ripe fruit contains more pectin than just-ripe fruit. Some fruits have more than others. Green apples and crab apples, for instance, are good sources. Strawberries are poor in natural pectin, raspberries much richer. For homemade jams and jellies you need to get a good balance between pectin levels, acid and sugar. Pectin needs an acidity between pH 3.3 and pH 3.2 to set. The level of sugar is important because if you add too much you'll get a syrup, and if there is too little you won't get a nice set. Around 40% sugar is as low as you can go. You can buy commercial pectin as a liquid (brand name Certo) or powder. It is extracted from apples and citrus peel mixed with a mineral acid. You will need to follow the manufacturer's advice for a good set.

For thickeners, see also Cornflour (page 219), Arrowroot (page 217) and Mustards (pages 262–3).

Vegetarians should be aware that gelatine is an animal product. There are

animal-free alternatives such as agar-agar (see page 132) or the product

Gelzone. I find these give a slightly softer set, which is nice for mousses

but might prove tricky if you wanted to make a solid moulded jelly.

PUDDING BISCUITS

I add this little section here because dessert recipes may call for certain biscuits and in my experience some work better than others. *Trifle sponges* are very low-fat light, crisp cakes that are made to be soaked with sherry or juice. But I find they go very mushy. Instead may I recommend you track down the Italian *savoiardi sponges*, the correct biscuits for *tiramisu*, the reason being that you have to dunk the biscuits in a rum and coffee syrup, then layer them in a dish with the mascarpone cheese. Fine in principle, but trifle sponge fingers tend to fall apart when you lift them. Savoiardi biscuits at least hold their shape long enough for transfer, then turn deliciously soggy. *Amaretti* biscuits are crisp almond-flavoured macaroons that can be layered with whipped cream and fruit for simple sundaes. The dainty British *ratafia* biscuits are equally nice, especially in strawberry trifle (and, please, no jelly layer!). *Cantucci* biscuits, from Florence, look like thin squashed French bread slices but are rebaked sweet bread flavoured with oil and aniseed. Dunk them in a sweet dessert wine. *Panettone* is a rich dough cake with candied peel and dried fruit generally most popular at Christmas time. Heavenly served in thick wedges with a cappuccino or sliced and turned into a terrific bread and butter pudding: just follow a normal recipe but substitute panettone slices for ordinary bread and reduce the amount of sugar slightly (see recipe on page 229).

SWEET THINGS

For simplicity's sake, references to 'sugar' here refer to the product that is 99.9% sucrose, the world's most popular sweetener.

Sugar is refined commercially from two main plant sources: sugar cane, grown in the tropics and warm temperate climates, and sugar beet, grown in cool temperate climates, e.g. Europe, Russia and North America. Sugar is extracted from the stems of the sugar cane or from the roots of beets. Nutritionally speaking, we can do without sugar – there's not much in it except simple carbohydrates that give a quick burst of energy. But as we have taste buds on our tongues to detect sweetness we are obviously intended to consume it.

Sugars do play an important role in our diet as preservers (they can prevent the growth of bacteria and moulds) and to make our food more palatable in terms of both flavour and texture. Sugar is important in baking to make cakes soft and moist and in confectionery to give crisp, crunchy and chewy coatings. It assumes different properties according to temperature: at room temperature it is crystalline and free flowing; at 100°C it is runny and melted; at 160°C it becomes brittle and snaps. The flavour also changes when heat is applied: it becomes caramelised but, if burnt, tastes acrid and bitter. Sugar can soften icy textures and even prevent a liquid freezing if present in a high enough proportion.

HISTORY OF SUGAR

Sugar has changed the course of history but at a price. Once a rare luxury and treated variously as an exotic spice or a medicine, sugar is now firmly in position as a provider of pure energy and pleasure. Sugar cane was thought to have originated from India around the Bay of Bengal, but as there are no wild strains of the plant it is hard to track its origins. The earliest mention is from China nearly three thousand years ago. The Romans and Greeks used it as a medicine and it was largely due to the Moors that sugar cane was cultivated for food. The Venetians started up a lucrative trade and the Italians went wild for it, followed by the French, who used it like a spice and sprinkled it on almost anything edible, including cheese.

Certainly by the time Christopher Columbus sailed to the New World on his second trip sugar was well established as a Mediterranean crop because he took with him stems of sugar cane. Indirectly this started one of the greatest, and most shameful, migrations of all time – the slave trade, involving an estimated 10 million souls. For cane sugar is a labour-intensive crop and its production, based on very low labour costs, became highly profitable. Once a plentiful supply of consistent quality was available demand took off, changing the face of cooking.

Sugar beet was cultivated in Europe from the early 19th century onwards, largely encouraged by Napoleon, who wished to sidestep the import of sugar from British colonies.

Sugar lands were regarded as trophies of war: the British gained New York in return for handing Surinam back to the Dutch, and France swapped Canada for Guadeloupe.

CHARACTERISTICS OF SUGARS

Sugar is a generic name. We are most used to sucrose but other natural sweeteners include fructose from plants, lactose from milk, glucose and dextrose, and maltose (simple plant sugars). And, of course, there's also the range of artificial sweeteners. These different sugars have varying sweetening powers: fructose is the sweetest, followed by sucrose, then glucose, with lactose being the least sweet. Artificial sweeteners can be several hundred times sweeter by weight, which is why they are so small when pressed into tablets.

The rate at which sugar dissolves and can be detected by our taste buds also determines our perception of sweetness. Icing sugar, finely ground normal sucrose, is very fine and seems to taste sweeter than, say, coffee crystal sugar. It isn't, but because it dissolves quicker it tastes sweeter, which is one reason why bakers dust cakes and biscuits with icing sugar – instant pleasure.

SUGAR VARIETIES

Cane sugar is still regarded by experienced cooks as being of a slightly finer quality than *beet sugar* in that it does not foam on boiling (good for jams), but otherwise any differences are marginal. Cane sugar is sold in the UK under names such as Tate & Lyle and Billingtons: beet sugar under the Silver Spoon brand from the British Sugar Corporation.

In the early days of refining, most sugar was brown with a rich treacly flavour and white sugar was deemed to be more socially refined and desirable by the increasingly moneyed classes. Now the trend has gone full circle and brown is seen as 'better' while white is tarnished with the image of 'pure, white and deadly'. In fact, both are the same in calorific value and can have the same negative effects on dental hygiene. *Genuine brown sugars* (rather than white sugar with added colouring) have tiny amounts of trace minerals but too small to be of great significance. What genuine brown sugars are rich in is flavour and moisture. Look for the words *'unrefined'* on sugar packs for the best of both. Most unrefined sugar comes from Mauritius and is delicious. Look for supermarket own labels or Billingtons.

Granulated sugar: the all-purpose sugar of medium-sized crystals. Granulated sugar dissolves well when heated slowly so it's useful for certain puddings, stock syrups, jams and preserves. It is not ideal for baking because the crystal size does not dissolve well enough in the mixture, leaving a speckled effect on top of cakes caused by undissolved grains. Cakes made with granulated sugar also tend to be rather heavy in texture.

SUGAR SYRUP

Sugar syrup is used by chefs for many purposes and is very useful to have on hand in the fridge. Make up a big batch of syrup either plain or with added whole spices that can be discarded after steeping. Put 550g (1lb 4oz) of granulated sugar into a pan with 1 litre (1¾pt) of cold water and two strips of lemon peel. Dissolve slowly over a low heat, stirring occasionally until the liquid is quite clear and you can feel no grittiness in the pan. (When sugar is dissolved, it is said to be saturated.) Bring the syrup to the boil and simmer for 5 minutes – it's important not to raise the heat until every grain has dissolved otherwise the syrup can crystallise. Leave until cold, then remove the lemon peel and store the syrup in the fridge.

If you want to make a spicy syrup add 1 cinnamon stick, 4 whole cloves, 2 star anise and ½tsp of black peppercorns (yes, peppercorns!) during the initial dissolving.

Caster sugar is a fine-grain crystal sugar and as such dissolves quickly when beaten with fat. At college we were taught the principle of 'maximum specific volume', measuring the amount of air a creamed mixture of caster sugar and butter could hold. The creamier and more fluffy our sugar and butter became, the lighter by volume it weighed and the more air it incorporated. (See Raising agents, page 227.) This basically meant lighter sponges. I've never forgotten it and still beat my sugar and fat like crazy. Golden caster sugar crystals are a little larger than white.

Demerara sugar was originally developed in the town of the same name in Guyana, but little is exported from there now. It is a lovely, moist, pale golden-brown with a soft velvety texture. Or it should be if made in the old-fashioned way – some of it is now coarse crystal sugar with added molasses. So, buy unrefined Demerara for the real thing. It's good in sticky cakes like gingerbread or sprinkled on top of rice puds.

Molasses is the sticky dark syrup that drains from the raw sugar when it goes through the first stage of refining. If syrup is made with cane sugar it is rich in minerals and treacly in flavour. Cane sugar molasses can be added to other sugars to colour and enrich them. Beet sugar molasses is bitter and used only as a cattle feed.

Muscovado sugar is a delicious soft, moist sugar made from unrefined sugar with a little added molasses. The exact amount determines whether it is light brown or dark brown. It's wonderful in chocolate cakes and a must for Christmas cake and pud. Light muscovado makes the best ever butterscotch sauce for ice cream.

Soft brown sugar is also fine-grain moist brown sugars, light or dark. It's often made from refined white sugar with added molasses, but sometimes made with unrefined sugar. *Barbados sugar*, if you can find it, is a particularly fine dark sugar with a rum flavour.

Preserving sugar is a coarse crystal sugar that dissolves more easily than granulated sugar without forming a mass at the base of the pan. It's the best sugar to use for jams and marmalades when you want a bright texture and colour. Preserving sugar also gives off less foam during boiling, which means less skimming is needed and more jam remains for you to pot. Jam sugar, with added pectin and citric acid, is to help cooks who use low-pectin fruits like strawberries and cherries. It's ideal for homemade jam novices as it takes the guesswork out of judging a good set and cuts down the boiling time while retaining a good colour and flavour. Preserving sugars normally appear in our shops around the traditional jam-making months – January/February and June to September. But I get irritated when standard 500g packs of jam (and icing

sugar) have back-of-pack recipes using 450g sugar. What are you supposed
to do with the remaining 50g? Throw it away? Grrr…

Icing sugar is finely ground white sugar with a little anti-caking agent to
keep it free-flowing. There are many uses for it apart from making icing. Icing
sugar tastes sweeter than granulated sugar, because it dissolves quicker on
the tongue, so a little goes a long way. You can now buy a *golden icing sugar*
with a hint of molasses. *Royal icing sugar* is icing sugar with added dried
egg albumen. You just mix it with a little warm water. A good storecupboard
ingredient: I always have a box to hand for those quick little decorating jobs
like trickling over biscuits and buns.

Sugar cubes, rock sugar and *coffee crystals* are all forms of refined
sugar dampened and pressed into shapes, or crystals formed slowly from a
saturated sugar liquor. The French La Perruche cubes, produced on the island
of Réunion in the Indian Ocean, are pressed from white or amber brown sugar
syrups. Not a lot better for you than normal cubes, but oh so chic!

Loaf sugar is the old-fashioned way of selling pressed sugar: it was
designed for easy transport before the days of packaging. The solid sugar had
then to be pounded by hand. Parts of the Middle East still use loaf sugar,
pressed into tall conical shapes.

Jaggery (also known as gur) is a delicious aromatic sugar used in desserts
and savoury dishes. India is reputed to be the home of sugar cane and for
centuries villages have made their own crudely refined cane sugar pressed
into sticky balls or hard lumps. It makes wonderful toffee. Jaggery can also be
made with date palm syrup.

HOT BUTTERSCOTCH SAUCE

Just melt down equal quantities of muscovado and unsalted
butter (say 100g/3½oz of each) with a splash of added water
to help the dissolving, stirring until smooth. Add a pinch of
salt and a dash of vanilla extract. You can also add 2–3tbsp
of double cream, if wished, to make the sauce richer. Bubble
for a minute or two, allow to cool until warm, then trickle over
ice cream.

SYRUPS FROM REEDS AND TREES

Much of our sugar comes from refining natural sweet saps found in reeds (sugar cane) or trees.

Golden syrup is a by-product of sugar refining which was turned into a highly popular product in the late 19th century by Tate & Lyle and has been associated with the company ever since. The colour and butterscotch flavours are due to 'impurities' rather than caramelisation. It's the syrup for treacle tarts, steamed suet puds and roly-polys.

Black treacle is a blend of syrup and molasses and is less sweet than sugar. Treacle tart is actually made with golden syrup, not treacle. Just one of those cookery quirks …

Coconut sugar is made from the sap of coconut palm flower buds.

Corn syrup is popular in the United States. It's made from corn, is available clear or dark, and is not as sweet as golden syrup and rather more runny.

Cane syrup is another American syrup still popular in the old sugar states such as Louisiana. It's good for trickling over breakfast pancakes and indispensable for Creole and Cajun cooking.

Maple syrup can be produced only in North America because the climate has to be just right to cause the sap to flow in the maple trees, caused by alternate freezing and thawing. Quebec (Canada) and Vermont (US) are the main producers. Until the introduction of European bees and sugar cane to North America, maple syrup was the only known sweetener. The collecting season lasts just two months beginning with the first spring thaw. The sap tapped from the tree bark is then boiled down to concentrate and clarify. I never realised that there were grades of maple syrup until I visited one of the farmers' markets in the middle of New York City and found myself in front of a stall displaying a sparkling variety of golden and amber syrups. Nor did I realise that one could buy maple sugar and maple candy. Both Canadian and US maple syrups have strict definitions of the natural tree syrups used and are graded according to quality and colours: the lighter the colour, the finer the flavour. Grades run from Fancy Grade through to Grades A to C. Although it's expensive, it's worth buying a good light-coloured syrup. Maple syrup is sometimes blended with dark sugar syrup so check the label. I always have a bottle in the fridge to trickle over sliced fruits or ice cream.

Palm sugar looks like light soft brown sugar with a moist texture. Buy it from oriental stores. Ex-pats in the Far East come back addicted to it. Made from the sap of the palmyra, date or sugar palm trees. *Palm syrup* is obtained by the boiling of palm sap until reduced. This syrup has a slightly fudgy, almost woody flavour and is popular in the orient, India and the Middle East.

Liquid glucose is a really useful syrup as it does not crystallise. It's much used by confectioners and bakers – one of those tricksy ingredients chefs know about and forget to tell us! A small spoonful in a rich chocolate torte will help keep it soft without it melting. Buy it from chemists or mail-order kitchen ingredients catalogues.

Agave syrup, a syrup of fructose and glucose, is from the Mexican honey tree cactus varieties. It is sweeter and more runny than bees' honey, and sold in squeezy botles. It captured the attention of health-food devotees when categorised as a low glycaemic index food that is slowly absorbed in the bloodstream.

Other crude or raw sugars: there are speciality sugars in many parts of the world, mostly produced by extracting juice or sap from plants and boiling them down. They will have varying levels of sweetness and distinctive flavours. If you find unusual ones on your back-packing travels buy a pot and taste. Mexico produces a crude brown sugar called *piloncillo* or *panocha*.

TIP: USING MAPLE SYRUP

Maple syrup has many uses in the kitchen apart from simply trickling

over pancakes. I use it like a ready-made light syrup, except it has

a lot more flavour The viscosity is very runny so it coats fruits quickly

and evenly and is excellent as a quick ice cream sauce. It's good brushed

on grilled chicken or lamb chops and good over soft fruits, creamy

yogurts, breakfast cereals, on sausages and bacon, and particularly

banana sundaes!

HONEY

How brave was the first *Homo sapiens* who stuck his (or her) finger into a
hive and extracted the sticky sweet liquid. But the sheer delight at discovering
such nectar must have been worth the risk because, judging from early cave
paintings in Europe, mankind learned to harvest this wonder food to his
advantage thousands of years ago. The Saracens nicknamed honey 'the healer'
because when spread on war wounds it prevented the spread of infection,
presumably because it blocked out air-borne pathogens. Even today, when we
have a sore throat, we reach for a drink of hot lemon and honey, or suck on
honey and menthol lozenges.

Honey is actually a pre-digested food, made from flower nectar. In other
words, the bees eat the nectar, which passes through the digestive system to be
expelled as honey. It is the particular flower the bees feast on that determines
the character and quality of a honey. Some experts claim that the finest honey
can be made only from single flower varieties, others that a mixture of flowers
adds to the character. And now we have a delicious array of urban bees' honey.

Honey is divided into two categories: *blended honey*, which is good for
all-purpose uses, and the more delicate *flower honey*, for eating as it is. The
best quality will have the country of origin and flower variety on the label
(e.g. Mexican orange blossom honey). If no flower name is mentioned, you can
presume it's a blended honey.

Most honey is clear and runny, indicating it is freshly harvested. The setting
of honey depends on the balance of sugars – fructose, glucose and maltose –
plus a time factor. Honey with a higher percentage of glucose is more prone to
setting. Also, stirring encourages the glucose to granulate. When you gently
heat set honey it liquefies again and does not reset. Honey tastes sweeter than
sucrose because of the fructose – one and three-quarter times as sweet, in fact.

It's not just the flavour of honey that is affected by the flower nectar but
also the colour. Honey from buckwheat flowers is very dark: that made with
thyme flowers is light and clear. *Pine flower honey* has a predictably resinous
taste: *herb honeys* have aromatic depths. The *Greek Hymettus honey*, with
a predominant flavour of thyme, is deemed by some to be the world's best,
though many honey lovers have their own favourites. Many rate *Scottish
heather honey* as particularly fragrant; *acacia honey* is clear and delicate;
eucalyptus is pungent; and *lavender* is perfumed. I was once presented with
a jar of *desert honey* from the Yemen – musky, fragrant and highly prized by
Arab gourmets, almost like perfumed liquid toffee. This is after all, the land of
frankincense and myrrh. *Lime flower, lemon blossom* and *orange blossom*

honeys are light and flowery. Try New Zealand honeys too, like *manuka* (the tea-tree) or *borage flower*. New Zealand honeys are said to have particularly good anti-bacterial properties.

Native American bees were not great producers of honey, but with the introduction of more efficient European worker bees it was not long before some of the finest honey came from the New World – like Mexico and California.

Honeycomb (sometimes called raw honey) is honey still contained within the hexagonal wax framework. Some people love the sticky, chewy texture of wax and honey, others worry that the wax will cause digestive problems. It doesn't – it just passes through! It's highly prized by honey lovers because of the pure, unrefined flavour. Some supermarkets now categorise honey according to depth of flavour from 1 to 5 and give good flavour tasting notes on the labelling.

TIP: AN EASY WAY TO MEASURE HONEY

To measure syrup or honey you need a hot metal spoon. Heat one either in a basin of just-boiled water or hold the spoon bowl over a naked gas flame. Then dip into the syrup or honey and it will slip off again easily. If measuring several spoons of syrup you will need to reheat the spoon between measures. Incidentally, I have noticed that some syrups do thicken over a lengthy period of time. Not that it matters much.

ARTIFICIAL SWEETENERS

These are non-carbohydrate chemical substances that pass through the body unchanged thus adding no calories, nor indeed any nutrients, to our diet. For this reason they are useful to diabetics and those trying to control weight gain who still want to enjoy a sweet taste. They also play a part in dental hygiene as they leave nothing on the teeth for bacteria to feed on.

There are a number of types. The best known is sodium saccharin, first discovered by accident in 1879 during research on derivatives of coal tar. It's still in popular use today and is around four hundred times the sweetness of sucrose. Some sweeteners have been the subjects of health scares, such as cyclamates with studies linking it to possible causes of bladder cancer. But if sweeteners are used in normal moderation they should present no health problems at all. As they are so very sweet the chances of 'overdosing' on them are remote. Most people detect a very slight aftertaste with some sweeteners or find them too cloyingly sweet and certainly it does seem to take a little time to get used to them. Cooking and baking using sweeteners can be difficult as they become bitter when heated, so most are added after heating. Here is a resumé of the more available types.

Saccharin is said to have a more 'traditional' taste (whatever that is). It's the cheapest and most widely used sweetener. Brand names include Hermesetas and Sweetex.

Aspartame, also known as Nutrasweet, was developed in the early 1980s and is said to have a 'sugar-like' flavour. It does have a tiny, tiny calorific value (0.2 calorie per tablet) and is the most expensive of the sweeteners. Brands using aspartame are Canderel and supermarket own brands. Look for the Nutrasweet logo.

Acesulfame, also known as Sunett, was developed at the same time as aspartame. It is calorie-free and can be heated in cooking and baking. Look for the brand name Hermesetas Gold.

Thaumatin is another new sweetener, the sweetest of all. It's produced as sugary granules to sprinkle over food.

Some branded products are blends of the various sweeteners above.

COFFEE, TEA AND CHOCOLATE

A broad classification for tea, coffee and chocolate could be beverages that stimulate feelings of well-being. They perk us up and calm us down. They encourage conversation and social harmony. They have generated far-reaching trends and nourished many of our great institutions. Our modern lifestyles would be unthinkable without them. Yet these beverages were unknown to ancient Mediterranean and Asiatic civilisations and records of them date only from just over a thousand years ago.

COFFEE

With such a proliferation of coffee blends and varieties available it is helpful to have a basic background knowledge so you have some idea of what you are buying. There are several species of the coffee bush (actually a tree) native to a number of different areas of Africa. The most widely quoted fable of the discovery of the stimulating effect of coffee berries comes from Abyssinia (now Ethiopia). A goatherd called Kaldi noticed how frisky his goats became each time they nibbled red berries from certain trees. He reported his findings to the local holy man, who then passed the discovery on to the monastery, which presumably did something about it. By the time coffee filtered through to Arabia Islam had arrived and Moslems, forbidden the intoxicating pleasures of alcohol, engaged in lengthy debates about the acceptability of this bracing new brew that produced such animated conversation. Eventually distinctions were drawn between intoxication and stimulation and so coffee drinking became another of the great Arab contributions to civilisation, along with numerals, iced desserts and perfumery. The lush wadis of the Yemen highlands became one of the first areas of cultivation and for centuries Yemeni coffee has been synonymous with quality. Sadly, these days quality coffee trees are giving way to the growth of another stimulant, the quat plant.

Coffee is produced in a broad band around the world where there is abundant year-long rainfall, regular daily sunshine, a steady warm temperature and rich volcanic-style soils. A good altitude helps too, and coffee plantations are best located on hillsides for good drainage. Not a lot to ask really.

The two main species that produce berries of an edible quality are *Coffea arabica* and *Coffea robusta*, the latter a native of Uganda. *Arabica* trees are best suited to high altitudes (high grown) and *Robusta* to lowlands (low grown). The coffee tree has the ability to produce flowers and berries at the same time. The fragrance from the jasmine-scented coffee flowers is heavenly. The berries are known as cherries, with the beans or seeds inside, usually two per fruit. If a fruit contains just one seed this seed is known as peaberry. The husks and fruity pulp are removed by drying and husking (the simplest method), or by soaking in water and fermenting, deemed to give a higher quality coffee and used for *Arabica beans*. The raw green beans are then ready for shipping to coffee mills and roasting. When the beans are roasted, chemical changes take place that lead to the characteristic aroma. It is an essential part of the process and the level of roasting – light, medium or high/Continental – determines flavour too.

All the great mercantile European countries – Portugal, France, Holland, Austria, Italy and Britain – were prominent in the development of coffee drinking and manufacture. Coffee also had an indirect effect on the development of the business world. Eighteenth-century merchants and bankers would gather in the scores of coffee houses springing up to discuss their business over countless cups of coffee. Insurance and financing schemes were established leading to permanent institutions, Lloyd's of London being the most famous. Those European nations with colonies encouraged plantations, establishing many of the renowned varieties still in demand today – Java, Mysore (in India), Jamaica, Brazil, Central America and East Africa. Over the centuries, the Italians and Spaniards have perfected roasting and grinding machines, leading to a renaissance of coffee drinking and social manners. The Italians and Americans were responsible for popularising coffee drinking. The high-pressure espresso machine was perfected in 1946 by Achille Gaggia. A distant relative of Gaggia, Riservato, set up the first espresso coffee bar in London's Soho, the Moka Bar, leading the way for London's swinging Sixties boom and ultimately on to our current cappuccino cafe society.

Italian names proliferate in the quality coffee market but America has had the biggest impact on our everyday coffee-drinking habits, from the early days of instant coffee powder to the latest chic California- and Seattle-style bars and Internet cafes. Seattle boasts the title of coffee capital of the world through its popularisation of 'cappuccino to go' stores, mobile coffee carts, flavoured syrups and bran-high breakfast muffins.

Roasting coffee

The fruits of a coffee bush are berries, containing seeds. After picking, the flesh of the berries is stripped and the seeds fermented and then dried. Eventually, these become green coffee 'beans' ready for roasting. Much roasting is done at source or by speciality roasting companies, creating their own identity of high- to low-roast aromas, etc. Coffee purists often prefer to control their own roasting at home before grinding and brewing. It's an art.

Storing coffee

Aromas dissipate easily as the volatile oils evaporate quite quickly. So, unless you drink several cups a day, it is best to buy coffee little and often, whether grounds or instant. Experts advise that we store beans or grounds in the freezer for the best flavour retention. They can be used straight from frozen. Storage and ageing lessens the acidity in beans.

Instant coffees

Several attempts were made to make an easy-dissolving coffee but it wasn't until 1909 that an Anglo-Belgian chemist and entrepreneur called (ironically) George Washington launched a soluble coffee powder called Red E Coffee in America. Both world wars provided incentives for coffee manufacturers to produce quick-brew beverages that 'our boys on the front' could enjoy with just a pot of boiling water. Earliest methods involved spraying concentrated brews of coffee liquor from the top of tall high-temperature drying chambers to evaporate the water, leaving behind powdery solids. But more of the essential aroma of the coffee is captured with a newer process known as freeze-drying. Basically, brewed coffee is frozen and the moisture extracted by vacuum pressure, leaving behind granules with a purer flavour. Ground coffee and ready-roasted beans are also sold vacuum packed to retain the essential flavour of coffee.

Wholebean instant coffee is the latest upgrade to the world of quick-brewed coffee by the cup. Very finely ground fresh coffee beans are added to freeze-dried instant.

Decaffeinated coffee

Throughout its history coffee has been credited with many, some quite incredible, cures for ailments. But the one effect everyone is agreed on is the stimulation of the nervous system and mental alertness that caffeine in coffee causes. (It is also a diuretic but that's another matter.) For many people it can over-stimulate the brain just when it should be winding down preparing for sleep, so a way had to be found to isolate and remove caffeine. This can be achieved by three methods: the first involves treating soaked beans with chemical solvents; the second dissolves caffeine out of the green beans with carbon dioxide; and the third is a water treatment. There is a slight loss of flavour with decaffeination but it does mean many people can continue to enjoy a cup without losing sleep. For the record, ground coffee contains around 90g of caffeine per 150 ml, instant 60g and decaff 3g.

COFFEE VARIETIES AND BLENDS

Robusta coffees give stronger tasting, more full bodied blends: Arabica milder and more aromatic. Most coffee is blended because there are few beans totally balanced in terms of depths of flavour, aroma, acidity etc. However, some drinkers may find the quirkiness of a particular variety enjoyable so why blend it out? So, a few speciality coffees are single Arabicas from one region or even one grower. Single blends are known in the trade as self-drinkers.

The growth of the mail-order coffee business has brought a number of excellent speciality coffee merchants into the arena and it is now possible to be a real coffee aficionado anywhere so long as you are on a postal route. These businesses, run by enthusiasts with almost messianic devotion, are great sources of information and advice.

African coffees
Although it was the Arab and European colonists who set up plantations and reintroduced the beans from South America, Ethiopia in Africa was, nevertheless, the birthplace of the coffee plant.

Kenyan coffee growers (the Kenco brand, for example) are highly efficient and well supervised. The character of the beans is aromatic and acidic, and is best suited to a medium roast. Some growers now grow a *Kenyan Blue Mountain* variety, well worth sipping. Ethiopia stills exports wild berries with a distinctive two-tone colour providing intriguing speciality coffees. The *Yemen* also exports romantic and intriguing coffees – after all, the old town of Mocha gave its name to a bean with an almost chocolatey flavour, and so established a well-known culinary description.

Indonesian coffees
These are among the best in the world, especially their high-grown blends, and are greatly enjoyed by coffee lovers. More mellow than South American

coffees, Indonesian coffees are described as full-bodied and earthy. *Sumatra* coffees have a thick, rich body and less acidic sweet flavour. Perhaps the most notable coffee of recent years, described as a 'show stopper', is from the *Celebes* (also known as Sulawesi) – a coffee with a smooth nectar and a hint of spicy chocolate. If you come across a coffee called *Old Brown Java* (or Old Simbola) then at least try it and see if you agree that it's among the best in the world. It is buried in pits for up to twelve years, so it should be distinctive. Papua New Guinea, in the same region, produces high-quality gourmet blends with a fruity aroma.

South American coffees

Over a quarter of the world trade in coffee comes from just one country: Brazil. They've got an awful lot of coffee. Whatever happens in Brazil affects the rest of the world's trade. It is the largest producer in the world and exports its coffee from the port of Santos (which also gives its name to a well-known Brazilian blend). Brazilian coffee blends range from the everyday, mellow mild coffees through to the high-quality, high-roast Brazilian beans often used in blends with other South American beans.

Central American coffee production centres on *Costa Rica* and Colombia, both well-represented on supermarket shelves. Costa Rican beans are said to possess a perfect balance of aroma, acidity, body and flavour – the ultimate medium-roast coffee for many occasions. Colombian beans are described as 'bold' with a certain spiciness and slight nuttiness, certainly fuller in flavour than Brazilian. The best-known Colombian coffee region is Medellin. Other coffee countries are Guatemala, Honduras and Nicaragua.

TIP: DRINK YOUR COFFEE FRESH

Acidity is that sour coffee smell that hits you when you walk into a

hotel or pub with coffee that has stood for an hour or two until it is stewed

and undrinkable. Manufacturers advise that you let coffee stand on a

warming tray for no more than twenty minutes, and even then I think

that's too long.

Other countries

Mysore coffee from India is mild and often blended with stronger beans. But India also supplies a special aged Mysore coffee called *Monsoon Malabar*. *Jamaican* coffee is best known for what is thought to be the world's most prized variety – from the *Blue Mountains*. The original is pale and smooth with a slight sweetness best suited to a light roast. But if you want to taste this connoisseur's coffee then you will probably have to go to Japan: the Japanese are mad for Jamaican Blue Mountain and take much of the harvest.

ETHICAL TRADING

Much fresh produce grown in the tropical band of the World still carries with it the legacy of imperial colonialism that has now morphed into a form of commercial colonialism. No more so than tea, coffee and cocoa – still grown and harvested in vast estates and plantations controlled around central points of localised management and production. Millions of agricultural workers are employed in this field vulnerable to the vagaries of world trading markets, politics and company investment policies. The fruits of their labour are central to our Western lifestyles – our favourite cuppas, cappuccinos and indulgent chocolates. Yet during the latter half of the twentieth century it became clear to many of us who appreciated the quality and finesse of these foodstuffs that in terms of lifestyles there was an unfair imbalance and distribution of the profits. Millions of agricultural labourers in the Third World live subsistent lifestyles with poor sanitation, habitation and education whilst more affluent westernised consumers sipped and munched on what are essentially luxury foods. And so, organisations of this imbalance began to grow to encourage large and smaller companies involved in the trade and ensure higher percentages of the profit margins were used for the benefits of the agricultural workers to provide basic facilities that we in the West take for granted – health care centres, schools and colleges, passable roads, electricity and clean water. Homily over – just BUY FAIRTRADE (www.fairtrade.org.uk) or support small organic-style producers.

TEA

The Dutch first brought our favourite cuppa to Europe in 1610, and
we started drinking it in earnest in the mid-17th century. A whole new
style of entertaining and etiquette, complete with new designs of china,
trays and pots, sprang up which has been with us ever since. Until the
19th century all tea was imported from China because, although tea as
a wild plant originated in India, it wasn't reintroduced there by Major
Robert Bruce until the 1820s. By the end of the 19th century India was
not only one of the world's great exporters, it had also become a nation
of tea drinkers.

Tea changed our eating habits and, like coffee, can be brewed in several
ways, each nation having its own style. Afternoon tea as a social event was
the brainchild of the Duchess of Bedford in the 1840s, when she served
dainty cups of Darjeeling with sandwiches. Within a few years, the name
of a beverage had become synonymous with a meal. In Russia tea is drunk
with great ceremony and enjoyment, brewed fresh each time from elaborate
samovars. The Arabs and Indians like to boil their tea for two to three minutes
and serve it thick with milk and sugar. The Chinese sip their brew very weak
without milk or sugar (although, apparently, some add jam), while Tibetans are
said to mix yak butter into their cups.

Tea comes from a camellia tree, though because of constant picking
it never grows taller than a bush. The tips of the tea stalk (two leaves
and a bud) are considered the finest and are picked mostly by women
because they have delicate, thin fingers. Like fine wine, tea acquires
characteristics from the soil, climate and aspect of where it is grown. Some
tea plantations perched in lush hilly or mountainous regions are among the
most breathtaking scenery in the world. As with coffee, the altitude of tea
plantations affects the quality of tea.

TEA VARIETIES AND BLENDS

Tea can be processed in three styles (unfermented, part and fully fermented) each with a different final flavour. Tea blending is a complicated art requiring great skills and experience. Teas have varying characteristics. Some give strength, some astringency, some colour, brightness or aroma. Brewing time can vary too. Like coffee, there are single growths and blends. Leaf size effects tea flavour and large leaves take slightly longer to brew than fine leaves. Tea-bag tea is a very fine type called dust or fannings (and is not sweepings from the factory floor!). Most tea sold in the West is blended, and encased in one-cup bags.

Green tea is made simply from leaves that have been dried soon after picking, giving an astringent and refreshing flavour. If the leaves are left alone enzyme activity starts and they begin to ferment and oxidise and have to be dried to stop further oxidisation. This makes the familiar black teas. However, there is an in-between stage of half fermented, the best known example being Oolong, a distinctive and pleasant tea originally made in Taiwan, formerly known as Formosa. *Lapsang Souchong* is tea whose leaves have been dried over woodsmoke and Earl Grey is a black variety flavoured with oil of bergamot. The originator, the second Earl Grey, never thought to patent his favourite brew and now many brands sell an Earl Grey blend with variable results; a few are so flavoured they are almost perfumed.

Tea is best drunk newly harvested and freshly dried, sold in foil packs. Tea described as 'first flush' is a new season's tea. Loose tea gives a better brew because the leaves can swirl around a hot pot and release their aroma but then you have to use a tea strainer and dispose of wet leaves. The quality of water affects tea brews – hard water makes for a flatter flavour – and tea tasters have to take this into account when making their blends. They are aware of regional differences and one brand may have separate versions for hard- and soft-water areas. Tea used in bags must be of a small enough size to deliver a flavour within a minute or two of pouring on the water.

African teas

Kenyan teas have a good body, a brisk flavour and a warming copper-coloured hue. Over half the tea in our popular blends comes from Kenyan teas. Sold as pure Kenyan tea, it's similar to Ceylon tea. Ugandan tea is one to watch – the growing conditions are perfect – while blends from Malawi give full flavour.

Ceylon/Sri Lanka teas

Once one of the world's great producers with excellent tea grown in the beautiful mountains around Kandy. But political upheavals during the 1960s forced many of the tea planters to migrate to Kenya and start the thriving industry there. Tea production is dominated by big companies and it's hard for small-scale producers to break through, unless via expensive online mail order. Smaller producers may have an outlet via Fair Trade marketing. One exception is Dilmah, a fine example of what tea tasters call Single Origin Tea.

China teas

These are probably more eclectic. Not only are there variations in leaf size, fermentation and drying but also additions of volatile oils, dried flowers such as jasmine flowers, chrysanthemum blossoms and rose petals and even fruits. *Gunpowder* is a green tea, as is the fragrant *Jasmine* tea – both ideal for sipping at Chinese meals. *Keemum* is a delicate black tea, *Yunan* has a distinctive flavour used in blends, and is a large leaf tea popular in Europe.

Indian teas

The most popular brews from the biggest supplier. *Assam* in the north east of India is thought to have been the home of the wild tea bush. Now it is used in many blends and produces tea with body and strength and in great quantity. *Nilgiri* grows in the hills of south-west India and is a mild tea described as brisk, bright and even delectable. The best known is *Darjeeling* – the Champagne of teas – grown high in the Himalayas and fed by snow water. It has a unique muscatel fragrance and rich aroma. But, it does take a good seven minutes 'mashing' (brewing) time so it's not practical when you're dying for a cuppa. A nice after-dinner brew.

Japanese teas

These are rarely seen on sale because most Japanese tea is drunk in that country. However, as the trend for Japanese food and cooking continues to grow and sushi bars spring up in chic food halls and hotels, so we might get to taste a few. It is mostly green tea. *Bancha* is the most commonly drunk in Japan, usually served with rice. *Matcha* is powdered green tea used in tea ceremonies and whisked until smooth. *Kukicha* is mild and low in caffeine and *Gyokura* the best quality, consisting of the tips of the first pickings of leaves.

White tea

White tea is a Chinese tea from the Fujian province, which is not readily available except in speciality health food stores and delis. The tea bush tips are allowed to ripen and wrinkle before picking. The infusion is pale yellow, not white.

TIP: TEA AND RECIPES

All tea makes excellent sweet syrups for steeping dried fruit, especially prunes. Some of the more fragrant teas make delicious sorbets and ice cream. Earl Grey is increasingly a favourite but Jasmine tea is also nice, mixed with a lemon-flavoured syrup and trickled over fruit salads.

NON-TEA TEAS, TISANES AND INFUSIONS

This is becoming a very significant section of the market as we search for caffeine-free drinks or good alternatives to alcohol and fizzy drinks. Almost any aromatic twig or leaf, it seems, will make an infusion. Some 'teas' have been produced for years and are specialities of certain countries. They are drunk either alone or with milk, sugar or honey and sometimes lemon slices. *Rooibosch* (Boer bush tea) is dried leaves picked from a bush peculiar to Table Mountain in South Africa. I've drunk this sweet, fragrant tea at night for many years because it is caffeine free and because it is delicious. It is now sold blended with other flavours like vanilla but I prefer the more natural blends. *Mate tea* is leaves from a holly-type tree that grows along the upper reaches of the Paraguay river. It is said to be a cure-all, and is traditionally served from a gourd that is handed round communally. *Herbal vervaine* is one of the most popular tisanes in France. In the UK, we call it lemon verbena and it's easy to grow in pots on the patio. Wonderfully fragrant. Other varieties include *linden lime blossom tea, camomile tea* and *Turkish apple tea. New Jersey tea* was drunk by Bostonians during the American war against the British; now they enjoy *Lipton's black tea*. There is also an increasing range of sweet *fruit teas* as the market brings out more and more esoteric blends but apart from the flavouring one wonders what else is contained in the little white tea bags.

CHOCOLATE

The cocoa pod grows at an unusual angle straight out of the trunk of the cocoa tree. Inside the golden-ribbed shell are numerous seeds enclosed in a fleshy pulp. The seeds are scooped out and left to ferment in a large heap for about a week. This fermentation stops the seeds germinating and changes the colour to a rich dark brown. The beans are then spread out to dry for up to two weeks and exported. At the chocolate factory the beans are roasted to develop flavour then cracked into nibs and over half their content is broken down into a substance called cocoa butter. A bitter cocoa powder called cocoa mass is also pressed out. Together these are referred to as cocoa solids. Remember this phrase when you come to check on the quality of chocolate. Cocoa butter melts under the frictional heat of the machinery and makes smooth cocoa liquor that solidifies when cooled. In this raw state, the liquor is sharp so sugar is added to make it sweet. How much is added depends on the desired end chocolate.

MELTING CHOCOLATE

Take care – this can be tricky because the cocoa solids might overheat and 'seize' (go lumpy), then be almost impossible to restore to silky smoothness. The slower the melting, the better. Overnight in an airing cupboard is a foolproof method if you remember in time, or by the side of a very low-temperature range cooker. The classic way is to break the bar into squares in a bowl and stand it over a pan of water that is just below boiling. Do not let the water touch the bowl nor let water splash into the chocolate as it melts. However, if you add liquid such as brandy or cream to the chocolate before it starts melting it will incorporate nicely. Heating in the microwave is almost foolproof, so long as you follow pack instructions and the wattage is not too high.

Making chocolate

Chocolate making is very complicated and requires great skill and temperature
control because it melts at one degree under body temperature, which makes
handling tricky. To make chocolate easier to handle, manufacturers might mix
in extra cocoa butter, but UK companies can also add up to 5% vegetable fat.
Quality chocolate makers prefer to use all cocoa butter because vegetable fat
affects the feel of the chocolate in the mouth.

At one time the term 'cooking chocolate' meant a rather cheap inferior
product with a high percentage of vegetable fat that made it easier to melt.
It also made it taste quite greasy. Nowadays those products have to be called
chocolate coating, and the name cooking chocolate has taken on a completely
different meaning. It is frequently the best-quality chocolate you can buy.

Chocolate is graded according to the percentage of cocoa solids. The best
quality will have 70%, but sometimes that is too high for handling and chefs
and cooks prefer a slightly lower grade in the mid-sixties. Very bitter chocolate
can have up to 90%. Plain chocolate has to have a minimum of 40% (many
have more) and milk chocolate around 20–30%. White chocolate has no cocoa
mass, just cocoa butter plus sugar and milk. Chocolate does not need to be
sweetened – it's just that it's what we are now used to – but many brands can
have added vanilla. In parts of Central America (the native home of the cocoa
bean in the lands of the Aztecs, where it was called the food of the gods),
chocolate is used in stews, sauces mixed with chilli and other spices – the
classic Mexican savoury moles – and also used in relishes. The Americans
have a high-quality unsweetened baking chocolate. The French even add
squares of dark unsweetened chocolate to red wine sauces for venison.
I do encourage you to try experimenting too, but only with the best-quality
chocolate and in small amounts.

The flavour of chocolate is also affected by the variety of cocoa bean. *Criollo* is regarded as the finest but accounts for only a very small percentage of the world's supply, chiefly from the Americas. *Trinitario* is another fine bean from the Caribbean, along with **Forastero** from West Africa (which accounts for over 50% of world trade). Like coffee beans, they have varying characteristics that balance each other out when blended. Not that we have to make a detailed study of all this when buying chocolate, but it does illustrate just how involved a subject it can be. During manufacture, good chocolate has to undergo a number of differing processes including one called conching, where liquid chocolate is stirred for up to seven days then cooled rapidly (called tempering) to keep the cocoa butter crystals smooth. For straightforward bars the liquid chocolate is simply moulded, but to cover candy centres another complicated process is involved called enrobing.

By the mid-19th century the first solid confectionery chocolate was launched at a Birmingham trade fair but it was another fifty years before the first chocolate bar, made by the American Milton Hershey, was launched in 1900. Now, of course, Birmingham, or rather its satellite town Bournville, is the home of Cadbury's. It is an interesting fact that many of the great British chocolate families were great philanthropists and reformers, including the prison reformer Elizabeth Fry and the Rowntree family of York.

In the end though, what is considered to be the best chocolate is very much a case of personal preference. I brought my children up on dark chocolate with high cocoa solids. As teenagers they preferred dairy milk chocolate. A decade or so on, they enjoy 'proper' chocolate, as they call it. Americans hunt for Hershey bars in Europe and we crave English, Belgian or Dutch chocolate when we are abroad.

BRAND NAMES FOR QUALITY CHOCOLATE

Here is a resumé of those with a high cocoa solids content (60% plus): Lindt Excellence, Valrhona, Cocoa Barry, Feodora, Green and Black (organic), The Chocolate Society, Godiva, Rococo. Most of the leading supermarket chains – Marks & Spencer, Sainsbury, Waitrose – sell excellent chocolate under their own brand names.

Cocoa and drinking chocolate

During processing, if all the cocoa butter is extracted what is left is pure cocoa mass. This can be further roasted and ground to a fine powder. Chocolate processing started in Europe at the end of the 16th century in Spain, but only to produce a hot drink. Gradually the idea spread to England, France, Italy and Holland, where Conrad van Houten not only improved on the drinking chocolate of the day by pressing out more of the cocoa fat but also found that by treating this powder with an alkali he could make pure cocoa powder. A good drinking chocolate was then the only way of enjoying the fruits of the cocoa bean. Now drinking chocolate is a powder mixed with sugar and milk powder and can even be added to boiling water to make an instant low-fat drink. But still there are excellent high-quality drinking chocolates available: try Dutch and French brands or the Californian Ghirardelli, described as sweetened ground chocolate, and cocoa made in San Francisco.

USING COCOA

Treat the powder like flour when mixing, sifting it into dry ingredients as it can settle into fine lumps. When cocoa is mixed with a liquid you'll find it hard to blend because of the high surface tension, but just keep stirring briskly and it will soon come together as a paste.

To make old-fashioned hot cocoa, allow 2–3tsp of powder per 300ml (10fl oz) milk. Blend the cocoa powder first with a little of the milk and put the rest on to heat. When the milk starts to rise, pour it on to the cocoa paste, stirring well. (Not the other way round, as the paste might not incorporate well.) Return the blended liquid to the pan and bring it to the boil for just a second or two. Cocoa does need to be cooked out or it will taste pasty. Sweeten to taste.

If making a chocolate mousse with low cocoa solids chocolate, you can make it taste richer by adding some blended cocoa paste

---

Index

puddings
  Eton mess 181
  peachy 170
pulses 189–95
  cooking 194–5
pumpkin
  and ham pasta 128
  seed 206
  seed oil 286
purslane 138
Puy lentils 192

quick apricot tarts 145

rabbit 36
raclette 85
radicchio *see* red chicory
radishes 129
ragu bolognese 238
raising agents 227, 299
raisins 157–8
raita 106
  cucumber 249
rambutans 162–3
rapeseed oil 285
rashers 38
raspberries 177
raw milk 69
Red Leicester cheese 86
red onions 118–19
red peppercorn syrup
  pears in 171
red split lentils 192
redcurrants 155
reduced-fat spreads 77
rhubarb 178–9
  upside-down cake 179
rice 208–16
  American long-grain 209
  basmati 209–11
  brown 212
  easy-cook 208–9
  enriched 212
  glutinous 212
  Japanese 212–13
  *mangoes with sweet Thai
  coconut rice* 165
  pudding 213
  risotto 213
  Spanish 215
  Thai 215
  wild 216

rice noodles 240
rice wine vinegar 289
ricotta 82
risotto rices 213
  real risotto 214
rock salt 291
rocket 115
roes 58
rolled oats *see* oatflakes
root vegetable chips 99
Roquefort 81
rosemary 250
rye 224

saccharin 314
safflower oil 285
saffron 266–7
saffron rice 211
sage 250
sago 224
salad dressing, Thai-style
  272
salad, panzanella 135
salame di Fabriano 47
salame felino 47
salame finocchiona 47
salame genovese 48
salame napoletano 48
salame romano 47
salame toscano 47
salamis 47–8
salmon 51
  canned 57
  smoked 52–3
salsify 130
salt beef 41
salt cod 59
salted fish 52, 59–60
salted herrings 60
saltpetre 42
salts 290–1
samphire 131
sardines 57
saturated fats 75
sauces 270–8
  bean 270
  hot butterscotch 309
  hot pepper 277
  non-oriental 276–8
  oriental 270–6
  ragu bolognese 238
sauerkraut 295

sausages 43–8
saveloys 44
savoy cabbage 96
scallions *see* spring
  onions
scorzonera 130
sea bass 51
sea salt 291
sea vegetables 130
seafood 60–3
seakale beet 132
seam butchery 23
seasonality 10
seeds 206–7
  sprouting 93
self-raising flours 233
semolina 224, 234
Serrano ham 40
sesame seeds 206–7
setting agents 302–4
shallots 120
  shallot confit 120
Sharon fruit 172
sheep's milk 70
sherry vinegar 288
shiitakes 184
shortenings 78
shrimp pastes 273
Sichuan pepper 265
Sichuan preserved
  vegetables 295
single cream 71
sirloin 25
smetana 73
Smithfield ham 41
smoked cod's roe 58
smoked eel 55
smoked fish pâté 56
smoked haddock 54
smoked halibut 54
smoked mackerel 56
smoked salmon 52–3
smoked sturgeon 54
smoked trout 55
smoked venison 42
smoking 37
soba 218, 241
soda bread 227
soft cheese 81–2
sole 51
sorghum *see* mullet
sorrel 138